OpenCL Programming by Example

A comprehensive guide on OpenCL programming with examples

Ravishekhar Banger

Koushik Bhattacharyya

[PACKT] PUBLISHING

BIRMINGHAM - MUMBAI

OpenCL Programming by Example

First published: December 2013

Production Reference: 1161213

Published by Packt Publishing Ltd.
Livery Place
35 Livery Street
Birmingham B3 2PB, UK.

ISBN 978-1-84969-234-2

www.packtpub.com

Cover Image by Asher Wishkerman (a.wishkerman@mpic.de)

Credits

Authors
Ravishekhar Banger
Koushik Bhattacharyya

Reviewers
Thomas Gall
Erik Rainey
Erik Smistad

Acquisition Editors
Wilson D'souza
Kartikey Pandey
Kevin Colaco

Lead Technical Editor
Arun Nadar

Technical Editors
Gauri Dasgupta
Dipika Gaonkar
Faisal Siddiqui

Project Coordinators
Wendell Palmer
Amey Sawant

Proofreader
Mario Cecere

Indexers
Rekha Nair
Priya Subramani

Graphics
Sheetal Aute
Ronak Dhruv
Yuvraj Mannari
Abhinash Sahu

Production Coordinator
Conidon Miranda

Cover Work
Conidon Miranda

About the Authors

Ravishekhar Banger calls himself a "Parallel Programming Dogsbody". Currently he is a specialist in OpenCL programming and works for library optimization using OpenCL. After graduation from SDMCET, Dharwad, in Electrical Engineering, he completed his Masters in Computer Technology from Indian Institute of Technology, Delhi. With more than eight years of industry experience, his present interest lies in General Purpose GPU programming models, parallel programming, and performance optimization for the GPU. Having worked for Samsung and Motorola, he is now a Member of Technical Staff at Advanced Micro Devices, Inc. One of his dreams is to cover most of the Himalayas by foot in various expeditions. You can reach him at `ravibanger@gmail.com`.

Koushik Bhattacharyya is working with Advanced Micro Devices, Inc. as Member Technical Staff and also worked as a software developer in NVIDIA®. He did his M.Tech in Computer Science (Gold Medalist) from Indian Statistical Institute, Kolkata, and M.Sc in pure mathematics from Burdwan University. With more than ten years of experience in software development using a number of languages and platforms, Koushik's present area of interest includes parallel programming and machine learning.

We would like to take this opportunity to thank "PACKT publishing" for giving us an opportunity to write this book.

Also a special thanks to all our family members, friends and colleagues, who have helped us directly or indirectly in writing this book.

About the Reviewers

Thomas Gall had his first experience with accelerated coprocessors on the Amiga back in 1986. After working with IBM for twenty years, now he is working as a Principle Engineer and serves as Linaro.org's technical lead for the Graphics Working Group. He manages the Graphics and GPGPU teams. The GPGPU team is dedicated to optimize existing open source software to take advantage of GPGPU technologies such as OpenCL, as well as the implementation of GPGPU drivers for ARM based SoC systems.

Erik Rainey works at Texas Instruments, Inc. as a Senior Software Engineer on Computer Vision software frameworks in embedded platforms in the automotive, safety, industrial, and robotics markets. He has a young son, who he loves playing with when not working, and enjoys other pursuits such as music, drawing, crocheting, painting, and occasionally a video game. He is currently involved in creating the Khronos Group's OpenVX, the specification for computer vision acceleration.

Erik Smistad is a PhD candidate at the Norwegian University of Science and Technology, where he uses OpenCL and GPUs to quickly locate organs and other anatomical structures in medical images for the purpose of helping surgeons navigate inside the body during surgery. He writes about OpenCL and his projects on his blog, `thebigblob.com`, and shares his code at `github.com/smistad`.

www.PacktPub.com

Support files, eBooks, discount offers and more

You might want to visit www.PacktPub.com for support files and downloads related to your book.

Did you know that Packt offers eBook versions of every book published, with PDF and ePub files available? You can upgrade to the eBook version at www.PacktPub.com and as a print book customer, you are entitled to a discount on the eBook copy. Get in touch with us at service@packtpub.com for more details.

At www.PacktPub.com, you can also read a collection of free technical articles, sign up for a range of free newsletters and receive exclusive discounts and offers on Packt books and eBooks.

PACKTLIB

http://PacktLib.PacktPub.com

Do you need instant solutions to your IT questions? PacktLib is Packt's online digital book library. Here, you can access, read and search across Packt's entire library of books.

Why Subscribe?

- Fully searchable across every book published by Packt
- Copy and paste, print and bookmark content
- On demand and accessible via web browser

Free Access for Packt account holders

If you have an account with Packt at www.PacktPub.com, you can use this to access PacktLib today and view nine entirely free books. Simply use your login credentials for immediate access.

Table of Contents

Preface

This book is designed as a concise introduction to OpenCL programming for developers working on diverse domains. It covers all the major topics of OpenCL programming and illustrates them with code examples and explanations from different fields such as common algorithm, image processing, statistical computation, and machine learning. It also dedicates one chapter to Optimization techniques, where it discusses different optimization strategies on a single simple problem.

Parallel programming is a fast developing field today. As it is becoming increasingly difficult to increase the performance of a single core machine, hardware vendors see advantage in packing multiple cores in a single SOC. The **GPU (Graphics Processor Unit)** was initially meant for rendering better graphics which ultimately means fast floating point operation for computing pixel values. **GPGPU (General purpose Graphics Processor Unit)** is the technique of utilization of GPU for a general purpose computation. Since the GPU provides very high performance of floating point operations and data parallel computation, it is very well suited to be used as a co-processor in a computing system for doing data parallel tasks with high arithmetic intensity.

Before NVIDIA® came up with **CUDA (Compute Unified Device Architecture)** in February 2007, the typical GPGPU approach was to convert general problems' data parallel computation into some form of a graphics problem which is expressible by graphics programming APIs for the GPU. CUDA first gave a user friendly small extension of C language to write code for the GPU. But it was a proprietary framework from NVIDIA and was supposed to work on NVIDIA's GPU only.

With the growing popularity of such a framework, the requirement for an open standard architecture that would be able to support different kinds of devices from various vendors was becoming strongly perceivable. In June 2008, the Khronos compute working group was formed and they published OpenCL1.0 specification in December 2008. Multiple vendors gradually provided a tool-chain for OpenCL programming including NVIDIA OpenCL Drivers and Tools, AMD APP SDK, Intel® SDK for OpenCL application, IBM Server with OpenCL development Kit, and so on. Today OpenCL supports multi-core programming, GPU programming, cell and DSP processor programming, and so on.

In this book we discuss OpenCL with a few examples.

What this book covers

Chapter 1, Hello OpenCL, starts with a brief introduction to OpenCL and provides hardware architecture details of the various OpenCL devices from different vendors.

Chapter 2, OpenCL Architecture, discusses the various OpenCL architecture models.

Chapter 3, OpenCL Buffer Objects, discusses the common functions used to create an OpenCL memory object.

Chapter 4, OpenCL Images, gives an overview of functions for creating different types of OpenCL images.

Chapter 5, OpenCL Program and Kernel Objects, concentrates on the sequential steps required to execute a kernel.

Chapter 6, Events and Synchronization, discusses coarse grained and fine-grained events and their synchronization mechanisms.

Chapter 7, OpenCL C Programming, discusses the specifications and restrictions for writing an OpenCL compliant C kernel code.

Chapter 8, Basic Optimization Techniques with Case Studies, discusses various optimization techniques using a simple example of matrix multiplication.

Chapter 9, Image Processing and OpenCL, discusses Image Processing case studies. OpenCL implementations of Image filters and JPEG image decoding are provided in this chapter.

Chapter 10, OpenCL-OpenGL Interoperation, discusses OpenCL and OpenGL interoperation, which in its simple form means sharing of data between OpenGL and OpenCL in a program that uses both.

Chapter 11, Case studies – Regressions, Sort, and KNN, discusses general algorithm-like sorting. Besides this, case studies from Statistics (Linear and Parabolic Regression) and Machine Learning (K Nearest Neighbourhood) are discussed with their OpenCL implementations.

What you need for this book

The prerequisite is proficiency in C language. Having a background of parallel programming would undoubtedly be advantageous, but it is not a requirement. Readers should find this book compact yet a complete guide for OpenCL programming covering most of the advanced topics. Emphasis is given to illustrate the key concept and problem-solution with small independent examples rather than a single large example. There are detailed explanations of the most of the APIs discussed and kernels for the case studies are presented.

Who this book is for

Application developers from different domains intending to use OpenCL to accelerate their application can use this book to jump start. This book is also good for beginners in OpenCL and parallel programming.

Conventions

In this book, you will find a number of styles of text that distinguish between different kinds of information. Here are some examples of these styles, and an explanation of their meaning.

Code words in text are shown as follows: " Each OpenCL vendor, ships this library and the corresponding `OpenCL.dll` or `libOpenCL.so` library in its SDK."

A block of code is set as follows:

```
void saxpy(int n, float a, float *b, float *c)
{
    for (int i = 0; i < n; ++i)
        y[i] = a*x[i] + y[i];
}
```

When we wish to draw your attention to a particular part of a code block, the relevant lines or items are set in bold:

```
#include <CL/cl.h>
#endif
#define VECTOR_SIZE 1024


//OpenCL kernel which is run for every work item created.
const char *saxpy_kernel =
"__kernel                                       \n"
"void saxpy_kernel(float alpha,     \n"
"                  __global float *A,           \n"
"                  __global float *B,           \n"
"                  __global float *C)           \n"
"{                                              \n"
"    //Get the index of the work-item           \n"
"    int index = get_global_id(0);              \n"
"    C[index] = alpha* A[index] + B[index];     \n"
"}                                              \n";

int main(void) {
  int i;
```

Any command-line input or output is written as follows:

```
# cp /usr/src/asterisk-addons/configs/cdr_mysql.conf.sample
     /etc/asterisk/cdr_mysql.conf
```

New terms and **important words** are shown in bold. Words that you see on the screen, in menus or dialog boxes for example, appear in the text like this: "clicking on the **Next** button moves you to the next screen".

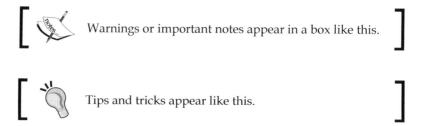

[Warnings or important notes appear in a box like this.]

[Tips and tricks appear like this.]

Reader feedback

Feedback from our readers is always welcome. Let us know what you think about this book—what you liked or may have disliked. Reader feedback is important for us to develop titles that you really get the most out of.

To send us general feedback, simply send an e-mail to `feedback@packtpub.com`, and mention the book title via the subject of your message.

If there is a topic that you have expertise in and you are interested in either writing or contributing to a book, see our author guide on `www.packtpub.com/authors`.

Customer support

Now that you are the proud owner of a Packt book, we have a number of things to help you to get the most from your purchase.

Downloading the example code

You can download the example code files for all Packt books you have purchased from your account at `http://www.packtpub.com`. If you purchased this book elsewhere, you can visit `http://www.packtpub.com/support` and register to have the files e-mailed directly to you.

Errata

Although we have taken every care to ensure the accuracy of our content, mistakes do happen. If you find a mistake in one of our books—maybe a mistake in the text or the code—we would be grateful if you would report this to us. By doing so, you can save other readers from frustration and help us improve subsequent versions of this book. If you find any errata, please report them by visiting `http://www.packtpub.com/submit-errata`, selecting your book, clicking on the **errata submission form** link, and entering the details of your errata. Once your errata are verified, your submission will be accepted and the errata will be uploaded on our website, or added to any list of existing errata, under the Errata section of that title. Any existing errata can be viewed by selecting your title from `http://www.packtpub.com/support`.

Piracy

Piracy of copyright material on the Internet is an ongoing problem across all media. At Packt, we take the protection of our copyright and licenses very seriously. If you come across any illegal copies of our works, in any form, on the Internet, please provide us with the location address or website name immediately so that we can pursue a remedy.

Please contact us at `copyright@packtpub.com` with a link to the suspected pirated material.

We appreciate your help in protecting our authors, and our ability to bring you valuable content.

Questions

You can contact us at `questions@packtpub.com` if you are having a problem with any aspect of the book, and we will do our best to address it.

1
Hello OpenCL

Parallel Computing has been extensively researched over the past few decades and had been the key research interest at many universities. Parallel Computing uses multiple processors or computers working together on a common algorithm or task. Due to the constraints in the available memory, performance of a single computing unit, and also the need to complete a task quickly, various parallel computing frameworks have been defined. All computers are parallel these days, even your handheld mobiles are multicore platforms and each of these parallel computers uses a parallel computing framework of their choice. Let's define Parallel Computing.

The Wikipedia definition says that, Parallel Computing is a form of computation in which many calculations are carried out simultaneously, operating on the principle that large problems can often be divided into smaller ones, which are then solved concurrently (in parallel).

There are many Parallel Computing programming standards or API specifications, such as OpenMP, OpenMPI, Pthreads, and so on. This book is all about OpenCL Parallel Programming. In this chapter, we will start with a discussion on different types of parallel programming. We will first introduce you to OpenCL with different OpenCL components. We will also take a look at the various hardware and software vendors of OpenCL and their OpenCL installation steps. Finally, at the end of the chapter we will see an OpenCL program example *SAXPY* in detail and its implementation.

Advances in computer architecture

All over the 20th century computer architectures have advanced by multiple folds. The trend is continuing in the 21st century and will remain for a long time to come. Some of these trends in architecture follow Moore's Law. "Moore's law is the observation that, over the history of computing hardware, the number of transistors on integrated circuits doubles approximately every two years". Many devices in the computer industry are linked to Moore's law, whether they are DSPs, memory devices, or digital cameras. All the hardware advances would be of no use if there weren't any software advances. Algorithms and software applications grow in complexity, as more and more user interaction comes into play. An algorithm can be highly sequential or it may be parallelized, by using any parallel computing framework. Amdahl's Law is used to predict the speedup for an algorithm, which can be obtained given `n` threads. This speedup is dependent on the value of the amount of strictly serial or non-parallelizable code (`B`). The time `T(n)` an algorithm takes to finish when being executed on `n` thread(s) of execution corresponds to:

$$T(n) = T(1)\,(B + (1-B)/n)$$

Therefore the theoretical speedup which can be obtained for a given algorithm is given by :

$$Speedup(n) = 1/(B + (1-B)/n)$$

Amdahl's Law has a limitation, that it does not fully exploit the computing power that becomes available as the number of processing core increase.

Gustafson's Law takes into account the scaling of the platform by adding more processing elements in the platform. This law assumes that the total amount of work that can be done in parallel, varies linearly with the increase in number of processing elements. Let an algorithm be decomposed into `(a+b)`. The variable `a` is the serial execution time and variable `b` is the parallel execution time. Then the corresponding speedup for `P` parallel elements is given by:

$$(a + P*b)$$

$$Speedup = (a + P*b) / (a + b)$$

Now defining α as `a/(a+b)`, the sequential execution component, as follows, gives the speedup for `P` processing elements:

$$Speedup(P) = P - a *(P - 1)$$

Given a problem which can be solved using OpenCL, the same problem can also be solved on a different hardware with different capabilities. Gustafson's law suggests that with more number of computing units, the data set should also increase that is, "fixed work per processor". Whereas Amdahl's law suggests the speedup which can be obtained for the existing data set if more computing units are added, that is, "Fixed work for all processors". Let's take the following example:

Let the serial component and parallel component of execution be of one unit each.

In Amdahl's Law the strictly serial component of code is B (equals 0.5). For two processors, the speedup `T(2)` is given by:

$T(2) = 1 / (0.5 + (1 - 0.5) / 2) = 1.33$

Similarly for four and eight processors, the speedup is given by:

$T(4) = 1.6$ *and* $T(8) = 1.77$

Adding more processors, for example when `n` tends to infinity, the speedup obtained at max is only 2. On the other hand in Gustafson's law, Alpha = 1(1+1) = 0.5 (which is also the serial component of code). The speedup for two processors is given by:

$Speedup(2) = 2 - 0.5(2 - 1) = 1.5$

Similarly for four and eight processors, the speedup is given by:

$Speedup(4) = 2.5$ *and* $Speedup(8) = 4.5$

The following figure shows the work load scaling factor of Gustafson's law, when compared to Amdahl's law with a constant workload:

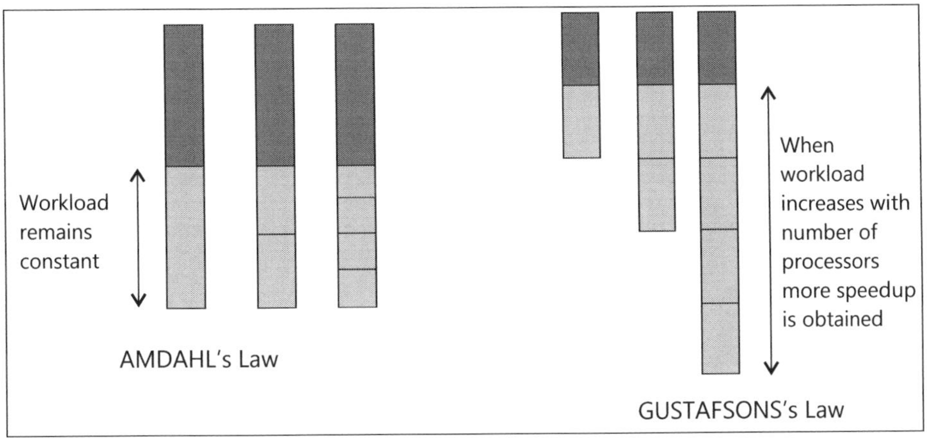

Comparison of Amdahl's and Gustafson's Law

OpenCL is all about parallel programming, and Gustafson's law very well fits into this book as we will be dealing with OpenCL for data parallel applications. Workloads which are data parallel in nature can easily increase the data set and take advantage of the scalable platforms by adding more compute units. For example, more pixels can be computed as more compute units are added.

Different parallel programming techniques

There are several different forms of parallel computing such as bit-level, instruction level, data, and task parallelism. This book will largely focus on data and task parallelism using heterogeneous devices. We just now coined a term, heterogeneous devices. How do we tackle complex tasks "in parallel" using different types of computer architecture? Why do we need OpenCL when there are many (already defined) open standards for Parallel Computing?

To answer this question, let us discuss the pros and cons of different Parallel computing Framework.

OpenMP

OpenMP is an API that supports multi-platform shared memory multiprocessing programming in C, C++, and Fortran. It is prevalent only on a multi-core computer platform with a shared memory subsystem.

A basic OpenMP example implementation of the OpenMP Parallel directive is as follows:

```
#pragma omp parallel
{
  body;
}
```

When you build the preceding code using the OpenMP shared library, `libgomp` would expand to something similar to the following code:

```
void subfunction (void *data)
{
    use data;
    body;
}

setup data;
```

```
GOMP_parallel_start (subfunction, &data, num_threads);
subfunction (&data);
GOMP_parallel_end ();
void GOMP_parallel_start (void (*fn)(void *), void *data,
  unsigned num_threads)
```

The OpenMP directives make things easy for the developer to modify the existing code to exploit the multicore architecture. OpenMP, though being a great parallel programming tool, does not support parallel execution on heterogeneous devices, and the use of a multicore architecture with shared memory subsystem does not make it cost effective.

MPI

Message Passing Interface (**MPI**) has an advantage over OpenMP, that it can run on either the shared or distributed memory architecture. Distributed memory computers are less expensive than large shared memory computers. But it has its own drawback with inherent programming and debugging challenges. One major disadvantage of MPI parallel framework is that the performance is limited by the communication network between the nodes.

Supercomputers have a massive number of processors which are interconnected using a high speed network connection or are in computer clusters, where computer processors are in close proximity to each other. In clusters, there is an expensive and dedicated data bus for data transfers across the computers. MPI is extensively used in most of these compute monsters called supercomputers.

OpenACC

The **OpenACC Application Program Interface** (**API**) describes a collection of compiler directives to specify loops and regions of code in standard C, C++, and Fortran to be offloaded from a host CPU to an attached accelerator, providing portability across operating systems, host CPUs, and accelerators. OpenACC is similar to OpenMP in terms of program annotation, but unlike OpenMP which can only be accelerated on CPUs, OpenACC programs can be accelerated on a GPU or on other accelerators also. OpenACC aims to overcome the drawbacks of OpenMP by making parallel programming possible across heterogeneous devices. OpenACC standard describes directives and APIs to accelerate the applications. The ease of programming and the ability to scale the existing codes to use the heterogeneous processor, warrantees a great future for OpenACC programming.

CUDA

Compute Unified Device Architecture (**CUDA**) is a parallel computing architecture developed by NVIDIA for graphics processing and **GPU** (**General Purpose GPU**) programming. There is a fairly good developer community following for the CUDA software framework. Unlike OpenCL, which is supported on GPUs by many vendors and even on many other devices such as IBM's Cell B.E. processor or TI's DSP processor and so on, CUDA is supported only for NVIDIA GPUs. Due to this lack of generalization, and focus on a very specific hardware platform from a single vendor, OpenCL is gaining traction.

CUDA or OpenCL?

CUDA is more proprietary and vendor specific but has its own advantages. It is easier to learn and start writing code in CUDA than in OpenCL, due to its simplicity. Optimization of CUDA is more deterministic across a platform, since less number of platforms are supported from a single vendor only. It has simplified few programming constructs and mechanisms. So for a quick start and if you are sure that you can stick to one device (GPU) from a single vendor that is NVIDIA, CUDA can be a good choice.

OpenCL on the other hand is supported for many hardware from several vendors and those hardware vary extensively even in their basic architecture, which created the requirement of understanding a little complicated concepts before starting OpenCL programming. Also, due to the support of a huge range of hardware, although an OpenCL program is portable, it may lose optimization when ported from one platform to another.

The kernel development where most of the effort goes, is practically identical between the two languages. So, one should not worry about which one to choose. Choose the language which is convenient. But remember your OpenCL application will be vendor agnostic. This book aims at attracting more developers to OpenCL.

There are many libraries which use OpenCL programming for acceleration. Some of them are MAGMA, clAMDBLAS, clAMDFFT, BOLT C++ Template library, and JACKET which accelerate MATLAB on GPUs. Besides this, there are C++ and Java bindings available for OpenCL also.

Once you've figured out how to write your important "kernels" it's trivial to port to either OpenCL or CUDA. A kernel is a computation code which is executed by an array of threads. CUDA also has a vast set of CUDA accelerated libraries, that is, CUBLAS, CUFFT, CUSPARSE, Thrust and so on. But it may not take a long time to port these libraries to OpenCL.

Renderscripts

Renderscripts is also an API specification which is targeted for 3D rendering and general purpose compute operations in an Android platform. Android apps can accelerate the performance by using these APIs. It is also a cross-platform solution. When an app is run, the scripts are compiled into a machine code of the device. This device can be a CPU, a GPU, or a DSP. The choice of which device to run it on is made at runtime. If a platform does not have a GPU, the code may fall back to the CPU. Only Android supports this API specification as of now. The execution model in Renderscripts is similar to that of OpenCL.

Hybrid parallel computing model

Parallel programming models have their own advantages and disadvantages. With the advent of many different types of computer architectures, there is a need to use multiple programming models to achieve high performance. For example, one may want to use MPI as the message passing framework, and then at each node level one might want to use, OpenCL, CUDA, OpenMP, or OpenACC.

Besides all the above programming models many compilers such as Intel ICC, GCC, and Open64 provide auto parallelization options, which makes the programmers job easy and exploit the underlying hardware architecture without the need of knowing any parallel computing framework. Compilers are known to be good at providing instruction-level parallelism. But tackling data level or task level auto parallelism has its own limitations and complexities.

Introduction to OpenCL

OpenCL standard was first introduced by Apple, and later on became part of the open standards organization "Khronos Group". It is a non-profit industry consortium, creating open standards for the authoring, and acceleration of parallel computing, graphics, dynamic media, computer vision and sensor processing on a wide variety of platforms and devices.

The goal of OpenCL is to make certain types of parallel programming easier, and to provide vendor agnostic hardware-accelerated parallel execution of code. **OpenCL** (**Open Computing Language**) is the first open, royalty-free standard for general-purpose parallel programming of heterogeneous systems. It provides a uniform programming environment for software developers to write efficient, portable code for high-performance compute servers, desktop computer systems, and handheld devices using a diverse mix of multi-core CPUs, GPUs, and DSPs.

OpenCL gives developers a common set of easy-to-use tools to take advantage of any device with an OpenCL driver (processors, graphics cards, and so on) for the processing of parallel code. By creating an efficient, close-to-the-metal programming interface, OpenCL will form the foundation layer of a parallel computing ecosystem of platform-independent tools, middleware, and applications.

We mentioned vendor agnostic, yes that is what OpenCL is about. The different vendors here can be AMD, Intel, NVIDIA, ARM, TI, and so on. The following diagram shows the different vendors and hardware architectures which use the OpenCL specification to leverage the hardware capabilities:

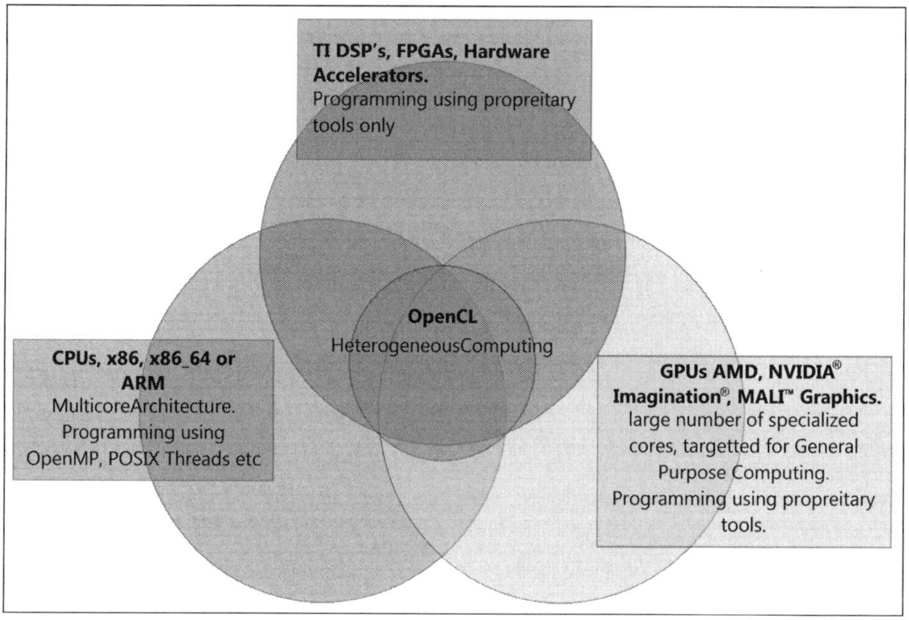

The heterogeneous system

The OpenCL framework defines a language to write "kernels". These kernels are functions which are capable of running on different compute devices. OpenCL defines an extended C language for writing compute kernels, and a set of APIs for creating and managing these kernels. The compute kernels are compiled with a runtime compiler, which compiles them on-the-fly during host application execution for the targeted device. This enables the host application to take advantage of all the compute devices in the system with a single set of portable compute kernels.

Based on your interest and hardware availability, you might want to do OpenCL programming with a "host and device" combination of "CPU and CPU" or "CPU and GPU". Both have their own programming strategy. In CPUs you can run very large kernels as the CPU architecture supports out-of-order instruction level parallelism and have large caches. For the GPU you will be better off writing small kernels for better performance. Performance optimization is a huge topic in itself. We will try to discuss this with a case study in *Chapter 8, Basic Optimization Techniques with Case Studies*

Hardware and software vendors

There are various hardware vendors who support OpenCL. Every OpenCL vendor provides OpenCL runtime libraries. These runtimes are capable of running only on their specific hardware architectures. Not only across different vendors, but within a vendor there may be different types of architectures which might need a different approach towards OpenCL programming. Now let's discuss the various hardware vendors who provide an implementation of OpenCL, to exploit their underlying hardware.

Advanced Micro Devices, Inc. (AMD)

With the launch of AMD A Series APU, one of industry's first **Accelerated Processing Unit (APU)**, AMD is leading the efforts of integrating both the x86_64 CPU and GPU dies in one chip. It has four cores of CPU processing power, and also a four or five graphics SIMD engine, depending on the silicon part which you wish to buy. The following figure shows the block diagram of AMD APU architecture:

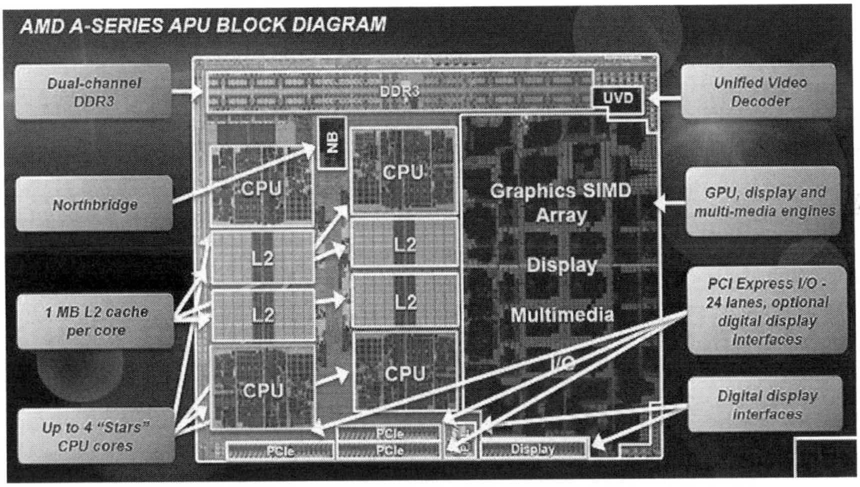

AMD architecture diagram—© 2011, Advanced Micro Devices, Inc.

An AMD GPU consist of a number of **Compute Engines (CU)** and each CU has 16 ALUs. Further, each ALU is a VLIW4 SIMD processor and it could execute a bundle of four or five independent instructions. Each CU could be issued a group of 64 work items which form the work group (wavefront). AMD Radeon ™ HD 6XXX graphics processors uses this design. The following figure shows the HD 6XXX series Compute unit, which has 16 SIMD engines, each of which has four processing elements:

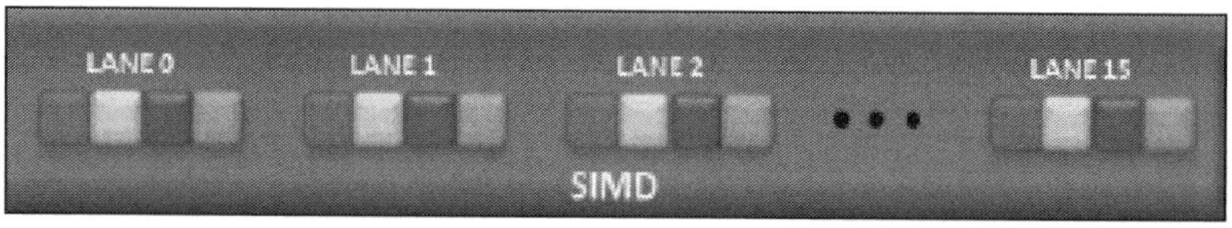

AMD Radeon HD 6xxx Series SIMD Engine – © 2011, Advanced Micro Devices, Inc.

Starting with the AMD Radeon HD 7XXX series of graphics processors from AMD, there were significant architectural changes. AMD introduced the new **Graphics Core Next (GCN) architecture**. The following figure shows an GCN compute unit which has 4 SIMD engines and each engine is 16 lanes wide:

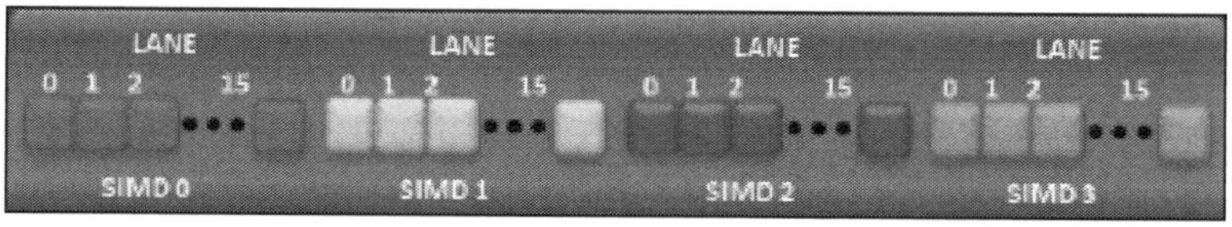

GCN Compute Unit – © 2011, Advanced Micro Devices, Inc.

A group of these Compute Units forms an AMD HD 7xxx Graphics Processor. In GCN, each CU includes four separate SIMD units for vector processing. Each of these SIMD units simultaneously execute a single operation across 16 work items, but each can be working on a separate wavefront.

Apart from the APUs, AMD also provides discrete graphics cards. The latest family of graphics card, HD 7XXX, and beyond uses the GCN architecture. We will discuss one of the discrete GPU architectures in the following chapter, where we will discuss the OpenCL Platform model. AMD also provides the OpenCL runtimes for their CPU devices.

NVIDIA®

One of NVIDIA GPU architectures is codenamed "Kepler". GeForce® GTX 680 is one Kepler architectural silicon part. Each Kepler GPU consists of different configurations of **Graphics Processing Clusters (GPC)** and streaming multiprocessors. The GTX 680 consists of four GPCs and eight SMXs as shown in the following figure:

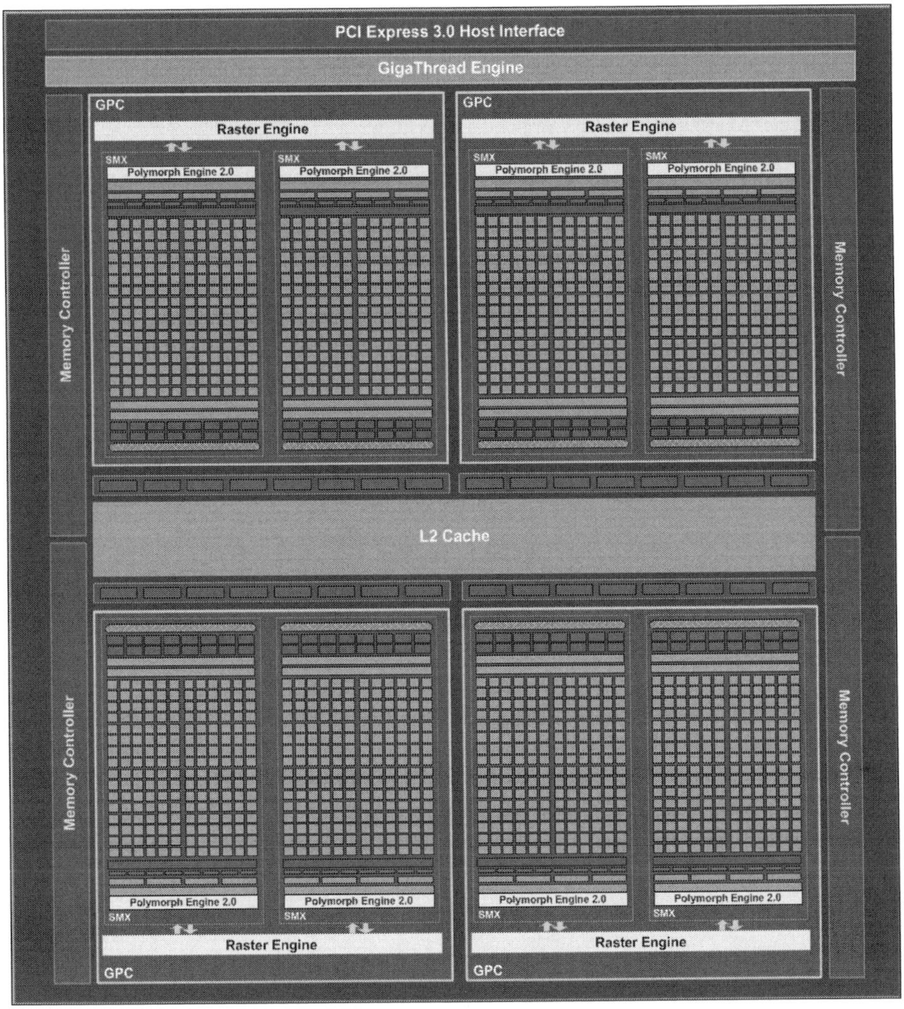

NVIDIA Kepler architecture—GTX 680, © NVIDIA®

Kepler architecture is part of the GTX 6XX and GTX 7XX family of NVIDIA discrete cards. Prior to Kepler, NVIDIA had Fermi architecture which was part of the GTX 5XX family of discrete and mobile graphic processing units.

Intel®

Intel's OpenCL implementation is supported in the Sandy Bridge and Ivy Bridge processor families. Sandy Bridge family architecture is also synonymous with the AMD's APU. These processor architectures also integrated a GPU into the same silicon as the CPU by Intel. Intel changed the design of the L3 cache, and allowed the graphic cores to get access to the L3, which is also called as the last level cache. It is because of this L3 sharing that the graphics performance is good in Intel. Each of the CPUs including the graphics execution unit is connected via Ring Bus. Also each execution unit is a true parallel scalar processor. Sandy Bridge provides the graphics engine HD 2000, with six **Execution Units (EU)**, and HD 3000 (12 EU), and Ivy Bridge provides HD 2500(six EU) and HD 4000 (16 EU). The following figure shows the Sandy bridge architecture with a ring bus, which acts as an interconnect between the cores and the HD graphics:

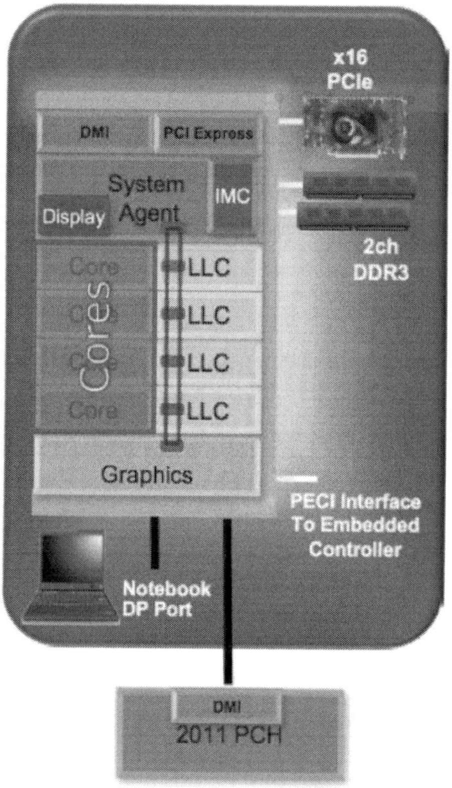

Intel Sandy Bridge architecture – © Intel®

ARM Mali™ GPUs

ARM also provides GPUs by the name of Mali Graphics processors. The Mali T6XX series of processors come with two, four, or eight graphics cores. These graphic engines deliver graphics compute capability to entry level smartphones, tablets, and Smart TVs. The below diagram shows the Mali T628 graphics processor.

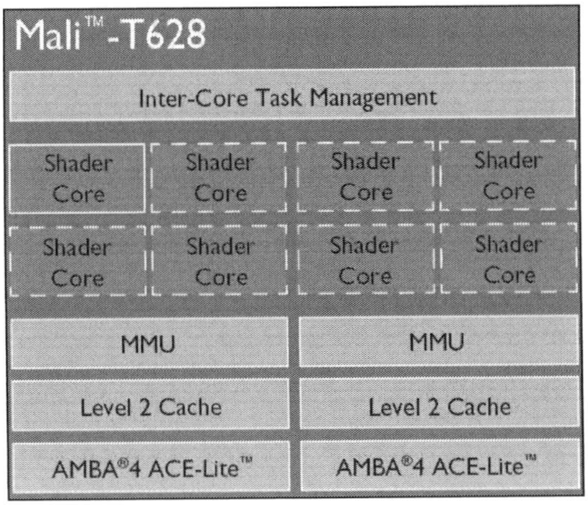

ARM Mali—T628 graphics processor, © ARM

Mali T628 has eight shader cores or graphic cores. These cores also support Renderscripts APIs besides supporting OpenCL.

Besides the four key competitors, companies such as TI (DSP), Altera (FPGA), and Oracle are providing OpenCL implementations for their respective hardware. We suggest you to get hold of the benchmark performance numbers of the different processor architectures we discussed, and try to compare the performance numbers of each of them. This is an important first step towards comparing different architectures, and in the future you might want to select a particular OpenCL platform based on your application workload.

OpenCL components

Before delving into the programming aspects in OpenCL, we will take a look at the different components in an OpenCL framework. The first thing is the OpenCL specification. The OpenCL specification describes the OpenCL programming architecture details, and a set of APIs to perform specific tasks, which are all required by an application developer. This specification is provided by the Khronos OpenCL consortium. Besides this, Khronos also provides OpenCL header files. They are `cl.h`, `cl_gl.h`, `cl_platform.h`, and so on.

An application programmer uses these header files to develop his application and the host compiler links with the `OpenCL.lib` library on Windows. This library contains the entry points for the runtime DLL `OpenCL.dll`. On Linux the application program is linked dynamically with the `libOpenCL.so` shared library. The source code for the `OpenCL.lib` file is also provided by Khronos. The different OpenCL vendors shall redistribute this `OpenCL.lib` file and package it along with their OpenCL development SDK. Now the application is ready to be deployed on different platforms.

The different components in OpenCL are shown in the following figure:

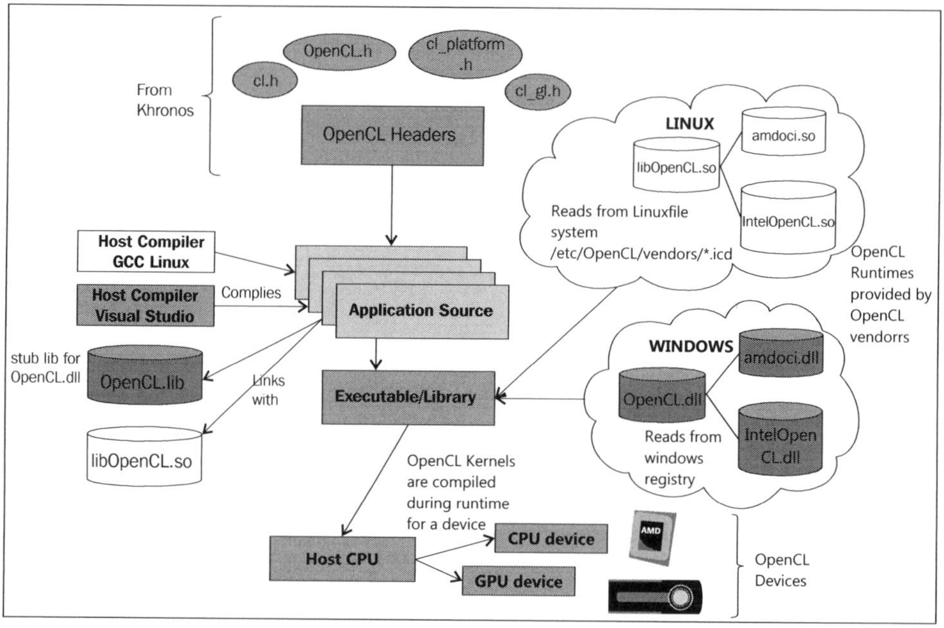

Different components in OpenCL

On Windows, at runtime the application first loads the `OpenCL.dll` dynamic link library which in turn, based on the platform selected, loads the appropriate OpenCL runtime driver by reading the Windows registry entry for the selected platform (either of `amdocl.dll` or any other vendor OpenCL runtimes). On Linux, at runtime the application loads the `libOpenCL.so` shared library, which in turn reads the file `/etc/OpenCL/vendors/*.icd` and loads the library for the selected platform. There may be multiple runtime drivers installed, but it is the responsibility of the application developers to choose one of them, or if there are multiple devices in the platforms, he may want to choose all the available platforms. During runtime calls to OpenCL, functions queue parallel tasks on OpenCL capable devices. We will discuss more on OpenCL Runtimes in *Chapter 5, OpenCL Program and Kernel Objects*.

An example of OpenCL program

In this section we will discuss all the necessary steps to run an OpenCL application.

Basic software requirements

A person involved in OpenCL programming should be very proficient in C programming, and having prior experience in any parallel programming tool will be an added advantage. He or she should be able to break a large problem and find out the data and task parallel regions of the code which he or she is trying to accelerate using OpenCL. An OpenCL programmer should know the underlying architecture for which he/she is trying to program. If you are porting an existing parallel code into OpenCL, then you just need to start learning the OpenCL programming architecture.

Besides this a programmer should also have the basic system software details, such as compiling the code and linking it to an appropriate 32 bit or 64 bit library. He should also have knowledge of setting the system path on Windows to the correct DLLs or set the `LD_LIBRARY_PATH` environment variable in Linux to the correct shared libraries.

The common system requirements for Windows and Linux operating systems are as follows:

Windows

- You should have administrative privileges on the system
- Microsoft Windows XP, Vista, or 7
- Microsoft Visual Studio 2005, 2008, or 2010
- Display Drivers for AMD and NVIDIA GPUs. For NVIDIA GPUs you will need display drivers R295 or R300 and above

Linux

- You should have root permissions to install the SDK
- With the vast number of flavors of Linux, practically any supported version which has the corresponding graphic device driver installed for the GPU

The GCC compiler tool chain

Installing and setting up an OpenCL compliant computer

To install OpenCL you need to download an implementation of OpenCL. We discussed about the various hardware and software vendors in a previous section. The major graphic vendors, NVIDIA and AMD have both released implementations of OpenCL for their GPUs. Similarly AMD and Intel provide a CPU-only runtime for OpenCL. OpenCL implementations are available in so-called **Software Development Kits (SDK)**, and often include some useful tools such as debuggers and profilers. The next step is to download and install the SDK for the GPU you have on your computer. Note that not all graphic cards are supported.
A list of which graphics cards are supported can be found in the respective vendor specific websites. Also you can take a look at the Khronos OpenCL conformance products list. If you don't have a graphics card, don't worry, you can use your existing processor to run OpenCL samples on CPU as a device.

If you are still confused about which device to choose, then take a look at the list of supported devices provided with each release of an OpenCL SDK from different vendors.

Installation steps

- For NVIDIA installation steps, we suggest you to take a look at the latest installation steps for the CUDA software. First install the GPU computing SDK provided for the OS. The following link provides the installation steps for NVIDIA platforms:

  `http://developer.download.nvidia.com/compute/cuda/3_2_prod/sdk/docs/OpenCL_Release_Notes.txt`

- For AMD **Accelerated Parallel Processing** (**APP**) SDK installation take a look at the AMD APP SDK latest version installation guide. The AMD APP SDK comes with a huge set of sample programs which can be used for running. The following link is where you will find the latest APP SDK installation notes:

  `http://developer.amd.com/download/AMD_APP_SDK_Installation_Notes.pdf`

- For INTEL SDK for OpenCL applications 2013, use the steps provided in the following link:

  `http://software.intel.com/en-us/articles/intel-sdk-for-opencl-applications-2013-release-notes`

Note these links are subject to change over a period of time.

AMD's OpenCL implementation is OpenCL 1.2 conformant. Also download the latest AMD APP SDK version 2.8 or above.

For NVIDIA GPU computing, make sure you have a CUDA enabled GPU. Download the latest CUDA release 4.2 or above, and the GPU computing SDK release 4.2 or above.

For Intel, download the Intel SDK for OpenCL Applications 2013.

We will briefly discuss the installation steps. The installation steps may vary from vendor to vendor. Hence we discuss only AMD's and NVIDIA's installation steps. Note that NVIDIA's CUDA only supports GPU as the device. So we suggest that if you have a non NVIDIA GPU then it would be better that you install AMD APP SDK, as it supports both the AMD GPUs and CPUs as the device. One can have multiple vendor SDKs also installed. This is possible as the OpenCL specification allows runtime selection of the OpenCL platform. This is referred to as the **ICD (Installable Client Driver)** dispatch mechanism. We will discuss more about this in a later chapter.

Installing OpenCL on a Linux system with an AMD graphics card

1. Make sure you have root privileges and remove all previous installations of APP SDK.
2. Untar the downloaded SDK.
3. Run the Install Script `Install-AMD-APP.sh`.
4. This will install the developer binary, and samples in folder `/opt/AMPAPP/`.
5. Make sure the variables `AMDAPPSDKROOT` and `LD_LIBRARY_PATH` are set to the locations where you have installed the APP SDK.

For latest details you can refer to the Installation Notes provided with the APP SDK. Linux distributions such as Ubuntu, provide an OpenCL distribution package for vendors such as AMD and NVIDIA. You can use the following command to install the OpenCL runtimes for AMD:

```
sudo apt-get install amd-opencl-dev
```

For NVIDIA you can use the following command:

```
sudo apt-get install nvidia-opencl-dev
```

Note that `amd-opencl-dev` installs both the CPU and GPU OpenCL implementations.

Installing OpenCL on a Linux system with an NVIDIA graphics card

1. Delete any previous installations of CUDA.
2. Make sure you have the CUDA supported version of Linux, and run `lspci` to check the video adapter which the system uses. Download and install the corresponding display driver.
3. Install the CUDA toolkit which contains the tools needed to compile and build a CUDA application.
4. Install the GPU computing SDK. This includes sample projects and other resources for constructing CUDA programs.

You system is now ready to compile and run any OpenCL code.

Installing OpenCL on a Windows system with an AMD graphics card

1. Download the AMD APP SDK v2.7 and start installation.
2. Follow the onscreen prompts and perform an express installation.
3. This installs the AMD APP samples, runtime, and tools such as the APP Profiler and APP Kernel Analyser.
4. The express installation sets up the environment variables `AMDAPPSDKROOT` and `AMDAPPSDKSAMPLESROOT`.
5. If you select custom install then you will need to set the environment variables to the appropriate path.

Go to the `samples` directory and build the OpenCL samples, using the Microsoft Visual Studio.

Installing OpenCL on a Windows system with an NVIDIA graphics card

1. Uninstall any previous versions of the CUDA installation.
2. CUDA 4.2 or above release toolkit requires version R295, R300, or newer of the Windows Vista or Windows XP NVIDIA display driver.
3. Make sure you install the display driver and then proceed to the installation.
4. Install the Version 4.2 release of the NVIDIA CUDA toolkit `cudatoolkit_4.2_Win_[32|64].exe`.

5. Install the Version 4.2 release of the NVIDIA GPU computing SDK by running `gpucomputingsdk_4.2_Win_[32|64].exe`.

Verify the installation by compiling and running some sample codes.

Apple OSX

Apple also provides an OpenCL implementation. You will need XCode developer tool to be installed. Xcode is a complete tool set for building OSX and iOS applications. For more information on building OpenCL application on OSX visit at the following link:

`https://developer.apple.com/library/mac/documentation/Performance/Conceptual/OpenCL_MacProgGuide/Introduction/Introduction.html`

Multiple installations

As we have stated earlier, there can be multiple installations of OpenCL in a system. This is possible in OpenCL standard, because all OpenCL applications are linked using a common library called the OpenCL ICD library. Each OpenCL vendor, ships this library and the corresponding `OpenCL.dll` or `libOpenCL.so` library in its SDK. This library contains the mechanism to select the appropriate vendor-specific runtimes during runtime. The application developer makes this selection. Let's explain this with an example installation of an AMD and Intel OpenCL SDK. In the following screenshot of the Windows Registry Editor you can see two runtime DLLs. It is one of these libraries which is loaded by the `OpenCL.dll` library, based on the application developers selection. The following shows the Regedit entry with AMD and Intel OpenCL installations:

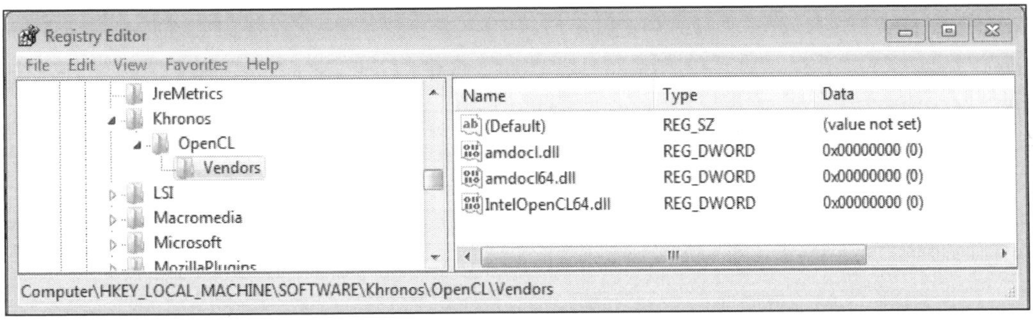

Registry Editor screenshot, showing multiple installations

During runtime, the `OpenCL.dll` library will read the registry details specific to `HKEY_LOCAL_MACHINE\SOFTWARE\Khronos` (or `libOpenCL.so` in Linux, will read the value of the vendor-specific library in the ICD file in folder `/etc/OpenCL/vendors/*.icd`), loads the appropriate library, and assigns the function pointers to the loaded library. An application developer can consider `OpenCL.dll` or `libOpenCL.so` as the wrapper around different OpenCL vendor libraries. This makes the application developers life easy and he can link it with `OpenCL.lib` or `libOpenCL.so` during link time, and distribute it with his application. This allows the application developer to ship his code for different OpenCL vendors/implementations easily.

Implement the SAXPY routine in OpenCL

SAXPY can be called the "Hello World" of OpenCL. In the simplest terms, the first OpenCL sample shall compute `A = alpha*B + C`, where `alpha` is a constant and `A`, `B`, and `C` are vectors of an arbitrary size `n`. In linear algebra terms, this operation is called **SAXPY (Single precision real Alpha X plus Y)**. You might have understood by now, that each multiplication and addition operation is independent of the other. So this is a data parallel problem.

A simple C program would look something like the following code:

```
void saxpy(int n, float a, float *b, float *c)
{
  for (int i = 0; i < n; ++i)
    y[i] = a*x[i] + y[i];
}
```

OpenCL code

An OpenCL code consists of the host code and the device code. The OpenCL kernel code is highlighted in the following code. This is the code which is compiled at run time and runs on the selected device. The following sample code computes `A = alpha*B + C`, where `A`, `B`, and `C` are vectors (arrays) of size given by the `VECTOR_SIZE` variable:

```
#include <stdio.h>
#include <stdlib.h>
#ifdef __APPLE__
#include <OpenCL/cl.h>
#else
#include <CL/cl.h>
#endif
#define VECTOR_SIZE 1024
```

```
//OpenCL kernel which is run for every work item created.
const char *saxpy_kernel =
"__kernel                                    \n"
"void saxpy_kernel(float alpha,     \n"
"                   __global float *A,      \n"
"                   __global float *B,      \n"
"                   __global float *C)      \n"
"{                                           \n"
"    //Get the index of the work-item       \n"
"    int index = get_global_id(0);          \n"
"    C[index] = alpha* A[index] + B[index]; \n"
"}                                           \n";

int main(void) {
  int i;
  // Allocate space for vectors A, B and C
  float alpha = 2.0;
  float *A = (float*)malloc(sizeof(float)*VECTOR_SIZE);
  float *B = (float*)malloc(sizeof(float)*VECTOR_SIZE);
  float *C = (float*)malloc(sizeof(float)*VECTOR_SIZE);
  for(i = 0; i < VECTOR_SIZE; i++)
  {
    A[i] = i;
    B[i] = VECTOR_SIZE - i;
    C[i] = 0;
  }

  // Get platform and device information
  cl_platform_id * platforms = NULL;
  cl_uint     num_platforms;
  //Set up the Platform
  cl_int clStatus = clGetPlatformIDs(0, NULL, &num_platforms);
  platforms = (cl_platform_id *)
  malloc(sizeof(cl_platform_id)*num_platforms);
  clStatus = clGetPlatformIDs(num_platforms, platforms, NULL);

  //Get the devices list and choose the device you want to run on
  cl_device_id     *device_list = NULL;
  cl_uint           num_devices;

  clStatus = clGetDeviceIDs( platforms[0], CL_DEVICE_TYPE_GPU, 0,
    NULL, &num_devices);
  device_list = (cl_device_id *)
  malloc(sizeof(cl_device_id)*num_devices);
```

```
clStatus = clGetDeviceIDs( platforms[0],
  CL_DEVICE_TYPE_GPU, num_devices, device_list, NULL);

// Create one OpenCL context for each device in the platform
cl_context context;
context = clCreateContext( NULL, num_devices, device_list,
  NULL, NULL, &clStatus);

// Create a command queue
cl_command_queue command_queue = clCreateCommandQueue(
  context, device_list[0], 0, &clStatus);

// Create memory buffers on the device for each vector
cl_mem A_clmem = clCreateBuffer(context, CL_MEM_READ_ONLY,
  VECTOR_SIZE * sizeof(float), NULL, &clStatus);
cl_mem B_clmem = clCreateBuffer(context, CL_MEM_READ_ONLY,
  VECTOR_SIZE * sizeof(float), NULL, &clStatus);
cl_mem C_clmem = clCreateBuffer(context, CL_MEM_WRITE_ONLY,
  VECTOR_SIZE * sizeof(float), NULL, &clStatus);

// Copy the Buffer A and B to the device
clStatus = clEnqueueWriteBuffer(command_queue, A_clmem,
  CL_TRUE, 0, VECTOR_SIZE * sizeof(float),
  A, 0, NULL, NULL);
clStatus = clEnqueueWriteBuffer(command_queue, B_clmem,
  CL_TRUE, 0, VECTOR_SIZE * sizeof(float),
  B, 0, NULL, NULL);

// Create a program from the kernel source
cl_program program = clCreateProgramWithSource(context, 1,
  (const char **)&saxpy_kernel, NULL, &clStatus);

// Build the program
clStatus = clBuildProgram(program, 1, device_list, NULL,
  NULL, NULL);

// Create the OpenCL kernel
cl_kernel kernel = clCreateKernel(program, "saxpy_kernel",
  &clStatus);

// Set the arguments of the kernel
clStatus = clSetKernelArg(kernel, 0, sizeof(float),
  (void *)&alpha);
clStatus = clSetKernelArg(kernel, 1, sizeof(cl_mem),
  (void *)&A_clmem);
clStatus = clSetKernelArg(kernel, 2, sizeof(cl_mem),
  (void *)&B_clmem);
```

```
    clStatus = clSetKernelArg(kernel, 3, sizeof(cl_mem),
      (void *)&C_clmem);

    // Execute the OpenCL kernel on the list
    size_t global_size = VECTOR_SIZE; // Process the entire lists
    size_t local_size = 64;           // Process one item at a time
    clStatus = clEnqueueNDRangeKernel(command_queue, kernel, 1,
      NULL, &global_size, &local_size, 0, NULL, NULL);

    // Read the cl memory C_clmem on device to the host variable C
    clStatus = clEnqueueReadBuffer(command_queue, C_clmem,
      CL_TRUE, 0, VECTOR_SIZE * sizeof(float), C, 0, NULL, NULL);

    // Clean up and wait for all the comands to complete.
    clStatus = clFlush(command_queue);
    clStatus = clFinish(command_queue);

    // Display the result to the screen
    for(i = 0; i < VECTOR_SIZE; i++)
      printf("%f * %f + %f = %f\n", alpha, A[i], B[i], C[i]);

    // Finally release all OpenCL allocated objects and
      host buffers.
    clStatus = clReleaseKernel(kernel);
    clStatus = clReleaseProgram(program);
    clStatus = clReleaseMemObject(A_clmem);
    clStatus = clReleaseMemObject(B_clmem);
    clStatus = clReleaseMemObject(C_clmem);
    clStatus = clReleaseCommandQueue(command_queue);
    clStatus = clReleaseContext(context);
    free(A);
    free(B);
    free(C);
    free(platforms);
    free(device_list);
    return 0;
}
```

Downloading the example code

You can download the example code files for all Packt books you have purchased from your account at `http://www.PacktPub.com`. If you have purchased this book elsewhere, you can visit `http://www.PacktPub.com/support` and register to have the files e-mailed directly to you.

The preceding code can be compiled on command prompt using the following command:

Linux:

```
gcc -I $(AMDAPPSDKROOT)/include -L $(AMDAPPSDKROOT)/lib -lOpenCL saxpy.
cpp -o saxpy
./saxpy
```

Windows:

```
cl /c saxpy.cpp /I"%AMDAPPSDKROOT%\include"
link  /OUT:"saxpy.exe" "%AMDAPPSDKROOT%\lib\x86_64\OpenCL.lib"
  saxpy.obj
saxpy.exe
```

If everything is successful, then you will be able to see the result of *SAXPY* being printed in the terminal. For more ease in compiling the code for different OS platforms and different OpenCL vendors, we distribute the examples in this book with a CMAKE build script. Refer to the documentation of building the samples using the CMAKE build uitility.

By now you should be able to install an OpenCL implementation which your hardware supports. You can now compile and run any OpenCL sample code, on any OpenCL compliant device. You also learned the various parallel programming models and solved a data parallel problem of *SAXPY* computation.

Next you can try out some exercises on the existing code. Modify the existing program to take different matrix size inputs. Try to use a 2D matrix and perform a similar computation on the matrix.

OpenCL program flow

Every OpenCL code consists of the host-side code and the device code. The host code coordinates and queues the data transfer and kernel execution commands. The device code executes the kernel code in an array of threads called NDRange. An OpenCL C host code does the following steps:

1. Allocates memory for host buffers and initializes them.
2. Gets platform and device information. This is discussed in detail in *Chapter 2, OpenCL Architecture*.
3. Sets up the platform.
4. Gets the devices list and chooses the type of device you want to run on.

5. Creates an OpenCL context for the device.
6. Creates a command queue.
7. Creates memory buffers on the device for each vector.
8. Copies the Buffer A and B to the device.
9. Creates a program from the kernel source.
10. Builds the program and creates the OpenCL kernel.
11. Sets the arguments of the kernel.
12. Executes the OpenCL kernel on the device.
13. Reads back the memory from the device to the host buffer. This step is optional, you may want to keep the data resident in the device for further processing.
14. Cleans up and waits for all the commands to complete.
15. Finally releases all OpenCL allocated objects and host buffers.

We will discuss the details of each step in the subsequent chapters. Platform and device selection, along with context and command queue creation will be discussed in *Chapter 2, OpenCL Architecture*. OpenCL buffers are integral parts of any OpenCL program. The creation of these buffers and transferring (copying) buffer data between the host and the device is discussed in *Chapter 3, Buffers and Image Objects – Image Processing*. Creating an OpenCL kernel object from an OpenCL program object, and setting the kernel arguments is discussed in *Chapter 5, OpenCL Program and Kernel Objects*.

Run on a different device

To make OpenCL run the kernel on the CPU, you can change the enum `CL_DEVICE_TYPE_GPU` to `CL_DEVICE_TYPE_CPU` in the call to `clGetDeviceIDs`. This shows how easy it is to make an OpenCL program run on different compute devices. The first sample source code is self-explanatory and each of the steps are commented. If you are running a multi GPU hardware system, then you will have to modify the code to use the appropriate device ID.

The OpenCL specification is described in terms of the following four models:

- **Platform model**: This model specifies the host and device specification. The host-side code coordinates the execution of the kernels in the devices.
- **Memory model**: This model specifies the global, local, private, and constant memory. The OpenCL specification describes the hierarchy of memory architecture, regardless of the underlying hardware.

- **Execution model**: This model describes the runtime snapshot of the host and device code. It defines the work-items and how the data maps onto the work-items.
- **Programming model**: The OpenCL programming model supports data parallel and task parallel programming models. This also describes the task synchronization primitives.

We will discuss each model in detail in *Chapter 2, OpenCL Architecture*.

Finally to conclude this chapter, General Purpose GPU Computing (GPGPU or just GPU computing) is undeniably a hot topic in this decade. We've seen diminishing results in CPU speeds in the past decade compared to the decade before that. Each successive manufacturing node presents greater challenges than the preceding one. The shrink in process technology is nearing an end, and we cannot expect exponential improvements in serial program execution. Hence, adding more cores to the CPU is the way to go, and thereby parallel programming. A popular law called Gustafson's law suggests that computations involving large data sets can be efficiently parallelized.

Summary

In this chapter we got a brief overview of what an OpenCL program will look like. We started with a discussion of various parallel programming techniques, and their pros and cons. Different components of an OpenCL application were discussed. Various vendors providing OpenCL capable hardware were also discussed in this chapter. Finally, we ended the chapter with a discussion of a simple OpenCL example, *SAXPY*. In the following few chapters, we will discuss about the different OpenCL objects. We start with a discussion on the OpenCL architecture and various OpenCL models in the following chapter.

References

- http://www.khronos.org/conformance/adopters/conformant-products
- http://www.khronos.org/opencl/resources
- http://gcc.gnu.org/onlinedocs/libgomp.pdf
- http://developer.amd.com/tools/hc/AMDAPPSDK/documentation/Pages/default.aspx
- http://developer.nvidia.com/cuda/nvidia-gpu-computing-documentation
- http://www.amd.com/jp/Documents/GCN_Architecture_whitepaper.pdf
- http://www.geforce.com/Active/en_US/en_US/pdf/GeForce-GTX-680-Whitepaper-FINAL.pdf
- http://en.wikipedia.org/wiki/Amdahl's_law
- http://en.wikipedia.org/wiki/Gustafson's_law

2

OpenCL Architecture

Heterogeneous computing is all about exploiting computing resources in a platform to maximize performance. Many developers have begun to realize that heterogeneous multi-core computer systems can provide significant performance opportunities to a range of applications. OpenCL specification targets expert programmers who want to run their code on various heterogeneous platforms. Unlike NVIDIA® CUDA framework, which is capable of running only on NVIDIA devices, library writers can provide acceleration on any parallel hardware device using OpenCL. Thus OpenCL provides a low-level hardware abstraction and a programming model to support a variety of hardware architectures.

OpenCL describes a hierarchy of models to describe the OpenCL programming framework:

- Platform model
- Memory model
- Execution model
- Programming model

Platform model

In heterogeneous computing, knowledge about the architecture of the targeted device is critical to reap the full benefits of the hardware. We had discussed the hardware architectures from AMD, Intel, and NVIDIA in *Chapter 1, Hello OpenCL*. Though we will briefly discuss about the hardware from different vendors, we suggest you to take a deeper look at the underlying platform on which you will be working. In this section we will describe the OpenCL Platform model and map the AMD, NVIDIA, and Intel hardware architectures to the OpenCL Platform definitions.

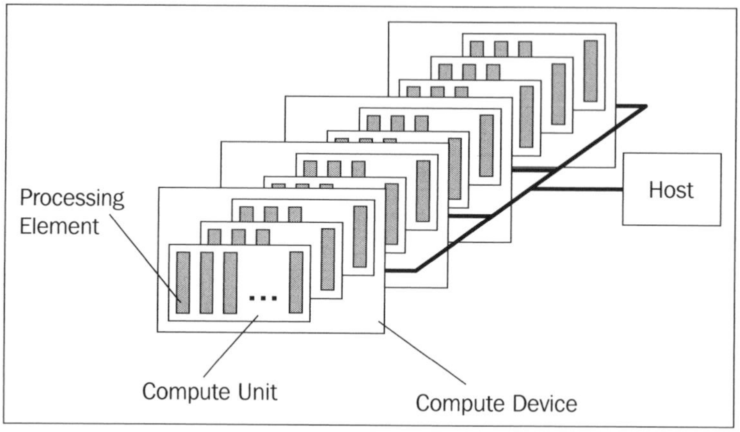

OpenCL platform model, Courtesy Khronos

An OpenCL Platform model consists of a host connected to one or more devices like CPU's, GPU's or hardware accelerators like DSP's. Each OpenCL device consists of one or more compute units, which in turn is further divided into one-to-many processing elements. Computations on a device that is the actual kernel (work item) execution occurs within these processing elements. We just coined the term **work item**. This we will discuss later in this chapter when we discuss about the OpenCL Execution model.

We will now discuss the four different architectures from different device vendors and try to map their architecture to the OpenCL Platform model. In the next diagram we have shown four different OpenCL architectures and their mappings to the Platform models.

AMD A10 5800K APUs

A10 5800K APU has four AMD x86_64 processor cores, which forms the host. Its graphics processor includes as many as six SIMD engines, each with four texture units and sixteen thread processors. There are four ALUs in each thread processor, adding up to 384 total shader cores or processing elements. The following diagram shows the relation of the Trinity APU to the OpenCL Platform model:

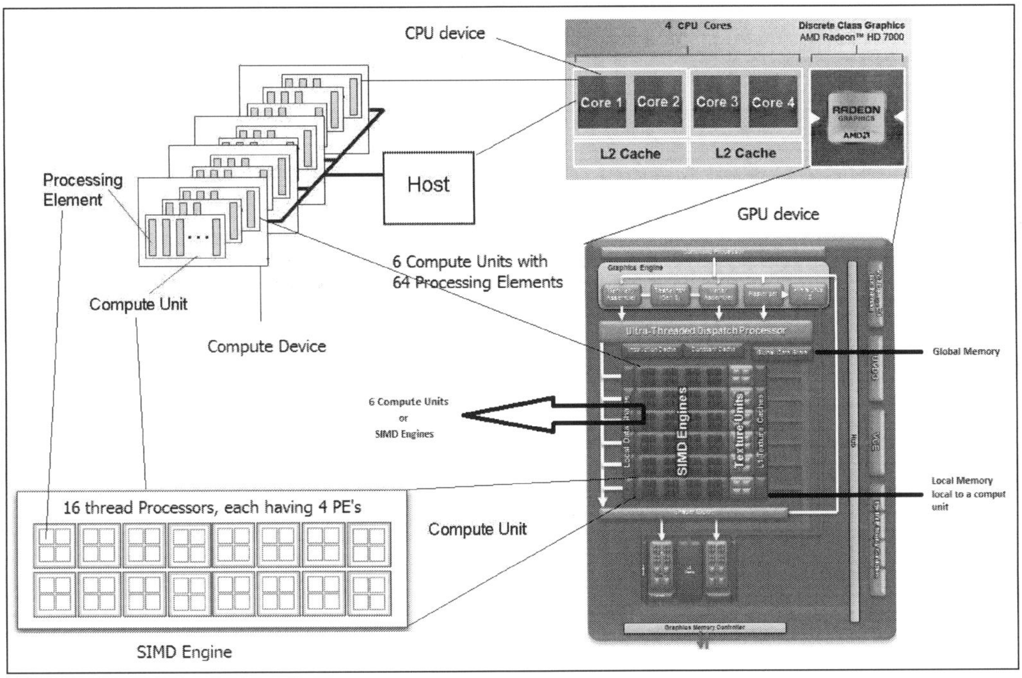

APU Showing the Platform Model and the Graphics Core. Courtesy AMD

This platform has two devices, the CPU device and the GPU device. The x86 CPU device is also the host. The OpenCL Platform model can be mapped as having four compute units and each having one processing element. The graphics processor connected to the host CPU also forms an OpenCL device of type GPU. The six SIMD engines form the six GPU device compute units in the platform. Each of the six compute elements have sixteen thread processors, each having four processing elements. In all there are 384 processing elements or shader cores in this platform for the GPU device.

AMD Radeon™ HD 7870 Graphics Processor

HD 7870 discrete card is a graphics processor based on the AMD GCN architecture. This compute device can be connected to any x86/x86_64 platform. The CPU forms the host and the GPU forms the device in the OpenCL platform. AMD Radeon HD 7870 GPU has a total of twenty compute units. With each compute unit having 64 shader cores a total of 1280 processing elements are there.

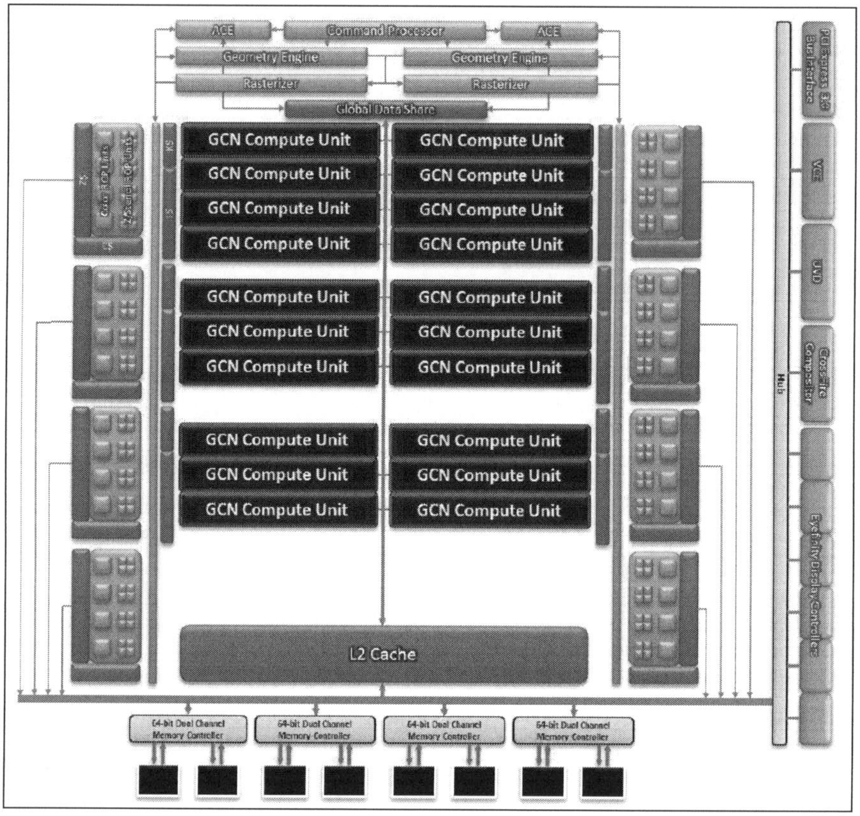

AMD Radeon™ HD 7870 Architecture diagram, © Advanced Micro Devices, Inc.

NVIDIA® GeForce® GTC 680 GPU

The NVIDIA GTX 680 graphics card architecture diagram is shown as follows. There are eight blocks of compute units in this graphics processor. Also referred to as the **Kepler Architecture**, the compute units are called the **Streaming Multiprocessors-X (SMX)**. This SMX compute unit is an advance over previous architectures and has 192 CUDA cores or processing elements. This is shown in the following diagram:

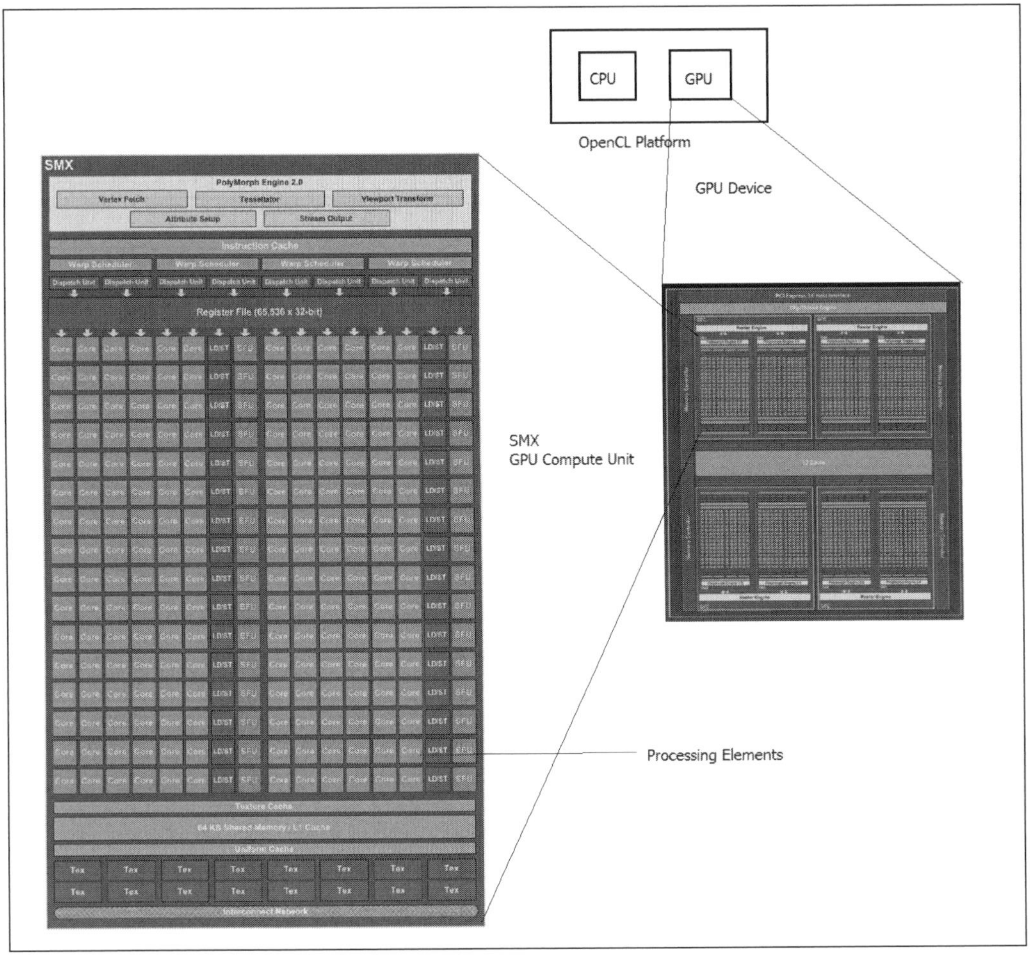

NVIDIA GeForce® GTX 680 Architecture. © NVIDIA

Intel® IVY bridge

The IVY bridge architecture is very similar to the sandy bridge architecture discussed in *Chapter 1, Hello OpenCL*. The CPU device can be mapped as any x86 CPU as discussed in the *AMD A10 5800K APU's* section. In the case of Intel hardware's, the GPU device offers what is called as the **Execution Units (EUs)**. These numbers vary across different SOC solutions provided by Intel. In Intel HD 4000 there are sixteen EUs. These sixteen EUs form the processing elements or sixteen compute unit, that is each execution unit is a compute unit.

For all the preceding OpenCL hardware architectures, which we have discussed till now an OpenCL application consists of a host program that runs according to the models native to the host platform. The host application submits commands to the device to which executes the OpenCL kernels on the processing elements in a compute device. The OpenCL specification describes the functions to create memory objects called buffers and run OpenCL kernels on an OpenCL device. The host queues the thread launch. Before processing the data the host application writes to device, and finally after processing it reads from device. It would be good if the data transfer bandwidth between the host and the device is good enough to hide the data transfer bottleneck with the highly parallel computing power of the device. Some computers may use a shared memory architecture between the host computer (CPU) and the OpenCL device (say a GPU). In such cases the memory transfer bottlenecks may be minimal.

Platform versions

The OpenCL is designed to support devices with different capabilities under a single platform. This includes devices which conform to different versions of the OpenCL specification. While writing an OpenCL based application one needs to query the implementation about the supported version in the platform. There are mainly two different types of version identifiers to consider.

- Platform Version: Indicates the version of the OpenCL runtime supported.
- Device Version: Indicates the device capabilities and attributes. The conformant version info provided cannot be greater than platform version.

Query platforms

Now let's write an OpenCL program to get the platform details. Use the `get_platform_property` example in this chapter.

The OpenCL standard specifies API interfaces to determine the platform configuration. To query the platform versions and details of the OpenCL implementation, the following two APIs are used:

```
cl_int clGetPlatformIDs (cl_uint num_entries,
  cl_platform_id *platforms,
  cl_uint *num_platforms);
cl_int clGetPlatformInfo(cl_platform_id platform,
  cl_platform_info param_name,
  size_t param_value_size,
```

```
    void *param_value,
    size_t *param_value_size_ret);
```

`clGetPlatformIDs` is used to obtain the total number of platforms available in the system. There can be more than one platform. If you install two OpenCL runtimes, one from AMD APP SDK and the other Intel OpenCL runtime for the CPU, you should be able to see two platforms in the system. Usually you don't want to pre-allocate the memory for storing the platforms. Before getting the actual platform, an application developer should query for the number of OpenCL implementations available in the platform. This is done using the following OpenCL call:

```
clError = clGetPlatformIDs(0, NULL, &num_platforms);
```

This call returns the total number of available platforms. Once we have obtained the number of available platforms we can allocate memory and query for the platform IDs for the various OpenCL implementations as follows:

```
platforms = (cl_platform_id *)malloc
                      (num_platforms*sizeof(cl_platform_id));
clError = clGetPlatformIDs (num_platforms, platforms, NULL);
```

Once the list of platforms is obtained, you can query for the platform attributes in a loop for each platform. In the example we have queried the following parameters using the API `clGetPlatformInfo`:

```
CL_PLATFORM_NAME
CL_PLATFORM_VENDOR
CL_PLATFORM_VERSION
CL_PLATFORM_PROFILE
CL_PLATFORM_EXTENSIONS
```

Example:

```
clError = clGetPlatformInfo (platforms[index], CL_PLATFORM_NAME, 1024,
&queryBuffer, NULL);
```

In the `get_device_property` example where we get device properties, we default to the first available platform and query the device property for all the devices in default platform obtained. Take a look at the `get_device_property` example for this chapter.

```
clError = clGetPlatformIDs(1, &platform, &num_platforms);
```

Note the difference in the calls to `clGetPlatformIDs` in the two examples discussed.

In this section we just wrote a small program to print the platform details. Take a look at how we allocate memory for platforms and how we get the details of the platform. As an exercise try to install multiple OpenCL implementations in your platform and see how many OpenCL platforms are enumerated by the function `clGetPlatformIDs`.

Multiple OpenCL implementations can be installed in the platform. You would question how would the application pick the appropriate runtime. The answer is OpenCL **Installable Client Driver (ICD)**. We will study this more in a later section.

Query devices

We shall now continue with getting the attributes and resource limitations of an OpenCL device. In the last program we were able to print all the platform information available. In this example we shall try to enhance the existing code to print some basic device attributes and resource information for the first available platform. We will implement a function `PrintDeviceInfo()`, which will print the device specific information. The following two OpenCL APIs are used in the example:

```
cl_int clGetDeviceIDs (cl_platform_id platform,
  cl_device_type device_type,
  cl_uint num_entries,
  cl_device_id *devices,
  cl_uint *num_devices);
cl_int clGetDeviceInfo (cl_device_id device,
  cl_device_info param_name,
  size_t param_value_size,
  void *param_value,
  size_t *param_value_size_ret);
```

In the same way as we did for platforms, we first determine the number of devices available, and then allocate memory for each device found in the platform.

```
clError = clGetDeviceIDs (platform,
  CL_DEVICE_TYPE_ALL,
  0, NULL, &num_devices);
```

The above call gives the number of available device of `CL_DEVICE_TYPE_ALL`. You can otherwise use `CL_DEVICE_TYPE_CPU` or `CL_DEVICE_TYPE_GPU`, if you want to list the number of available CPU or GPU devices.

To understand better we we have added the `PrintDeviceInfo` function:

```
void PrintDeviceInfo(cl_device_id device)
{
  char queryBuffer[1024];
  int queryInt;
  cl_int clError;
  clError = clGetDeviceInfo(device, CL_DEVICE_NAME,
    sizeof(queryBuffer),
    &queryBuffer, NULL);
  printf("CL_DEVICE_NAME: %s\n", queryBuffer);
  queryBuffer[0] = '\0';
  clError = clGetDeviceInfo(device, CL_DEVICE_VENDOR,
    sizeof(queryBuffer), &queryBuffer,
    NULL);
  printf("CL_DEVICE_VENDOR: %s\n", queryBuffer);
  queryBuffer[0] = '\0';
  clError = clGetDeviceInfo(device, CL_DRIVER_VERSION,
    sizeof(queryBuffer), &queryBuffer,
    NULL);
  printf("CL_DRIVER_VERSION: %s\n", queryBuffer);
  queryBuffer[0] = '\0';
  clError = clGetDeviceInfo(device, CL_DEVICE_VERSION,
    sizeof(queryBuffer), &queryBuffer,
    NULL);
  printf("CL_DEVICE_VERSION: %s\n", queryBuffer);
  queryBuffer[0] = '\0';
  clError = clGetDeviceInfo(device, CL_DEVICE_MAX_COMPUTE_UNITS,
    sizeof(int), &queryInt, NULL);
  printf("CL_DEVICE_MAX_COMPUTE_UNITS: %d\n", queryInt);
}
```

Note that each of the `param_name` associated with `clGetDeviceInfo` returns a different data type. In the routine `PrintDeviceInfo` you can see that the `CL_DEVICE_MAX_COMPUTE_UNITS` `param_name` returns an integer type The `CL_DRIVER_VERSION` `param_name` returns a character buffer.

The preceding function prints the following information about the device:

```
CL_DEVICE_NAME
CL_DEVICE_VENDOR
CL_DRIVER_VERSION
CL_DEVICE_VERSION
CL_DEVICE_MAX_COMPUTE_UNITS
```

Following is the maximum number of compute units for different types of platforms when you query for the GPU type device:

For APU like processors:

```
AMD A10 5800K    - 6
```

AMD trinity has 6 SIMD engines (compute units) and each has 64 processing elements.

```
INTEL HD 4000 - 16
```

Intel HD 4000 has 16 compute units and each is a single thread processor.

For discrete graphics:

```
NVIDIA GTX 680 - 8
```

The NVIDIA GTX 680 has a total of eight Compute units; each compute unit has 192 processing elements.

```
AMD Radeon HD 7870 - 32
```

The AMD Radeon HD 7870 GPU has 32 compute units and each has 64 processing elements.

It is not the case that if you have more compute units in the GPU device type, the faster the processor is. The number of compute units varies across different computer architectures and across different hardware vendors. Sometimes even within the vendors there are different families like the NVIDIA Kepler and Fermi architectures or the AMD Radeon HD 6XXX and Radeon HD 7XXX Architecture. The OpenCL specification is targeted at programming these different kinds of devices from different vendors. As an enhancement to the sample program print all the device related attributes and resource sizes for some of the `param_name` instances listed as follows:

- `CL_DEVICE_TYPE`
- `CL_DEVICE_MAX_CLOCK_FREQUENCY`
- `CL_DEVICE_IMAGE_SUPPORT`
- `CL_DEVICE_SINGLE_FP_CONFIG`

Besides these there are many more device attributes which can be queried. Take a look at the different `param_name` instances provided in the OpenCL specification 1.2, table 4.3. You should try out all the `param_name` instances and try to understand each device property.

Execution model

The two main execution units in OpenCL are the kernels and the host program. The kernels execute on the so called OpenCL device and the host program runs on the host computer. The main purpose of the host program is to create and query the platform and device attributes, define a context for the kernels, build the kernel, and manage the execution of these kernels.

On submission of the kernel by the host to the device, an *N* dimensional index space is created. *N* is at least *1* and not greater than *3*. Each kernel instance is created at each of the coordinates of this index space. This instance is called as the "work item" and the index space is called as the **NDRange**. In the following screenshot we have shown the three scenarios for 1, 2 and 3 dimensional NDRange:

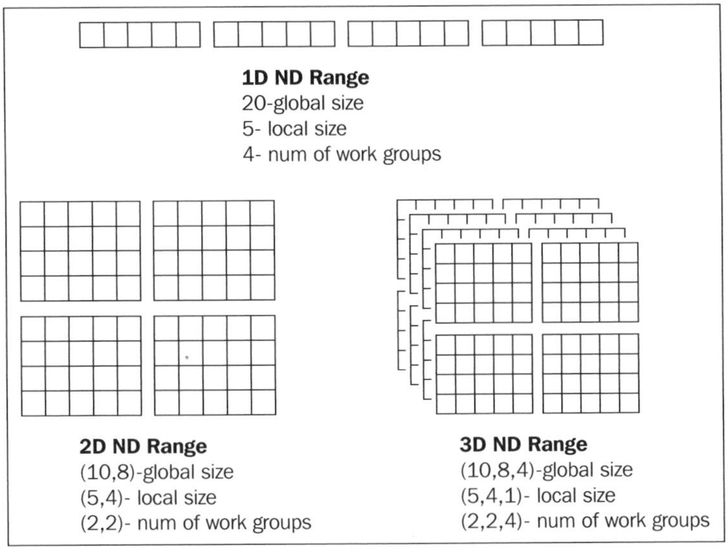

OpenCL NDRange

In the saxpy example which we discussed in the previous chapter, we have taken a global size of *1024* and a local size of *64*. Each work item computes the corresponding:

```
C[local id] = alpha* A[local id] + B[local id];
```

A total of sixteen work groups are spawned. When the `clEnqueueNDRange` function is executed, a 1 Dimensional NDRange is created for the `saxpy_kernel` function. The explanation of `clEnqueueNDRange` function is given in the next section. Since in `saxpy` every data `C[...]` can be calculated independently, all the work items can run in a parallel way. We divide the problem of 1024 element saxpy into work groups, so that a group of contiguous elements can work on a separate OpenCL capable compute unit.

NDRange

An NDRange is the kernel execution index in an N-dimensional index space. The values which *N* can take are *1*, *2*, or *3*. An NDRange value is given by an array of integers of length *N* specifying the index's extent in each dimension. Starting OpenCL 1.2 an offset index value can also be specified for each dimension, which gives the starting offset for an NDRange. If this offset is not specified then its value is *0* by default in each dimension. The extent of a work group is specified by `local_work_size` in the `clEnqueueNDRangeKernel` function below. Global ID and Local ID are *N* tuple values. The `global_work_size` function defines the total number of work items, which can be spawned for the OpenCL kernel. The global ID components are values in the range from offset *X*, to *X* plus the `global_work_size` function in their corresponding dimensions.

A group of work items are organized in OpenCL work groups. Take a look at the following diagram of a 2D NDRange. The work groups provide a coarse-grained decomposition of the index space. Each work group is assigned a unique ID with the same number of dimensions as the global index space used to define the work items. Every work item in a work group is assigned a unique local ID, so that every work item can be uniquely addressed during the kernel execution within a work group scope. Similarly work items are also assigned a unique global ID in the NDRange and can be uniquely addressed during the kernel execution.

Work groups are also assigned work group IDs. This is also an array of *N* integers, where each integer defines the number of work groups in each dimension. The work groups' IDs are assigned in the same manner as it is done for assigning global IDs. See equation 2 later in the section. Every work item has an associated work group ID and a local ID. It's easy to calculate the global ID of the work item, when we are given a work group ID and a local-ID. See equation 1 later in this section. Each work item can be identified in two ways; global index, and work group index plus a local index in each of its respective dimensions.

Let's explain the following with an equation: *N=2 NDRange*:

We will be using the following terms for defining the Execution model:

- `work-item`: It is the individual kernel execution instance
- `work-group`: It is a group of work items form a work group
- `global-id`: A unique global ID given to each work item in the global NDRange
- `local-id`: A unique local ID given to each work item within a work group

Consider a *(12,12)* NDRange as shown in the following figure. Each of the smallest box is a work item. As you can see there are twelve of them in each row and there are twelve such rows.

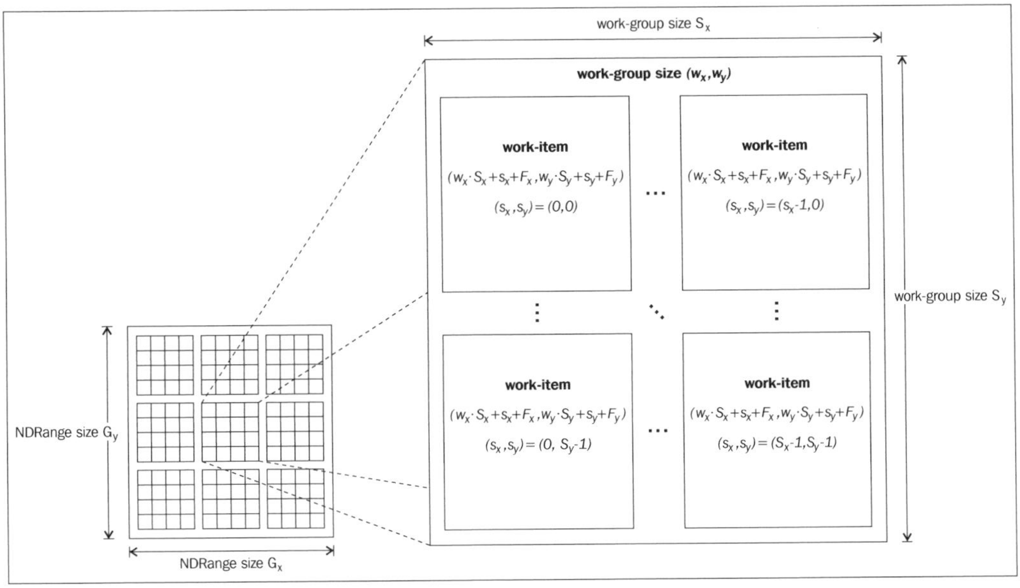

Execution model, Courtesy Khronos

In the preceding diagram the global size is defined by *(12, 12) ~ (Gx, Gy)*. The extent of *Gx* and *Gy* is *0* to *11*. The total number of work items is given by the product of *Gx* and *Gy*, which amounts to a total of 144 work items.

The size of each work group is *(4, 4) ~ (Sx, Sy)*. The extent of *Sx* and *Sy* is *0* to *3*. The total number of work items in a work group is given by the product of *Sx* and *Sy*. In this example there are sixteen work items in the work group.

From the extent of the global work items *(Gx, Gy)* and the extent of the local work items *(Sx, Sy)*, we can compute the number of work groups *(Wx, Wy)* in the NDRange.

Each work item is identified by its global ID `(gx, gy)` or local ID `(sx, sy)`. The work items in a work group belong to a work group ID `(wx, wy)` defined in the following equation 3. Similarly the global ID can be computed using a combination of local ID `(sx, sy)` and work group ID `(wx, wy)`, as shown in the equation:

$$(gx, gy) = (wx * Sx + sx, wy * Sy + sy) \qquad (1)$$

The number of work groups can be computed using the equation:

$$(Wx, Wy) = (Gx / Sx, Gy / Sy) \qquad (2)$$

The work-group ID for a work item is computed the using equation:

$$(wx, wy) = ((gx - sx) / Sx, (gy - sy) / Sy) \qquad (3)$$

Till now we have discussed about the work item, work group, local ID, and global ID. All these values can be determined inside a kernel execution at runtime using the built-in functions, which are listed as follows:

- `get_global_id(int dim);`
- `get_local_id(int dim);`
- `get_num_groups(int dim);`
- `get_group_size(int dim);`
- `get_group_id(int dim);`

The NDRange execution space is defined by the OpenCL API. The associated parameters should all be created in an OpenCL context as follows:

```
cl_int clEnqueueNDRangeKernel(cl_command_queue command_queue,
  cl_kernel          kernel,
  cl_uint            work_dim,
  const size_t     * global_work_offset,
  const size_t     * global_work_size,
  const size_t     * local_work_size,
  cl_uint            num_events_in_wait_list,
  const cl_event   * event_wait_list,
  cl_event         * event)
```

This function enqueue's a command to execute a kernel on the device associated with the `command_queue` function. Of all the OpenCL functions that run on the host, `clEnqueueNDRangeKernel` is the most important to understand. Not only does it deploys kernels to devices, it also specifies how many work items should be generated to execute the kernel (`global_work_size`) and the number of work items in each work group (`local_work_size`). The following list represents certain objects:

- `command_queue`: Every `command_queue` is associated with one device. kernel will be enqueued for execution on this device. The `command_queue` object is created using the `clCreateCommandQueue` function.
- `kernel`: It refers to an OpenCL kernel object. This kernel object would have been created using the OpenCL program object.
- `work_dim`: It specifies the dimension of the NDRange (index space). The value can be *1*, *2* or *3*.
- `global_work_offset`: This is a `size_t` pointer to the `work_dim` elements. If set to `NULL` all the values in each dimension take the default value as `0`. Otherwise this is used to calculate the global ID of a work item.
- `global_work_size`: This is a `size_t` pointer to the `work_dim` elements, which specifies the extent of the global work items in every dimensions.
- `local_work_size`: This is also a `size_t` pointer to the `work_dim` elements and specifies the extent of local work items in every dimension.
- `event_wait_list` and `num_events_in_wait_list`: The `event_wait_list` object contains handles to events, which an OpenCL implementation will wait for before enqueuing this command.
- `event`: Every enqueued command returns an OpenCL event object that is the reference to the command in the queue. Here the kernel's execution handle is returned in the `event` pointer. This `cl_event` object can be used later on for reference to the execution status.

The OpenCL supports two of these execution models; the data parallel programming model and the task parallel programming model. The `clEnqueueNDRangeKernel` function is a kind of data parallel execution model, the task parallel programming model will be discussed in *Chapter 5, OpenCL Program and Kernel Objects*.

We just coined the term "enqueues a command", let's explain what a queue has to do with the OpenCL. Before that, let's discuss the OpenCL context.

OpenCL context

A context defines the entire OpenCL environment, including the devices, the program objects, the OpenCL kernels, memory objects, command queues, and so on. A context can be associated with multiple devices or with only one device. The OpenCL context associated with command queue and the kernel should be the same. They cannot be from different contexts.

Before we can create a context we must first query the OpenCL runtime to determine which vendor platforms are available in the system. After you have selected a vendor platform, the first step is to initialize the OpenCL implementation in order to create a context. The rest of the OpenCL work like creating devices and memory, compiling, and running programs is performed within this context. A context can have a number of associated devices, which can be either of CPU or GPU or both, and, within a context. Contexts in the OpenCL are referenced by a `cl_context` object, which must be initialized using the following OpenCL API:

```
cl_context clCreateContext (const cl_context_properties *properties,
                    cl_uint num_devices,
                    const cl_device_id *devices,
                    void (CL_CALLBACK *pfn_notify)
                           (const char *errinfo,
                            const void *private_info,
                            size_t cb, void *user_data),
                    void *user_data,
                    cl_int *errcode_ret)
```

The following is the list of few contexts of the OpenCL along with its description:

- `properties`: It is a list of name and its corresponding value. The name is the context property name like `CL_CONTEXT_PLATFORM` and this is followed by the property value. An example of the same is as follows:

  ```
  cl_context_properties props[3] =
  {
      CL_CONTEXT_PLATFORM,
      (cl_context_properties)platforms,
      0
  };
  ```

  One can add more property values based on the requirements of the application.

- `num_devices`: It is the number of devices one wants to associate with the context. The devices pointer should have at least `num_devices, cl_device_id` instance
- `devices`: It is a pointer to a `num_devices` list of `cl_device_id` instances, which will be associated with the context.
- `errcode_ret`: The error code returned by the OpenCL implementation associated with a call to this function.
- `pfn_notify`: It is a function pointer to the callback function, which an application can register. The underlying OpenCL implementation will call this function to asynchronously report errors for context creation. If set to `NULL` then no callback function is registered. The prototype of a callback function is as follows:

```
void OpenCL_Context_Callback(const char *errinfo,
  const void *private_info,
  size_t cb, void *user_data);
```

- `user_data`: This is the pointer to the data, which will be passed to the callback function if registered by the application. If no callback function is registered this should be set to `NULL`.

OpenCL command queue

The OpenCL command queue is an object where OpenCL commands are queued to be executed by the device. The command queue is created for every usable OpenCL device for kernel execution. One can have multiple command queues for different tasks in applications. This way an application developer can run tasks independently on different command queues. We will discuss about the various synchronization mechanisms using multiple command queues in *Chapter 6, Events and Synchronization*. The following code snippet creates a command queue and a write (`clEnqueueWriteBuffer`), and NDRange execution of the kernel commands are queued on to the device:

```
cl_command_queue command_queue =
  clCreateCommandQueue(context, device_list[0],
    0, &clStatus);
clStatus = clEnqueueWriteBuffer(command_queue, A_clmem,
                  CL_TRUE, 0,
                    VECTOR_SIZE * sizeof(float), A, 0, NULL, NULL);
clStatus = clEnqueueNDRangeKernel(command_queue, kernel,
                  1, NULL, &global_size,
                    &local_size, 0, NULL, NULL);
```

The host program creates this command queue. The snapshot of the queue anytime shall give you the list of enqueued commands. These commands can be of data transfer, or kernel execution commands or barriers within the command queue. The host enqueues these commands to the command queue. Each command or task is associated with an OpenCL event. These events can be used as a synchronization mechanism to coordinate execution between the host and the device.

There can be multiple queues associated within a context. They can dispatch commands independently and concurrently with no explicit mechanism to synchronize between them.

Queues can be in-order of the execution queues. The commands are dequeued in **first in first out (FIFO)** manner. Hence application can send commands to the queue and be ensured that they execute in order.

Out of order command queues are also supported by the OpenCL. The commands are issued in order, but do not wait for the previous command to complete before the next command executes. We will discuss more about this in *Chapter 5, OpenCL Program and Kernel Objects*.

Memory model

The OpenCL Memory model guarantees a relaxed memory consistency between devices. This means that different work items may see a different view of global memory as the computation progresses. This leads to a bigger challenge for the developers to partition data and splitting computation tasks into different work items. Synchronization is required to ensure data consistency within the work items of a work group. One needs to make sure that the data the work item is accessing is always correct. This makes the application developers task a little complicated to write applications with relaxed consistency, and hence explicit synchronization mechanisms are required.

The x86/x86_64 CPU cache coherent architecture is different from the OpenCL relaxed memory architecture. In cache coherent systems, data that resides in the local processor caches is guaranteed to be consistent across processors. The programmer need not worry about the data partitioning in cache coherent architectures. This results in a lot of memory bandwidth at the back of the cache, and makes the task of an application programmer easier. The OpenCL Memory model scales well across cache coherent memory architectures also. An OpenCL programmer must have knowledge of partitioning the data across his application work load, to achieve the highest performance in massively parallel heterogeneous systems. The standard defines four distinct memory regions. Each region can be accessed by the work items executing a kernel. The following are the different types of memory.

Global memory

Every OpenCL device has an associated global memory. This is the largest size memory subsystem. Memory accesses can be coalesced, to ensure contiguous memory reads and thereby increasing the performance. All the work items in all the work groups can read or write into this memory buffer. This memory can be cached depending on the OpenCL device. Take a look at the following OpenCL kernel prototype:

```
__kernel
void histogram_kernel(__global const uint* data,
  __local uchar* sharedArray,
  __global uint* binResultR,
  __global uint* binResultG,
  __global uint* binResultB)
```

The `__global` or `global` keyword identifies this buffer region. This memory region is device wide and changes made in this region are visible to all the work items in the NDRange.

Constant memory

An OpenCL device has a region of memory called the constant memory, which is initialized by the host. This is similar to creating an OpenCL buffer with `CL_MEM_READ_ONLY` flag. This is the region of memory that remains constant throughout the execution time of the kernel.

Local memory

For high performance every OpenCL device has an associated local memory. This is the memory closest to the OpenCL processing element. Every work item in a work group can use this buffer and is shared amongst them that is if one work item modifies a local memory then the changes are visible across all the work items in a work group. As shown in the diagram the local memory is associated with one OpenCL compute unit. This means that the work items in a work group should all run on one compute unit. The `__local` or `local` keyword identifies this memory region.

Private memory

Memory region or processing element scratch registers are all referred to as the private region. This region of memory is used by the OpenCL device complier to allocate all the local variables in the kernel code. Any modifications done to this memory region are not visible to the other work items. As shown in the following diagram every processing element has a private memory. This is the default memory attribute in an OpenCL kernel:

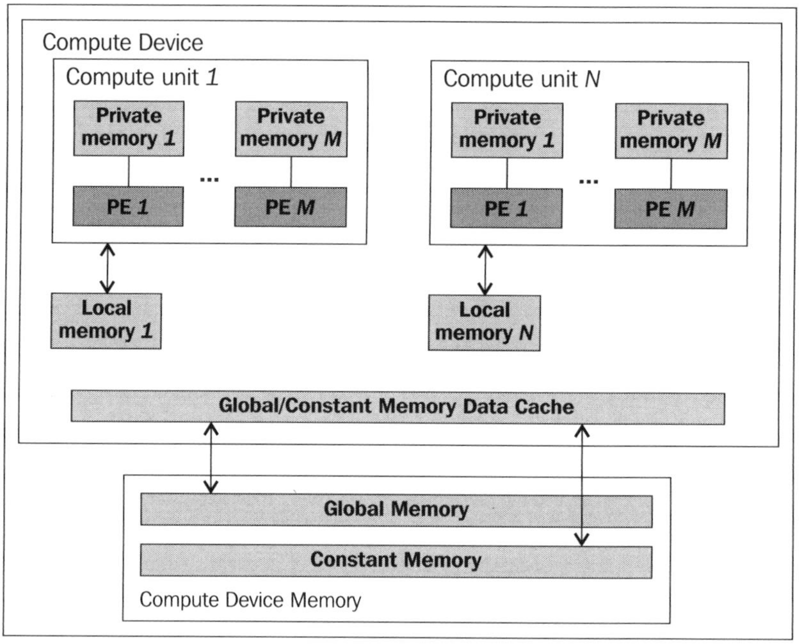

OpenCL Memory Model, Courtesy Khronos

Based on the underlying architecture the work items in a given work group execute concurrently on the processing elements of a single compute unit. This means that one work group is associated with one compute unit of the hardware in OpenCL. This is because most of the hardware architectures have high speed memory local to the compute unit. In the context of OpenCL we refer to private memory as high speed memory.

The private memory can be shared among all the work items in the work group. For example in some graphics architectures, every compute unit has a large private memory say of the size 64 KB. When all the work items in the work group run on the device this 64 KB is shared among all the work items. For example a work group of size *64* work items will allocate 1 KB of private memory for each work item. This makes the application programmer create the OpenCL kernels, which use small number of registers and the hardware scheduler should be able to launch many work items or wave fronts at a time.

OpenCL ICD

The OpenCL function `clGetPlatformIDs` is used to determine the different OpenCL implementations available in the platform. There can be multiple OpenCL implementations installed in the system. Let's define an OpenCL platform.

An OpenCL platform is a host computing machine and a collection of heterogeneous devices managed by OpenCL implementations, which allow an application to share hardware resources and execute kernels on different devices in the platform. Devices from different vendors will have their own OpenCL runtimes in the platform. Let's consider a system with an AMD graphics card and an NVIDIA graphics card. Now an AMD OpenCL implementation is not going to work on NVIDIA OpenCL devices. Remember only the code is portable not the underlying OpenCL runtime. So how does an application solve this problem of using the multiple OpenCL runtimes or use multiple platforms. The answer is OpenCL ICD.

What is an OpenCL ICD?

The OpenCL **Installable Client Driver (ICD)** is a means of allowing multiple OpenCL implementations to co-exist and applications to select between them at runtime. With this it is now the applications responsibility for querying which OpenCL platform is present in the system and which one the application should use, instead of just requesting the default like we did in our first few example wherein we chose the first available platform as default.

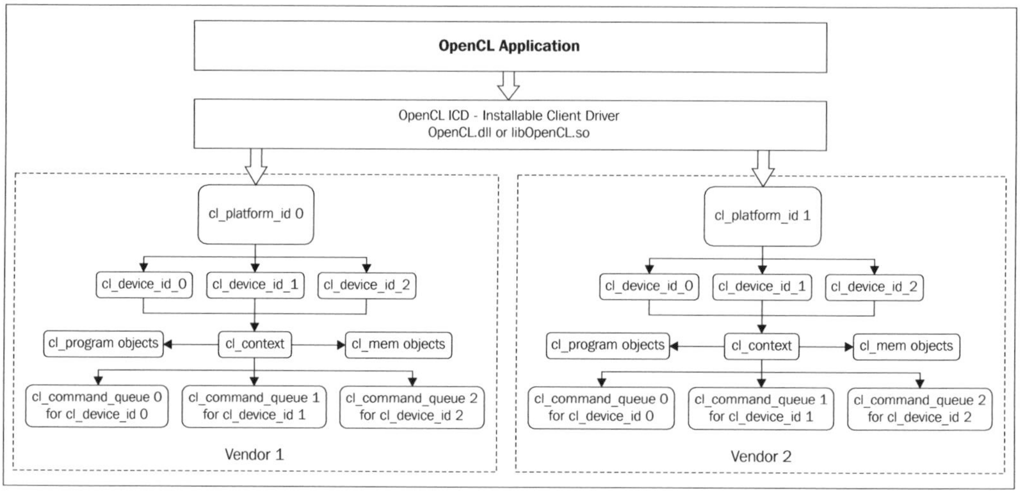

OpenCL ICD and different vendors

In the preceding diagram, an OpenCL application is linked with the OpenCL ICD library. At runtime this ICD shared library (`OpenCL.dll` in windows and `libOpencl.so` in Linux) will query the registry and load the appropriate shared library as selected by the application. An application may want to use both the platforms available. The application developer can create a context for each device in the platform, and appropriately execute his algorithm on the device. It is not possible to pass device buffers between two different OpenCL contexts. It is the host applications responsibility to share, transfer, and synchronize data consumption between two contexts.

Application scaling

A multithreaded program is partitioned into blocks of threads that execute independently from each other, so that a GPU with more cores will automatically execute the program in less time than a GPU with fewer cores. This is important since we can see here two levels of nested data parallelism or data parallelism nested within task parallelism. The upper level parallelism partitions a given problem into blocks of threads. Each block of thread will run on a compute unit, for example, a SIMD engine in the AMD APUs. Beyond this high level parallelism there is lower level parallelism, where a group of threads run cooperatively within the thread block. Each of these threads runs on the processing elements of the compute unit.

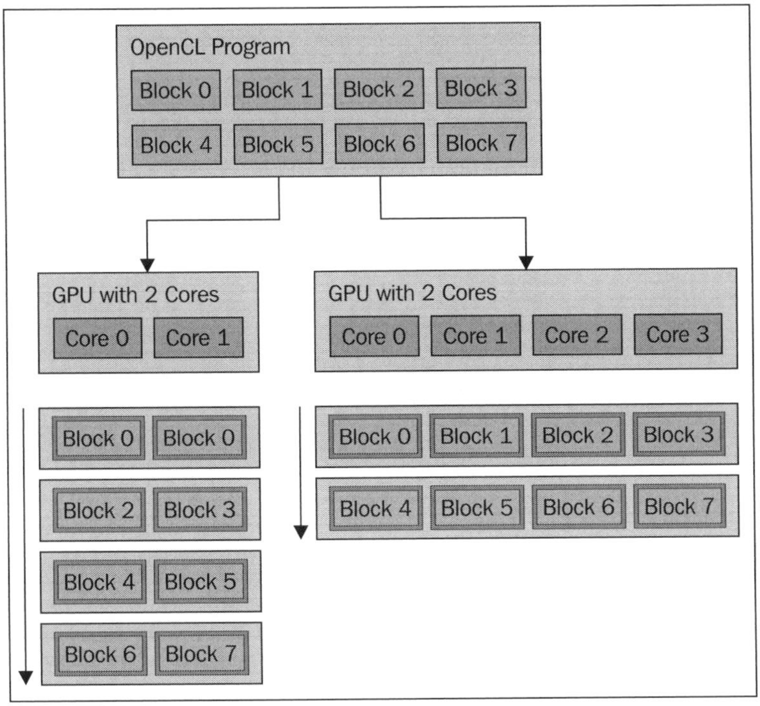

Less cores more time, Courtesy NVIDIA®

Summary

In this chapter we started with the discussion of OpenCL Platform model, and briefly explained the various hardware from different vendors and tried to map the OpenCL terminologies to the devices which we discussed. We also discussed the Execution and Memory model of OpenCL. This chapter forms the foundation for any OpenCL programmer.

Till now we discussed about the OpenCL architecture and the OpenCL ecosystem in general. From here on we will study the OpenCL objects such as, buffers, images, programs, kernels, and so on in detail. In the next chapter we will start our discussion about the OpenCL buffers, and the mechanisms of data transfer between the host and the OpenCL devices.

3

OpenCL Buffer Objects

In the previous chapter we discussed about the OpenCL Architectural models, and also understood the device context and command queue creation. This forms the first step towards the OpenCL language programming. In *Chapter 1, Hello OpenCL*, we implemented a simple `saxpy` OpenCL example, which created memory objects (buffers in this case) and the kernel performed the `saxpy` operation on these buffers. These memory objects were created and transferred to and from the device's memory. Computations were performed on these memory objects by every instance of the kernel execution created in the NDRange. OpenCL memory objects form the most fundamental architectural unit in the OpenCL programming.

In this chapter we will study the OpenCL buffer memory object and the functions and characteristics related to these buffer objects. This is referred to as the `cl_mem` object for contiguous memory locations. We will discuss the following in this chapter:

- Create buffer objects
- Create subbuffer objects
- Use these buffer objects to compute the image histogram
- Transferring the buffer data to and from the device
- Mapping and querying the buffer objects

Besides this there is another form of OpenCL `cl_mem` object called the image buffer. The image buffer represents the various raw formats of an image. We will discuss the image objects in the next chapter.

Memory objects

Memory objects are encapsulated by `cl_mem` data structure. The two important functions to create a memory object are as follows:

```
cl_mem clCreateBuffer (cl_context context,
  cl_mem_flags flags,
    size_t size,
      void *host_ptr,
        cl_int *errcode_ret)
cl_mem clCreateImage (cl_context context,
  cl_mem_flags flags,
    const cl_image_format *image_format,
      const cl_image_desc *image_desc,
        void *host_ptr,
          cl_int *errcode_ret)
```

Note that both the buffer and image data objects are of type `cl_mem` and these objects form the most important basic component in OpenCL. Both these functions return the `cl_mem` objects and the type of memory is specified by the flags variable of type `cl_mem_flags`. For comparison purpose the `clCreateImage` function is shown here. More details of this will be discussed in the next chapter. The possible values for the `cl_mem_flags` flags are shown in the following table:

cl_mem_flags	Description
`CL_MEM_READ_WRITE`	The buffer is created in the device global memory and can be read and written by the kernel.
`CL_MEM_WRITE_ONLY`	The buffer is created in the device global memory and will be written by the compiler.
`CL_MEM_READ_ONLY`	The buffer created with this memory attribute can only be read by the kernel code. This is also referred to as the constant memory in the OpenCL memory architecture.
`CL_MEM_USE_HOST_PTR`	The `cl_mem` object to be created uses the memory referred by the `host_ptr`.
`CL_MEM_ALLOC_HOST_PTR`	The `cl_mem` object to be created allocates the memory from the host accessible memory, that is, the memory allocated at the device can be mapped to the host memory.
`CL_MEM_COPY_HOST_PTR`	The `cl_mem` object will allocate memory at the device and copy the data specified by the host pointer.
`CL_MEM_HOST_WRITE_ONLY`	This `cl_mem` object can only be written by the host.
`CL_MEM_HOST_READ_ONLY`	This `cl_mem` object can only be read by the host.
`CL_MEM_HOST_NO_ACCESS`	This `cl_mem` object will neither be read nor written to.

The cl_mem_flags flag specifies the property of the cl_mem object created. The first three memory flags create memory at the device and specify the constraints for the device and not the host. It can either be set as a single property or with multiple properties by applying bitwise OR to the different flag combinations, like (CL_MEM_READ_WRITE |CL_MEM_USE_HOST_PTR). There may be different combinations possible, but each combination is restricted by the flag definition. The cl_mem_flags flag specification specifies some mutually exclusive combinations. For example (CL_MEM_USE_HOST_PTR |CL_MEM_COPY_HOST_PTR) is not possible, because the CL_MEM_COPY_HOST_PTR flag allocates memory at the device and copies the data pointed to by the host pointer. But CL_MEM_USE_HOST_PTR flag does not allocate any memory at the device; instead it uses the already existing buffer pointed by host_ptr to be used by the device. The host_ptr must be specified when we use the flag CL_MEM_USE_HOST_PTR. It cannot be NULL.

The following are the ways in which COPY/HOST/ALLOC can be used:

- CL_MEM_COPY_HOST_PTR: This can be used when an application developer wants to create new device memory, and you are sure that any modifications on the created buffer object in the device side are not required at the host side.
- CL_MEM_USE_HOST_PTR: This is used when an application developer wants to process the buffer at the device, the input to which comes from the host and also wants the modified buffer back on the host.
- CL_MEM_ALLOC_HOST_PTR: This buffer is used when the host uses the data which is first filled by the device. For example, the device generates random numbers in the allocated buffer and this buffer will be used by the host. This is like performing malloc and not filling the memory, instead device fills the buffer.

The performance of the three flags we just saw are OpenCL implementation defined, for example CL_MEM_USE_HOST_PTR uses the host memory as a buffer location, but when it comes to accessing the data at the device side, the OpenCL implementation may pin this memory and then transfer the data over the memory bus interface (PCIe in the case of discrete graphics cards). But in the case of CL_MEM_ALLOC_HOST_PTR the OpenCL implementation may allocate memory directly on the pinned memory location which the OS uses for data transfer using the DMA. This may be faster when compared to CL_MEM_USE_HOST_PTR.

The cl_mem object or buffer refers to any type of contiguous data location which can be used by the kernel during execution. Image objects data are sampled in a different way and will be discussed in *Chapter 4, OpenCL Images*. The parameters passed to the clCreateBuffer API are described in the following table:

Parameter name	Description
`context`	A valid context object for which the buffer is allocated.
`flags`	The `flags` parameter is a bit field specifying buffer allocation and usage information. Multiple flags can be specified by OR'ing the different flag values.
`size`	Size of the buffer to be allocated, in bytes.
`host_ptr`	A pointer to data, allocated by the application; its use in a call to `clCreateBuffer` is determined by the flags parameter. The size of the data pointed to by `host_ptr` must be at least that of the requested allocation, that is, greater than or equal to the `size` bytes.
`errcode_ret`	Error code, if any, will be set in this variable if it's a non-NULL parameter.

Creating subbuffer objects

There may be situations when you may want to create a subbuffer out of the existing buffer object. For this purpose OpenCL provides the API.

```
cl_mem clCreateSubBuffer (cl_mem buffer,
  cl_mem_flags flags,
    cl_buffer_create_type buffer_create_type,
      const void *buffer_create_info,
        cl_int *errcode_ret)
```

The `clCreateSubBuffer` function can be used to create a new partial buffer object (referred to as a subbuffer object) from an existing OpenCL `cl_mem` buffer object.

Parameter name	Description
`buffer`	Must be a valid buffer object created using the `clCreateBuffer` API and cannot itself be a subbuffer object.
`flags`	This parameter takes the same values as described in the table of `cl_mem_flags` shown earlier. The values taken by the flags variable should not get into any mutual exclusion condition with the `flags` of the original `buffer`. For example, if the original `cl_mem` object buffer is created with `CL_MEM_HOST_WRITE_ONLY` and the flag specified is `CL_MEM_HOST_READ_ONLY`, then the API shall return `CL_INVALID_VALUE` in the `errcode_ret` pointer.
`buffer_create_type`	Size of the buffer to be allocated, in bytes.

Parameter name	Description

`buffer_create_info`	This is a pointer to the `cl_buffer_region` structure shown:
	`typedef struct _cl_buffer_region {`
	`size_t origin;`
	`size_t size;`
	`} cl_buffer_region;`

`errcode_ret`	Error code if any will be set in this variable if it's a non-NULL parameter.

The `buffer_create_info` and `buffer_create_type` parameters describe the type of buffer object to be created. The only value which can be specified for `buffer_create_type` is `CL_BUFFER_CREATE_TYPE_REGION`. The region specified is given by the `cl_buffer_region` object. The `cl_buffer_region` structure member `origin` is the offset in bytes in the `cl_mem` buffer object. The `size` is the size of the `buffer` object in bytes. Good care should be taken while specifying the size of the subbuffer. It should not go outside of the boundaries of `buffer`. There can be overlaps in the memory region, but writing to the overlapped region by two different kernels simultaneously is undefined.

Take a look at the following code snippet. The code creates three subbuffer `cl_mem` objects `subuffer1`, `subBuffer2` and `subBuffer3` from a larger `cl_mem` `buffer`. Note the overlap region as shown in the following diagram.

```
buffer = clCreateBuffer(
  context,
    CL_MEM_READ_ONLY,
      sizeof(float) * 100, /*buffer of 100 floats*/
        NULL,
          &status);
cl_buffer_region region;
region.size   = 50*sizeof(float);
region.origin = 0;
//Create first subBuffer with origin at the start of
// buffer and of size 50 floats
cl_mem subBuffer1 = clCreateSubBuffer(
  buffer,
    CL_MEM_READ_ONLY,
      CL_BUFFER_CREATE_TYPE_REGION,
        &region,
          &err);
```

```
region.origin = 50*sizeof(float);

cl_mem subBuffer2 = clCreateSubBuffer(
  buffer,
    CL_MEM_READ_ONLY,
      CL_BUFFER_CREATE_TYPE_REGION,
        &region,
          &err);

region.origin = 40*sizeof(float);

cl_mem subBuffer3 = clCreateSubBuffer(
  buffer,
    CL_MEM_READ_ONLY,
      CL_BUFFER_CREATE_TYPE_REGION,
        &region,
          &err);
```

The following figure explains the code we just saw and shows the overlap region:

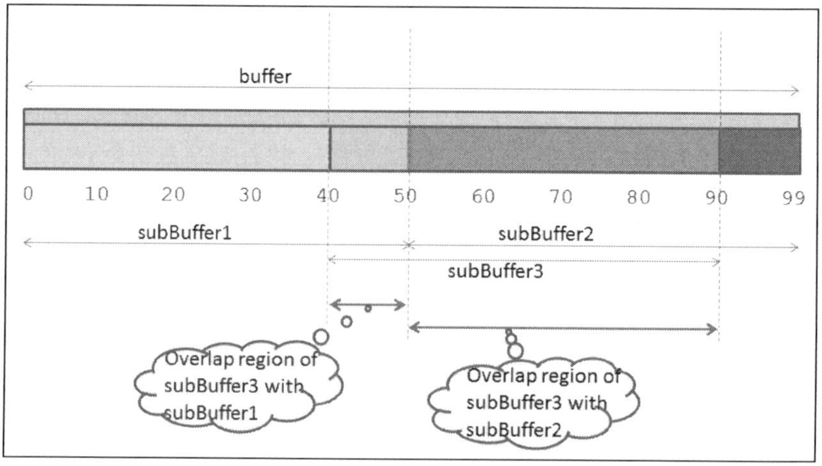

Diagram showing overlap of buffers

An example usage of subbuffers may be that you want to divide the buffer across multiple devices and launch kernels for each buffer on a separate command-queue. An OpenCL developer can enqueue map commands on overlapped regions in the memory. These map commands should be done for reading purpose only using the `CL_MAP_READ` flag. It is an invalid operation if the memory mapping is done for writing purpose. We will discuss more about Mapping Buffers in a section later in this chapter.

Histogram calculation

Histogram is a graphical representation of tonal distribution of a digital image. It plots the number of pixels for each tonal value. In this example we find the histogram of each of the RGB color components in the color image.

In this section, we will discuss the `histogram` sample. The sample code has two parts the host code and the device code which is defined as a `const char *histogram_kernel`. For understanding purpose, we will discuss the OpenCL kernel code that follows. For an OpenCL application programmer most of the effort goes in writing the OpenCL kernel. The majority of the host code is that of setting up the OpenCL platform to run that kernel. We now start with the discussion of the kernel code.

Algorithm

The input image of size X height and Y width is divided into the small linear chunks of size `BIN_SIZE=256`. Each thread shall process 256 pixel values and compute the RGB histogram. Also the total number of threads in a work group which we have selected is 16. The 16 threads are chosen so that the code works well for all the available OpenCL hardware vendors. Ideally, one should query the device properties using `clGetDeviceInfo` with the `param_name` variable set to value `CL_DEVICE_MAX_WORK_GROUP_SIZE` function and appropriately select the work group size for the algorithm.

One more factor which limits the number of work items in a work group is the local memory size. In this example we have created a local memory `sharedArray` of size 16 * 256 = 4 KB of local memory per work group. On AMD graphics cards which have a local memory size of 32 KB across all GPU devices, you can launch upto 64 work items per work group or multiples of 64 work items upto 256. This local memory is used by all the work items in the work group. Application developer can query the available local memory size using the function `clGetDeviceInfo` with the `param_name CL_DEVICE_LOCAL_MEM_SIZE`.

In a work group the kernel operates on the image area which is equal to 256*16 pixels linear image buffer. The histogram is computed for each of this local image area by a work group independently. So basically in the kernel we compute

$(X * Y) / (256 * 16)$

sub histograms. The computed sub-histograms are stored in the `uint *` buffer pointed by `binResultR`, `binResultG` and `binResultB` for R, G, and B components respectively. This buffer is a global memory in the device.

Each of the work items in a work group shall compute the histogram and store in its local buffer pointed by `sharedArray`. The pixel value used by each work-item is in the range:

`(globalId * BIN_SIZE)` to `(globalId * BIN_SIZE + 255)`

OpenCL Kernel Code

We first discuss the OpenCL kernel code for the histogram example. The kernel `histogram_kernel` is built by the OpenCL runtime compiler and is shown in the following code. This kernel computes the block histogram of 256*16 pixel values, each for R, G, and B components. Each work-item first computes the histogram of the 256 elements, into the local memory `sharedArray`. After each work-item has computed the histogram which is confirmed by a local barrier in the kernel code, the last loop in the kernel accumulates all the histogram values into a block level histogram that is, finally the `binResultX` will contain the histogram of 256*16 pixel values of each of the color components.

```
#define BIN_SIZE 256
#pragma OPENCL EXTENSION cl_khr_byte_addressable_store : enable
__kernel
void histogram_kernel(__global const uint* data,
  __local uchar* sharedArray,
    __global uint* binResultR,
      __global uint* binResultG,
        __global uint* binResultB)
{
    size_t localId = get_local_id(0);
    size_t globalId = get_global_id(0);
    size_t groupId = get_group_id(0);
    size_t groupSize = get_local_size(0);
    __local uchar* sharedArrayR = sharedArray;
    __local uchar* sharedArrayG = sharedArray +
                                  groupSize * BIN_SIZE;
    __local uchar* sharedArrayB = sharedArray +
                                  2 * groupSize * BIN_SIZE;

    /* initialize shared array to zero */
    for(int i = 0; i < BIN_SIZE; ++i)
    {
        sharedArrayR[localId * BIN_SIZE + i] = 0;
        sharedArrayG[localId * BIN_SIZE + i] = 0;
        sharedArrayB[localId * BIN_SIZE + i] = 0;
    }
```

Till now in the `histogram_kernel`, we have initialized the local memory uchar pointer pointed by `sharedArray` to 0 and assigned pointers to each of the R, G, and B components. In the next for loop we compute the histogram of `BIN_SIZE` pixels. This is computed in each of the 16 work-items in the work group.

```
/* calculate thread-histograms */
for(int i = 0; i < BIN_SIZE; ++i)
{
  uint value = data[globalId * BIN_SIZE + i];
  uint valueR = value & 0xFF;
  uint valueG = (value & 0xFF00) >> 8;
  uint valueB = (value & 0xFF0000) >> 16;
  sharedArrayR[localId * BIN_SIZE + valueR]++;
  sharedArrayG[localId * BIN_SIZE + valueG]++;
  sharedArrayB[localId * BIN_SIZE + valueB]++;
}
    barrier(CLK_LOCAL_MEM_FENCE);
```

Note the `barrier` function in the code above . After the calculation of the histogram at each work-item, we need to count the number of pixels with the values 0, 1, and so on till 255. But before that each work-item must have computed its histogram count and stored the result in its corresponding `sharedArray` bins. To ensure that all the work-items in a work group have completed its execution we add a `barrier` function in the code. Every work-item in the work group shall wait for the `barrier` function to execute before proceeding further.

```
/* merge all thread-histograms into block-histogram */
for(int i = 0; i < BIN_SIZE / groupSize; ++i)
{
  uint binCountR = 0;
  uint binCountG = 0;
  uint binCountB = 0;
  for(int j = 0; j < groupSize; ++j)
  {
    binCountR +=
      sharedArrayR[j * BIN_SIZE + i * groupSize + localId];
    binCountG +=
      sharedArrayG[j * BIN_SIZE + i * groupSize + localId];
    binCountB +=
      sharedArrayB[j * BIN_SIZE + i * groupSize + localId];
  }
```

The for loop above adds up the local histogram computed. Finally we store the result from local memory `sharedArray` to global memory `binResult`.

```
binResultR[groupId * BIN_SIZE + i * groupSize + localId] =
  binCountR;
binResultG[groupId * BIN_SIZE + i * groupSize + localId] =
  binCountG;
binResultB[groupId * BIN_SIZE + i * groupSize + localId] =
  binCountB;
  }
}
```

By now you must have understood the histogram kernel implementation and may have thought of several more ways to implement the same. We will discuss a way to optimize this solution in *Chapter 8, Basic Optimization Techniques with Case Studies - Histogram calculation*.

The Host Code

The host side code involves the following steps:

1. **Read the BMP Image into a raw pixel buffer**: In a BMP image the pixel values are stored as interleaved RGB pixel values or as a reference to a palette table. We first read the image pixels into system memory. For this purpose, we create a simple `Image` object, which stores the buffer and the size of the image using the utility function.

   ```
   void ReadBMPImage(string filename, Image **image)
   ```

2. **Setup the OpenCL Platform**: Once we obtain the raw image pixel values in a contiguous system memory, we set up the OpenCL Platform and then pass this buffer to the OpenCL device. Setting up the OpenCL device involves selecting an available platform, selecting the device to execute the kernel, creating an execution context and an associated command queue.
3. **Create OpenCL Buffers**: For histogram computation we create as many as four OpenCL Buffers using the API `clCreateBuffer`. One is the input buffer which has the raw pixel values. This buffer needs to be written to the device memory using the `clEnqueueWriteBuffer`. The remaining three are the output buffers which after the histogram computation need to be read back to the host memory using the `clEnqueueReadBuffer` OpenCL runtime API. Take a look at the following code:

   ```
   //Create OpenCL device input buffer
   imageBuffer = clCreateBuffer(context,
     CL_MEM_READ_ONLY,
       sizeof(cl_uint) * image->width * image->height,
   ```

```
        NULL,
          &status);
LOG_OCL_ERROR(status, "clCreateBuffer Failed." );

//Set input data
cl_event writeEvt;
status = clEnqueueWriteBuffer(commandQueue,
  imageBuffer,
    CL_FALSE,
      0,
        image->width * image->height * sizeof(cl_uint),
          image->pixels,
            0,
              NULL,
                &writeEvt);
LOG_OCL_ERROR(status, "clEnqueueWriteBuffer Failed." );

status = clFinish(commandQueue);
LOG_OCL_ERROR(status, "clFinish Failed " );
```

The code snippet we just saw creates an OpenCL buffer. Once the buffer is created the application enqueues a command to write the buffer data pointed by `image->pixels` into the device associated with the `commandQueue`. It is at this point when the actual data transfer takes place to the device. Every command enqueued on the queue is associated with an event handle. The write operation results in the event `writeEvt` being returned by the application. The application can wait on this event to complete and continue with further processing. For now in this example we will use the `clFinish` function to complete all tasks in the queue.

There is one other way to create a buffer, which will not involve any data transfer, between the devices. (But instead have data transfer during the actual computation. This varies between different device architectures.) The buffer can be created with `CL_MEM_USE_HOST_PTR` flag. The OpenCL buffer is created using the existing host buffer. The maps and unmaps of OpenCL buffers will result in the same host pointer being returned. The creation of this buffer is shown in the following code snippet:

```
//Create OpenCL device input buffer
imageBuffer = clCreateBuffer(
  context,
  CL_MEM_READ_ONLY|CL_MEM_USE_HOST_PTR,
  sizeof(cl_uint) * image->width * image->height,
    image->pixels,
      &status);
LOG_OCL_ERROR(status, "clCreateBuffer Failed." );
```

The `LOG_OCL_ERROR` utility is a macro used in the sample programs of this book, and is not related to OpenCL specification.

The other three OpenCL buffers are created as follows:

```
//Create OpenCL device output buffer
intermediateHistR = clCreateBuffer(
  context,
    CL_MEM_WRITE_ONLY,
      sizeof(cl_uint) * binSize * subHistgCnt,
        NULL,
          &status);
LOG_OCL_ERROR(status, "clCreateBuffer Failed." );

intermediateHistG = clCreateBuffer(
  context,
    CL_MEM_WRITE_ONLY,
      sizeof(cl_uint) * binSize * subHistgCnt,
        NULL,
          &status);
LOG_OCL_ERROR(status, "clCreateBuffer Failed." );

intermediateHistB = clCreateBuffer(
  context,
    CL_MEM_WRITE_ONLY,
      sizeof(cl_uint) * binSize * subHistgCnt,
        NULL,
          &status);
LOG_OCL_ERROR(status, "clCreateBuffer Failed." );
```

The buffers `intermediateHistR`, `intermediateHistG`, and `intermediateHistB` will store the computed RGB histogram values. These buffers are characterized by `CL_MEM_WRITE_ONLY` flags. The input and output buffers are characterized by the `cl_mem_flags` values `CL_MEM_READ_ONLY` and `CL_MEM_WRITE_ONLY` respectively.

4. **Build the kernel**: The kernel `histogram_kernel` shown in the code snippet is compiled and we are ready to setup the kernel parameters.
5. **Setup the kernel arguments**: After a brief look at the kernel code you will immediately realize the relation/correspondence between the host-side OpenCL buffer object and the actual kernel-side global memory pointer.

```
Host side variable  -- Kernel parameter
imageBuffer   --     data
intermediateHistR  --     binResultR
intermediateHistG  --     binResultG
intermediateHistB  --     binResultB
```

```
// Set the arguments of the kernel
status = clSetKernelArg(kernel, 0, sizeof(cl_mem),
  (void*)&imageBuffer);
status = clSetKernelArg(kernel, 1, 3 * groupSize * binSize
  * sizeof(cl_uchar), NULL);
status = clSetKernelArg(kernel, 2, sizeof(cl_mem),
  (void*)&intermediateHistR);
status = clSetKernelArg(kernel, 3, sizeof(cl_mem),
  (void*)&intermediateHistG);
status = clSetKernelArg(kernel, 4, sizeof(cl_mem),
  (void*)&intermediateHistB);
```

In the code snippet we just saw, the kernel arguments are set. Note that the arguments 0, 2, 3, and 4 are set using the `cl_mem` objects. The argument number 1 is specified with a NULL parameter, which indicates a local memory and is characterized by `__local uchar*` in the kernel. We will discuss more about setting the kernel arguments and executing the kernel in *Chapter 5, OpenCL Program and Kernel Objects*

6. **Read the Buffer to the host memory**: After each thread has computed its share of 256 elements histogram into the shared memory the final sub-histogram result is computed as the sum of each pixel counts and stored into the `binResultR`, `binResultG`, and `binResultB` global memory. Finally on completion of the kernel execution, the results are read back to the host memory.

Run the histogram sample code and check the correctness of the computed histogram result.

Reading and writing buffers

By now you know how to create buffer objects and how to read them in the kernel. Before the kernel is launched you may want to write the buffer to the device memory using the API `clEnqueueWriteBuffer`. And after the kernel has completed processing, you will want to get the buffer back to the host from the device memory. This can be achieved by using the `clEnqueueReadBuffer` function.

```
cl_int clEnqueueWriteBuffer (cl_command_queue command_queue,
  cl_mem buffer,
    cl_bool blocking_write,
      size_t offset,
        size_t size,
          const void *ptr,
            cl_uint num_events_in_wait_list,
            const cl_event *event_wait_list,
              cl_event *event)
```

This function writes data from the host to the device memory. Following are the descriptions of the parameters passed.

Parameter name	Description
`command_queue`	The write command will be queued in this OpenCL queue. One should make sure that the `cl_mem` object buffer and the `command_queue` are created using the same context.
`buffer`	A valid `cl_mem` buffer object, which will be written to.
`blocking_write`	If this value is set to `CL_TRUE`, then `clEnqueueWriteBuffer` blocks until the data is written from `ptr`; otherwise it returns `immediately` and the user must query `event` to check the command's status.
`offset`	The `offset`, in bytes, into the destination buffer object. At this offset the first byte from the input source buffer is written to.
`size`	Total bytes to be written into the device memory pointed by buffer.
`ptr`	The host memory pointer from where the data will be read.
`num_events_in_wait_list`	The number of events to wait for before executing this command
`event_wait_list`	The pointer to the events wait list. The size of this is specified by `num_events_in_wait_list`. The OpenCL implementation shall queue this command only after the events in `event_wait_list` is completed.
`event`	A `cl_event` object is returned which describes this write command. This event can be used by any other OpenCL command for synchronization. If the `event_wait_list` and the event arguments are not NULL, then the event argument should not refer to any element of the `event_wait_list` array. Also if the `blocking_write` is set to `CL_TRUE` then this event may not be of any use, because it is known that the event has completed execution after the blocking read has completed.

Similarly the function `clEnqueueReadBuffer` reads data from the device to the host memory.

```
cl_int clEnqueueReadBuffer (cl_command_queue command_queue,
  cl_mem buffer,
    cl_bool blocking_read,
      size_t offset,
        size_t size,
          void *ptr,
            cl_uint num_events_in_wait_list,
              const cl_event *event_wait_list,
                cl_event *event)
```

The parameters passed to this function are similar in description to the write command. `command_queue`, `offset`, `size`, `ptr`, `num_events_in_wait_list`, `event_wait_list`, and `event` all have similar descriptions as discussed in the previous table.Other parameters are discussed further.

`buffer`: A valid `cl_mem` buffer object, which will be read from and written to `ptr`.

`blocking_read`: If set to `CL_TRUE`, then `clEnqueueReadBuffer` blocks until the data is read to the `ptr`; otherwise it returns directly and the user must query `event` to check the command's status.

`event`: An OpenCL event object is returned which describes this read command. This event can be used by any other OpenCL enqueue commands for synchronization by querying its state of execution.

Blocking_read and Blocking_write

Memory read/writes can be marked as blocked by setting it to CL_TRUE. This will cause the host thread to block, until the enqueued command has completed. OpenCL uses relaxed memory model. So it is up to the application programmer to make sure that the memory being written to by a particular device is updated across all the devices associated with the particular context. Similarly for the memory read operation. Some non-cache coherent devices may see different values for the same global address. Hence explicit synchronization is required by the application programmer.

If the read/write command is not blocking, then the host thread may return immediately before the enqueued task has completed, and the application cannot assume that the memory being written or read is ready to be consumed from. In such a case the host application can use OpenCL synchronization API `clFinish` or `clWaitForEvents` to ensure that the command has completed. We will discuss more on this in *Chapter 6, Events and Synchronization*.

Now let's go back to the histogram sample code. The read commands are provided in the following code snippet. All these read commands have the `blocking_read` argument set to `CL_FALSE`. The order of execution of these commands will be defined by the property of `commandQueue` created. Take a look at the following code:

```
cl_event readEvt[3];
status = clEnqueueReadBuffer(
  commandQueue,
    intermediateHistR,
      CL_FALSE,
        0,
          subHistgCnt * binSize * sizeof(cl_uint),
            midDeviceBinR,
              0,
                NULL,
                  &readEvt[0]);
LOG_OCL_ERROR(status, "clEnqueueReadBuffer of intermediateHistR
  Failed." );

status = clEnqueueReadBuffer(
  commandQueue,
    intermediateHistG,
      CL_FALSE,
        0,
          subHistgCnt * binSize * sizeof(cl_uint),
            midDeviceBinG,
              0,
                NULL,
                  &readEvt[1]);
LOG_OCL_ERROR(status, "clEnqueueReadBuffer of intermediateHist
  Failed." );

status = clEnqueueReadBuffer(
  commandQueue,
    intermediateHistB,
      CL_FALSE,
        0,
          subHistgCnt * binSize * sizeof(cl_uint),
            midDeviceBinB,
              0,
                NULL,
                  &readEvt[2]);
LOG_OCL_ERROR(status, "clEnqueueReadBuffer of intermediateHistB
  Failed." );
```

At the first read command the function clEnqueueReadBuffer enqueue's a command in the cl_command_queue commandQueue to read a device memory object pointed by intermediateHistR into the host memory midDeviceBinR. The size read by this command is equal to subHistgCnt * binSize * sizeof(cl_uint). The blocking_read variable is set to CL_FALSE. The last API clWaitForEvents waits for the three read events to complete. Once we have the result read into host memory, one final step computes the count of each pixel tonal value.

As an exercise for you modify the histogram sample code in the following way. We have created the cl_mem objects for each of the output buffers. Combine these three into a single buffer object, and use the API clCreateSubBuffer to create three different subbuffers. Pass these subbuffers as cl_mem object to the histogram_kernel and verify the execution of the histogram result.

Rectangular or cuboidal reads

OpenCL specification provides with an ability to read or write rectangular segments of data into host memory. The clEnqueueReadBufferRect function enqueues a command to read a rectangular 2D or 3D region from a cl_mem buffer object to host memory. This is shown in the following code:

```
cl_int
clEnqueueReadBufferRect(cl_command_queue command_queue,
  cl_mem buffer,
    cl_bool blocking_read,
      const size_t *buffer_origin,
        const size_t *host_origin,
          const size_t *region,
            size_t buffer_row_pitch,
              size_t buffer_slice_pitch,
                size_t host_row_pitch,
                  size_t host_slice_pitch,
                    void *ptr,
                      cl_uint num_events_in_wait_list,
                        const cl_event *event_wait_list,
                          cl_event *event)
```

Similarly OpenCL provides a function `clEnqueueWriteBufferRect` which enqueues the command to write rectangular piece of buffer. As shown in the following code:

```
cl_int
clEnqueueWriteBufferRect (cl_command_queue command_queue,
  cl_mem buffer,
    cl_bool blocking_write,
      const size_t *buffer_origin,
        const size_t *host_origin,
          const size_t *region,
            size_t buffer_row_pitch,
              size_t buffer_slice_pitch,
                size_t host_row_pitch,
                  size_t host_slice_pitch,
                    const void *ptr,
                      cl_uint num_events_in_wait_list,
                        const cl_event *event_wait_list,
                          cl_event *event)
```

The following figure helps explain the rectangular region in 2D space. Note that every OpenCL buffer is a one-dimensional contiguous memory location. These rectangular functions help to visualize or access the 2D or 3D equivalent memory regions in that 1D contiguous buffer.

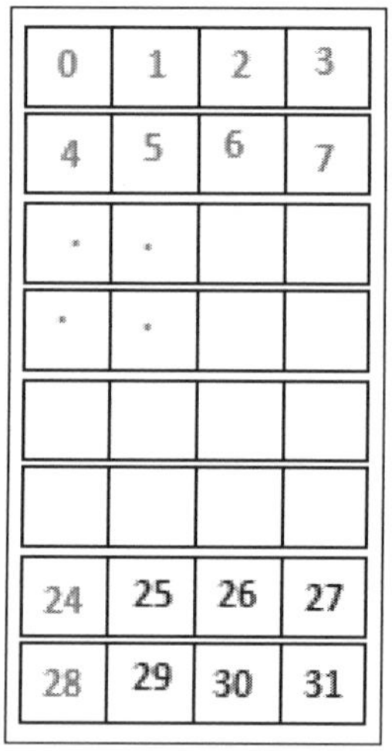

2D Image read marked with black color

The `buffer_row_pitch` and `buffer_slice_pitch` functions, define the 2D or 3D representation of the whole buffer.

The offset in bytes into the `cl_mem` object is computed as:

```
buffer_origin[2] * buffer_slice_pitch +
  buffer_origin[1] * buffer_row_pitch +
    buffer_origin[0];
```

Let's take an example array of size 32 elements in 1D. In 2D it can be visualized as 8 rows with `buffer_row_pitch` = 4 elements as described in the figure we just saw. In 3D it can be visualized as 4 slices of 4X2 each as shown in the following figure:

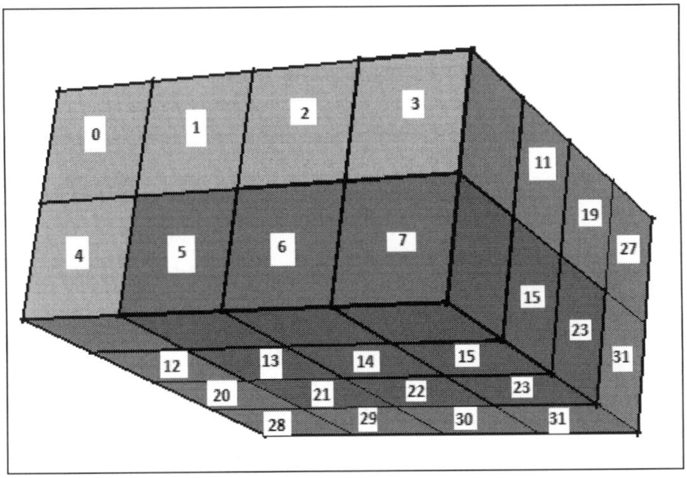

3D rectangular read

To explain the `clEnqueue{Write|Read}BufferRect` functions, we will discuss one of the sample codes. In the `bufferRectangularReads` sample code we create a buffer of size 32 elements and try to emulate a 2D and 3D buffer reads from the input 1D buffer (all OpenCL buffer objects store data in a linear contiguous location). We will perform two operations in the sample code. First we emulate a 2D buffer and read a 3X2 size 2D rectangular read.

We first create a buffer as follows:

```
clBuffer = clCreateBuffer(
  context,
    CL_MEM_READ_ONLY | CL_MEM_COPY_HOST_PTR,
      sizeof(cl_uint) * NUM_OF_ELEMENTS,
        hostBuffer, /*Pointer to 32 elements*/
          &status);
LOG_OCL_ERROR(status, "clCreateBuffer Failed..." );
```

The following code reads a 2D rectangular region as shown in the figure we just saw:

```
//Read a 2D rectangular object from the clBuffer of 32 elements
int hostPtr2D[6] = {0, 0, 0, 0, 0, 0};
size_t bufferOrigin2D[3] = {1*sizeof(int), 6, 0};
size_t hostOrigin2D[3] = {0 ,0, 0};
size_t region2D[3] = {3* sizeof(int), 2,1};
status =
    clEnqueueReadBufferRect(
        commandQueue,
        clBuffer,
        CL_TRUE,
        bufferOrigin2D, /*Start of a 2D buffer to read from*/
        hostOrigin2D,
        region2D,
        (NUM_OF_ELEMENTS / 8) * sizeof(int), /*buffer_row_pitch  */
        0,                                   /*buffer_slice_pitch*/
        0,                                   /*host_row_pitch    */
        0,                                   /*host_slice_pitch  */
        static_cast<void*>(hostPtr2D),
        0,
        NULL,
        NULL);
```

Next we emulate a 3D buffer and read 3 contiguous slices of 3X1 each. The following code reads 3D cuboid as shown in the figure we just saw.

```
//Read a 3D rectangular object from the clBuffer of 32 elements
int hostPtr3D[9] = {0, 0, 0, 0, 0, 0, 0, 0, 0};
size_t bufferOrigin3D[3] = {1*sizeof(int), 1, 0};
size_t hostOrigin3D[3] = {0 ,0, 0};
size_t region3D[3] = {3* sizeof(int), 1,3};
status =
    clEnqueueReadBufferRect(
      commandQueue,
      clBuffer,
      CL_TRUE,
      bufferOrigin3D, /*Start of a 2D buffer to read from*/
      hostOrigin3D,
      region3D,
      (NUM_OF_ELEMENTS / 8) * sizeof(int), /*buffer_row_pitch  */
      (NUM_OF_ELEMENTS / 4) * sizeof(int), /*buffer_slice_pitch*/
      0,                                   /*host_row_pitch    */
      0,                                   /*host_slice_pitch  */
      static_cast<void*>(hostPtr3D),
```

```
        0,
        NULL,
        NULL);
```

Compile and run the `bufferRectangularReads` project in the OpenCL examples and check the result. The code will print the highlighted sections in the figure.

Copying buffers

The two functions `clEnqueueCopyBuffer` and `clEnqueueCopyBufferRect` enable the application to copy data between two OpenCL buffer objects. It is equivalent to reading the buffer back from device to host and then writing it back to a destination `cl_mem` object. This mechanism is provided by these copy buffer routines:

```
cl_int
clEnqueueCopyBuffer(cl_command_queue command_queue,
  cl_mem src_buffer,
    cl_mem dst_buffer,
      size_t src_offset, size_t dst_offset,
        size_t size,
          cl_uint num_events_in_wait_list,
            const cl_event *event_wait_list,
              cl_event *event)
```

This OpenCL API enqueue's a command to copy a `cl_mem` buffer object identified by `src_buffer` to another `cl_mem` object destination buffer, `dst_buffer`. Remaining parameters like `offset` and `events` are similar to the one in `clEnqueue[Read|Write]Buffer` routines.

Similarly if one wants to copy only a small rectangular region in the `cl_mem` buffer then he can use the API:

```
cl_int
clEnqueueCopyBufferRect(cl_command_queue command_queue,
  cl_mem src_buffer,
    cl_mem dst_buffer,
      const size_t *src_origin,
        const size_t *dst_origin,
          const size_t *region,
            size_t src_row_pitch,
              size_t src_slice_pitch,
                size_t dst_row_pitch,
                  size_t dst_slice_pitch,
                    cl_uint num_events_in_wait_list,
                      const cl_event *event_wait_list,
                        cl_event *event)
```

Take a look at the `copyRectangular` project in the book examples for this chapter. This example gives an explanation of the function `clEnqueueCopyBufferRect`.

What is the difference between the `clEnqueueWriteBuffer` and `clEnqueueCopyBuffer`? Unlike `clEnqueueWriteBuffer` function, `clEnqueueCopyBuffer` copies the data between two `cl_mem` objects directly in the device memory or through the device memory interface across two devices. `clEnqueueReadBuffer` function will read the data from the device memory to the host memory. The following figure explains the difference:

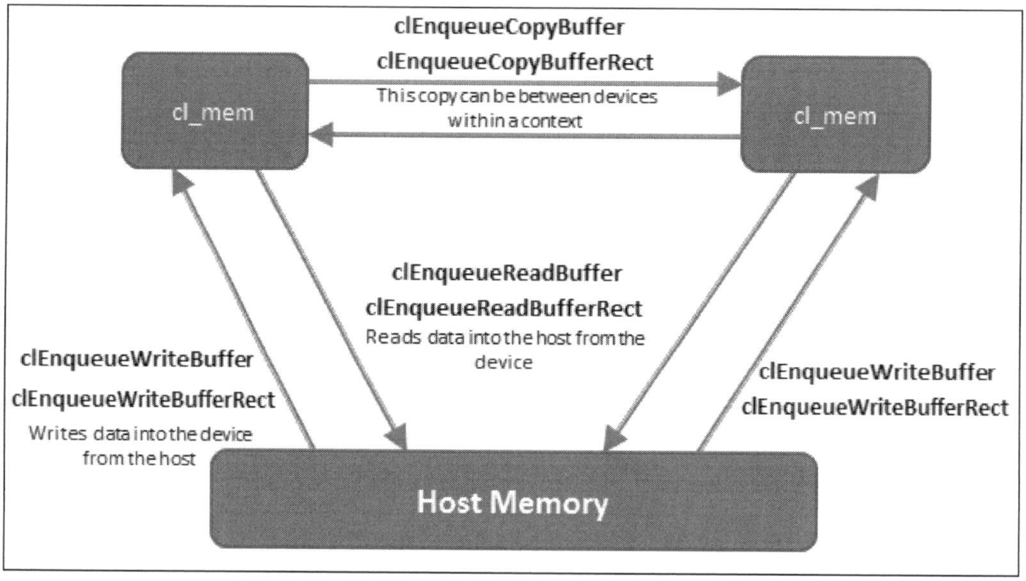

Difference between Copy Buffer and Read Write Buffer

Mapping buffer objects

OpenCL provides a mechanism to map a region of a buffer directly into host memory instead of using the `clEnqueue[Read|Write]Buffer` functions. These mapped regions can be returned to the application. The application can use this mapped memory region based on the `cl_map_flags` flag value which is set during mapping. Now the first question which would arise in the readers mind is that how different are the two APIs `clEnqueueMapBuffer` and `clEnqueueReadBuffer`.

The `clEnqueueReadBuffer` function reads into a memory location pre-allocated. But `clEnqueueMapBuffer` returns a pointer to the mapped region.

Other difference between clEnqueueReadBuffer and clEnqueueMapBuffer is the map_flags argument. If map_flags is set to CL_MAP_READ, the mapped memory will be read only, and if it is set as CL_MAP_WRITE the mapped memory will be write only, if you want both read and write, then set the flags as CL_MAP_READ|CL_MAP_WRITE. The importance of CL_MAP_READ lies when an unmap is called on the mapped region. An OpenCL implementation will optimize a CL_MAP_READ by quickly relinquishing the data held by the mapped region. It will not do a write back operation to the device. But in the case of CL_MAP_WRITE the OpenCL implementation will have to copy the modified mapped buffer back to the device.

```
void *
clEnqueueMapBuffer (cl_command_queue command_queue,
  cl_mem buffer,
    cl_bool blocking_map,
      cl_map_flags map_flags,
        size_t offset,
          size_t size,
             cl_uint num_events_in_wait_list,
              const cl_event *event_wait_list,
                cl_event *event,
                  cl_int *errcode_ret)
```

The following table describes the parameters passed to the clEnqueueMapBuffer.

Parameter name	Description
buffer	A valid cl_mem buffer object, which will be mapped from.
blocking_map	If set to CL_TRUE, then clEnqueueMapBuffer blocks until the data is mapped into host memory; otherwise it returns directly and the user must query event to check the command's status.
offset	The offset, in bytes, into the buffer object to begin reading from.
size	The number of bytes to be read from buffer.
num_events_in_wait_list	Number of events to wait for before executing this command.
event_wait_list	The pointer to the events wait list. The size of this is specified by num_events_in_wait_list. The OpenCL implementation shall queue this command only when num_events_in_wait_list events in the event_wait_list is completed.

Parameter name	Description
event	A cl_event object is returned which describes this map command. This event can be used by any other OpenCL command for synchronization. If event_wait_list and event arguments are not NULL, then the event argument should not be one of the events in event_wait_list array. Also if the blocking_map is set to CL_TRUE then this event may not be of any use, because it is known that the event has completed execution after the blocking read has completed.
errcode_ret	If non-NULL, the error code returned by the function will be returned in this parameter.

The clEnqueueMapBuffer function returns a pointer to the mapped host memory. This memory can later be unmapped using the function clEnqueueUnmapMemObject.

```
cl_int
clEnqueueUnmapMemObject (cl_command_queue command_queue,
  cl_mem memobj,
    void *mapped_ptr,
      cl_uint num_events_in_wait_list,
        const cl_event *event_wait_list,
          cl_event *event)
```

The mapped_ptr is the pointer to the mapped region returned by the clEnqueueMapBuffer function and the pointer.

It is a common consensus that memory mapping gives significant improvement in performance compared to regular read/write commands. The OpenCL driver can make use of DMA transfer to transfer data to the host. The efficiency of mapping the buffers is dependent on the OpenCL implementation. Compared to read/write functions, memory mapping is a three step process:

1. Use the function clEnqueueMapBuffer to map a device memory into the host.
2. Perform operations (read or write) on the mapped buffer.
3. Unmap the mapped buffer using clEnqueueUnmapObject.

Querying buffer objects

As any other OpenCL objects, cl_mem objects can be queried to return information regarding how they are constructed, their status, reference count, and so on. The OpenCL function `clGetMemObjectInfo` helps in this.

```
cl_int
clGetMemObjectInfo (cl_mem memobj,
  cl_mem_info param_name,
    size_t param_value_size,
      void *param_value,
        size_t *param_value_size_ret)
```

This function is similar to the `clGetDeviceInfo` discussed in *Chapter 2, OpenCL Architecture*. The `param_name` is a parameter specific to this function and is of type `cl_mem_info`. It can be used for both image and buffer type `cl_mem` objects. The following code snippet shows you how to retrieve the flags associated with a `cl_mem` object.

```
// Create memory buffers on the device for each vector
cl_mem A_clmem = clCreateBuffer(context,
  CL_MEM_READ_ONLY|CL_MEM_USE_HOST_PTR,
    VECTOR_SIZE * sizeof(float), A_ptr, &clStatus);
...
...
...
cl_mem_flags flags;
clStatus =
  clGetMemObjectInfo (A_clmem,
    CL_MEM_FLAGS,
      sizeof(cl_mem_flags),
        &flags,
          NULL);
```

We created a `cl_mem` object `A_clmem` using the host malloc'd buffer `A_ptr`. Somewhere down the code or in a function you want to retrieve the flags associated with the `cl_mem` object, then you can use the function `clGetMemObjectInfo` to retrieve this information. Note that `cl_mem_flags` is a bit field representation of the different flags. In the `cl.h` header file each flag is associated with a bit in a `cl_ulong` bit field, which is a 64 bit unsigned integer. For simplicity we have added the following code following code which shows the different flag values:

```
typedef cl_ulong            cl_bitfield;
typedef cl_bitfield         cl_mem_flags;
```

```
/* cl_mem_flags - bitfield */
#define CL_MEM_READ_WRITE                                  (1 << 0)
#define CL_MEM_WRITE_ONLY                                  (1 << 1)
#define CL_MEM_READ_ONLY                                   (1 << 2)
#define CL_MEM_USE_HOST_PTR                                (1 << 3)
#define CL_MEM_ALLOC_HOST_PTR                              (1 << 4)
#define CL_MEM_COPY_HOST_PTR                               (1 << 5)
```

The `cl_mem_info` function takes the following tabulated values.

cl_mem_info	Description
`CL_MEM_TYPE`	This determines the type of the buffer object.
`CL_MEM_FLAGS`	This returns the flags argument value specified when `memobj` is created with `clCreateBuffer`, `clCreateSubBuffer`, or `clCreateImage`.
`CL_MEM_HOST_PTR`	This function returns a `host_ptr` which was specified during the creation of the `memobj` using the `clCreateBuffer` or `clCreateImage` functions and `CL_MEM_USE_HOST_PTR` was specified in `mem_flags`. Otherwise a NULL ptr is returned.
`CL_MEM_SIZE`	Returns the actual size of the `memobj cl_mem` buffer in bytes.
`CL_MEM_CONTEXT`	Returns the context to which `memobj` belongs.
`CL_MEM_MAP_COUNT`	Returns an integer representing the number of times the buffer is currently mapped.
`CL_MEM_REFERENCE_COUNT`	Return reference count to `memobj`.
`CL_MEM_ASSOCIATED_MEMOBJECT`	Returns a memory object from which `cl_mem memobj` is created. This is used to get the `cl_mem` object from which subbuffer `memobj` was created with. Otherwise a NULL value is returned.
`CL_MEM_OFFSET`	Return offset of `memobj` from the original buffer from which `memobj` was created with. That is `memobj` should have been created using the function `clCreateSubBuffer` otherwise it would return 0.

Undefined behavior of the cl_mem objects

An OpenCL memory model, being a relaxed memory architecture, specifies some restrictions or undefined behavior around the `cl_mem` object. These undefined behaviors occur mostly when there is a simultaneous read and write to a buffer. Following are listed some undefined scenarios:

- If the buffer is created with `CL_MEM_WRITE_ONLY` flag and the kernel reads from this buffer pointer on the devices side, then it's an undefined behavior. That means reading from a `CL_MEM_WRITE_ONLY` buffer inside the kernel is undefined.
- Similarly writing to a buffer created using the flag `CL_MEM_READ_ONLY` is undefined inside the kernel.
- It is possible to create two OpenCL `cl_mem` buffers from the same host memory using the `CL_MEM_USE_HOST_PTR` flag. There may be an overlapping memory region. If one or more commands enqueued to the command queue operate on the two `cl_mem` objects but pointing to the same host memory `host_ptr`, then such an operation is not defined. It is the application programmer's responsibility to make sure that he is not writing and reading to the same `host_ptr` pointer simultaneously.
- Similarly reading from, writing to and copying between `cl_mem` buffer object and its corresponding subbuffer object is undefined.
- For `cl_mem` object created using `CL_MEM_USE_HOST_PTR` should meet the requirements that they contain the latest bits i.e. simultaneous writes from the host and the device kernel is undefined.

Summary

In this chapter we discussed about OpenCL `cl_mem` objects. There are two types of OpenCL buffers. In the next chapter we will study about the OpenCL Image buffers, and discuss similar characteristics which we have discussed in this chapter.

We also discussed an example of histogram computation of an image data with OpenCL buffers as an object. In the next chapter we will discuss the same sample example but with OpenCL Image Objects. Besides there were two more examples given in this chapter, one for copy rectangular regions and the other for rectangular reads from a buffer. Try the samples out and modify the kernel code at your will.

4
OpenCL Images

In the previous chapter, we discussed the OpenCL buffers, which are the most important OpenCL objects. They represent the handle to the OpenCL device memory. We discussed how to create a buffer, sub-buffer, transfer the host allocated data to the device, and mapping or un-mapping of the OpenCL buffer. The OpenCL buffers provide caching for regular linear buffers only in one dimension. Many OpenCL devices have a texture processor, which can cache pixels in an image which are its neighbor. So providing a separate interface for images is useful, and can be used to enhance the performance of applications.

In this chapter we will discuss the OpenCL image objects, which are also represented by `cl_mem`.

We will discuss the following topics:

- Creating image and sampler objects
- Performing histogram equalization using image objects. Mapping and querying the image objects.

Before we start, we need to mention that not all OpenCL devices support image computations. An OpenCL programmer can query whether the device supports image formats or not using the function `clGetDeviceInfo` and `param_name` as `CL_DEVICE_IMAGE_SUPPORT`. The image2d_t, image3d_t, image2d_array_t, `image1d_t`, `image1d_buffer_t`, `image1d_array_t`, and `sampler_t` types are only defined if the device supports images that is `clGetDeviceInfo` on `CL_DEVICE_IMAGE_SUPPORT` returns a true.

Let's start our discussion with how to create an image object.

Creating images

Image objects can be created using the following function call:

```
cl_mem clCreateImage (cl_context context,
  cl_mem_flags flags,
  const cl_image_format *image_format,
  const cl_image_desc *image_desc,
  void *host_ptr,
  cl_int *errcode_ret)
```

A single function call supports the creation of a 1D, 2D, and 3D image object, which can either be transferred to the device or can be formed in the device. Besides this, the same function call can be used to create an array of 1D and 2D image objects using the `cl_image_desc` data structure. We will discuss more on this later. In OpenCL 1.1 instead of one function `clCreateImage`, there were two different functions `clCreateImage2D` and `clCreateImage3D`.

The function call `clCreateImage` takes the usual four arguments as used in the `clCreateBuffer`. They are the `context`, `flags`, `host_ptr`, and `error_code`. The definition of these parameters is similar to that discussed in context with `clCreateBuffer`. If the `flags` parameter is specified as `0` then the default value is always `CL_MEM_READ_WRITE`. In the `clCreateBuffer` function, there is a `size` parameter. In the case of `clCreateImage`, the size field is embedded in the `cl_image_desc *image_desc` parameter, which is passed to this function. This describes the type and dimensions of the image to be created.

There is another parameter passed to this function `cl_image_format *image_format`, which describes the properties of the image which is to be created.

`host_ptr`: This is a pointer to the raw image data that is allocated by the host. This is used if the `flags` parameter is specified as `CL_MEM_COPY_HOST_PTR` or `CL_MEM_USE_HOST_PTR`.

Let's discuss about the `cl_image_format` and `cl_image_desc` format in more detail.

Image format descriptor cl_image_format

The `cl_image_format` image format descriptor is defined as follows:

```
typedef struct _cl_image_format {
  cl_channel_order image_channel_order;
  cl_channel_type image_channel_data_type;
  } cl_image_format;
```

The image_channel_data_type format specifies the size of the data type used to store each of the channel information. Most of these data types are of basic data types such as, int, unsigned int, short, unsigned short, and float. They can be CL_SNORM_INT8, CL_UNORM_INT8, CL_SNORM_INT16, CL_UNORM_INT16, CL_UNSIGNED_INT8, CL_UNSIGNED_INT16, CL_UNSIGNED_INT32, CL_SIGNED_INT8, CL_SIGNED_INT16, CL_SIGNED_INT32, CL_HALF_FLOAT, or CL_FLOAT.

The image_channel_order format describes the memory layout of the channel data, which represents the image in memory. The channel can be one of R, G, B, or A. The combination of these channels forms a channel type/order. The following table shows the different types of channel orders possible.

No of Channels	Enum values that specify the image_channel_order
Single channel format	CL_R, CL_Rx, or CL_A can be used with any channel data type other than the packed data types.
Dual channel format	CL_RG, CL_RGx, or CL_RA
Four channel format	CL_RGBA can be used with any data type discussed earlier other than the packed data types. This is the minimum required supported image format if an OpenCL device is supporting images.
	CL_ARGB and CL_BGRA can be used only with CL_UNORM_INT8, CL_SNORM_INT8, CL_SIGNED_INT8, or CL_UNSIGNED_INT8.
Packed format channel	CL_RGB or CL_RGBx. This format can be used only if the channel data type is CL_UNORM_SHORT_565, CL_UNORM_SHORT_555, or CL_UNORM_INT_101010.
Other formats	CL_INTENSITY and CL_LUMINANCE can be used if channel data type is CL_UNORM_INT8, CL_UNORM_INT16, CL_SNORM_INT8, CL_SNORM_INT16, CL_HALF_FLOAT, or CL_FLOAT.

There are some special forms of packed image_channel_data_type, which represents all the color components. They are CL_UNORM_SHORT_555, CL_UNORM_SHORT_565, and CL_UNORM_INT_101010.

The value of image_channel_order and image_channel_data_type is used to calculate the size of a pixel element. This is useful when the pitch values are specified as 0 in the clEnqueue{Read|Write|Copy|Fill}Image functions.

The CL_R, CL_A, CL_RG, CL_RA, and CL_RGBA channel order types can be represented using all the available channel data type, except the packed ones. While creating an OpenCL image object using clCreateImage, if the image format specified by image_channel_data_type and image_channel_order is not supported by the OpenCL implementation, then a NULL memory object is returned.

Image details descriptor cl_image_desc

The cl_image_desc structure contains fields with specifications required for the image to be created as follows:

```
typedef struct _cl_image_desc {
  cl_mem_object_type image_type,
  size_t image_width;
  size_t image_height;
  size_t image_depth;
  size_t image_array_size;
  size_t image_row_pitch;
  size_t image_slice_pitch;
  cl_uint num_mip_levels;
  cl_uint num_samples;
  cl_mem buffer;
}cl_image_desc;
```

The specifications are listed in the following bullet list with their description:

- image_type: It describes the type of the image 1D, 2D, 3D, or array types.
    - For 1D image, use CL_MEM_OBJECT_IMAGE1D. For 1D image from an OpenCL cl_mem buffer use the CL_MEM_OBJECT_IMAGE1D_BUFFER format. To create an array of 1D images use CL_MEM_OBJECT_IMAGE1D_ARRAY format.
    - For 2D image and an array of 2D images, use CL_MEM_OBJECT_IMAGE2D, CL_MEM_OBJECT_IMAGE2D_ARRAY respectively.
    - For creating 3D image use CL_MEM_OBJECT_IMAGE3D.
- image_width: It specifies the width of the image in pixels. This is specified for all of 1D, 2D and 3D images.

- `image_height`: It specifies the height of the image in pixels. This is specified for all of 2D and 3D images.
- `image_depth`: It specifies the depth of the image in pixels and is used only for 3D images.

> Note that the width, height, and depth are not the byte lengths, they are the pixel lengths.

- `image_array_size`: It is the total number of images (1D or 2D only) to be created in the image array. 3D image arrays cannot be created.

For specifying the pitch in bytes for the array types, use the following specifications:

- `image_row_pitch`: This is the pitch in bytes for a row in an image. If `host_ptr` is `NULL`, that is if you are creating a device resident buffer, then this value should be `0`. If the `host_ptr` pointer is not `NULL` and if this value is `0` then the value of row pitch is calculated as follows:

  *image_width * (size of pixel element in bytes)*

- `image_slice_pitch`: This is the size in bytes of a 2D slice in a 3D image. It can also represent the size in bytes of each image in an image array (both 1D or 2D). This value can be zero or a multiple of the `image_row_pitch` value. If not zero then it should be greater than or equal to `image_row_pitch * image_height`. If `host_ptr` is `NULL`, that is if you are creating a device resident buffer, then this value should be 0. If the `host_ptr` is not `NULL` and if this value is 0 then the of slice pitch is calculated as follows:

  *image_row_pitch * image_height*

  Remember that `num_mip_levels` and `num_samples` must be set to 0.

- `buffer`: This is a valid OpenCL `cl_mem` buffer created using the `clCreateBuffer` function. This must be specified, if the `image_type` is `CL_MEM_OBJECT_IMAGE1D_BUFFER`. The size of the buffers should be sufficiently large to hold `image_width * size of pixel element in bytes`. If the `image_row_pitch` specification is specified then it should be less than the `size of buffer object data store`. In all the other cases it should be set to `NULL`.

The following diagrams show the different types of images:

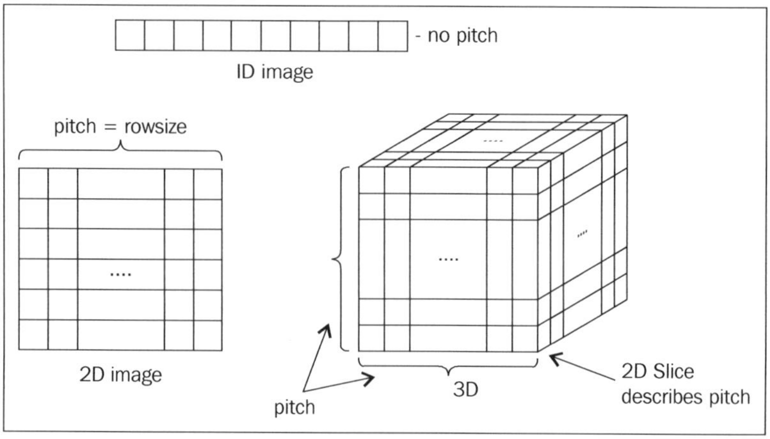

1D, 2D, and 3D image formats.

The following diagram depicts an array of 1D and 2D images:

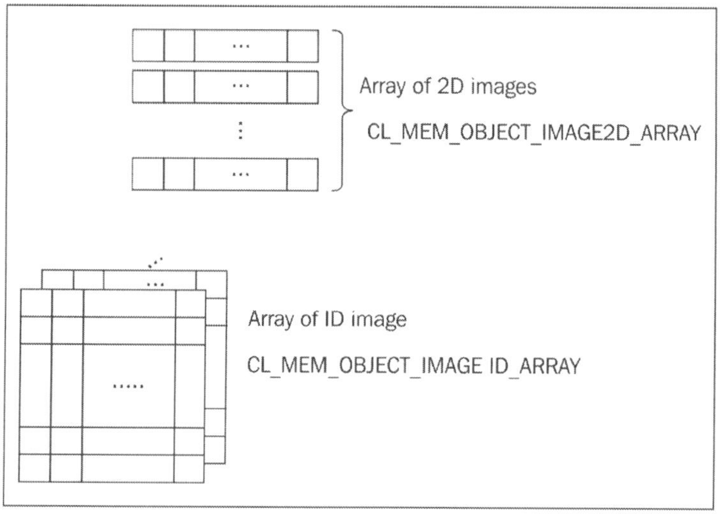

Array of 1D and 2D images.

`CL_MEM_OBJECT_IMAGE1D_BUFFER` is a special type of image representation. This image maps to the same buffer in the device, that is any modifications done on the buffer will reflect on the image also. Take a look at the following figure. Simultaneous writes at the image and buffer side are undefined.

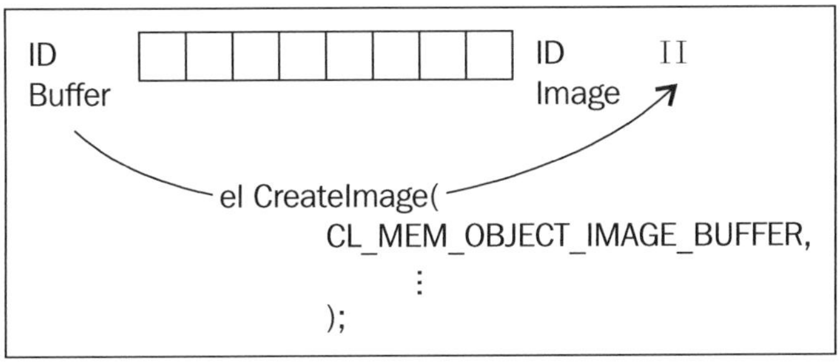

OpenCL provides a function `clGetSupportedImageFormats` to determine the different types of image formats image supported by an OpenCL implementation.

```
cl_int clGetSupportedImageFormats (cl_context context,
  cl_mem_flags flags,
  cl_mem_object_type image_type,
  cl_uint num_entries,
  cl_image_format *image_formats,
  cl_uint *num_image_formats)
```

The following code snippet helps you to determine the supported image formats.

```
cl_image_format *image_formats;
cl_uint num_image_formats;
clStatus= clGetSupportedImageFormats (context,
  CL_MEM_READ_ONLY,
  CL_MEM_OBJECT_IMAGE2D,
  0,
  NULL,
  &num_image_formats);
image_formats = (cl_image_format *)malloc(sizeof(cl_image_format)
  * num_image_formats);
clStatus= clGetSupportedImageFormats (context,
  CL_MEM_READ_ONLY,
  CL_MEM_OBJECT_IMAGE1D,
  num_image_formats,
  image_formats,
  &num_image_formats);
```

The input to the function is a valid OpenCL context. On return from the second call to `clGetSupportedImageFormats`, the `image_formats` buffer shall contain all the supported formats, Build and run the getSupportedImageFormats example code and see the out image formats supported by your platform.

Let's take some examples and see how an OpenCL image object is created:

```
cl_image_format image_format;
image_format.image_channel_data_type = CL_FLOAT;
image_format.image_channel_order = CL_R;

image_width = 5;
image_height = 5;
cl_image_desc image_desc;
image_desc.image_type = CL_MEM_OBJECT_IMAGE2D;
image_desc.image_width = image_width;
image_desc.image_height = image_height;
image_desc.image_depth = 1;
image_desc.image_array_size = 1;
image_desc.image_row_pitch = 0;
image_desc.image_slice_pitch = 0;
image_desc.num_mip_levels = 0;
image_desc.num_samples = 0;
image_desc.buffer= NULL;

clImage = clCreateImage(context, CL_MEM_WRITE_ONLY,
  &image_format, &image_desc,
  NULL, &status);
```

This will create a 2D image of width and height equal to five pixels. Note that pixel data is not yet filled in the image object. You can do so by using the `CL_MEM_USE_HOST_PTR`. Assume that you want to use the following array of pixels given by data:

```
float *data = (float *)malloc(image_width*
  image_height*sizeof(float));
float pixels[] = {              /* Pixel Values */
    10, 20, 30, 40, 50,
    10, 20, 30, 40, 50,
    10, 20, 30, 40, 50,
    10, 20, 30, 40, 50,
    10, 20, 30, 40, 50
};
memcpy(data, pixels, image_width*image_height*sizeof(float));
clImage = clCreateImage(context,
  CL_MEM_WRITE_ONLY| CL_MEM_USE_HOST_PTR,
  &image_format, &image_desc,
  data, &status);
```

You can also write the pixel data onto the destination image object using the `clEnqueueWriteImage` function as follows:

```
size_t origin[] = {0,0,0};
size_t region[] = {image_width,image_height,1};
status = clEnqueueWriteImage(command_queue, clImage, CL_TRUE,
  origin, region,
  image_width*sizeof(float), /*row pitch*/
  image_width*image_height*sizeof(float), /*slice pitch*/
  pixels, 0, NULL, NULL);
```

Passing image buffers to kernels

OpenCL C provides built-in image data types which can be used inside an OpenCL kernel. The following are the image argument types which correspond to the respective arguments in an image in the kernel:

- `image2d_t`: A 2D image created with `CL_MEM_OBJECT_IMAGE2D`
- `image3d_t`: A 3D image created with `CL_MEM_OBJECT_IMAGE3D`
- `image2d_array_t`: A 2D image array `CL_MEM_OBJECT_IMAGE2D_ARRAY`
- `image1d_t`: A 1D image created with `CL_MEM_OBJECT_IMAGE1D`
- `image1d_buffer_t`: A 1D image created from a buffer object using `CL_MEM_OBJECT_IMAGE1D_BUFFER`
- `image1d_array_t`: A 1D image array created with `CL_MEM_OBJECT_IMAGE1D_ARRAY`.

All the preceding image data types can be used as a `datatype` in a kernel argument. An image function kernel argument cannot be modified or read from directly. Every image argument should be declared with `__read_only` or `__write_only` qualifiers. `__read_only` images can only be read from and `__write_only` images can only be written to. OpenCL specification provides for built-in functions, which can be used to read or write pixel elements. They are `read_image{f|u|i}` and `write_image{f|u|i}`. Also note that the calls to `read_image` and `write_image` to the same image memory object in a kernel are not supported.

Samplers

One of the parameters passed to `read_image` and `write_image` built-ins is the image sampler object. Sampler variables in a program are declared to be of type `sampler_t` and enable the read and write routines to sample an input pixel value. The samplers are created inside a kernel by using the OR operator for the normalized coordinates, the addressing modes, and the filtering modes. Example is as follows:

```
const sampler_t sampler = CLK_NORMALIZED_COORDS_FALSE |
  CLK_ADDRESS_NONE |
  CLK_FILTER_NEAREST;
```

Normalized coordinates can be set to either of the following two:

- `CLK_NORMALIZED_COORDS_TRUE`: The pixel coordinate values are in the range of 0 to 1.0.
- `CLK_NORMALIZED_COORDS_FALSE`: The pixel coordinate values will be having an extent of image dimensions. That is **0** for **Height - 1** and **0** for **WIDTH - 1**. The following diagram shows a 3D-coordinate system when it is normalized or non-normalized:

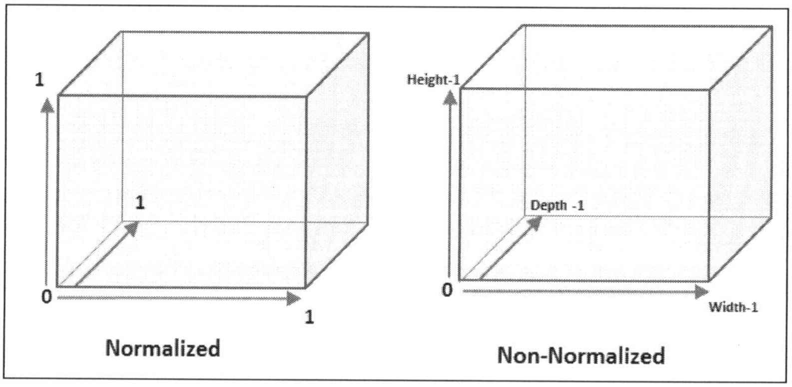

The addressing mode can be one of: `CLK_ADDRESS_MIRRORED_REPEAT`, `CLK_ADDRESS_REPEAT`, `CLK_ADDRESS_CLAMP_TO_EDGE`, `CLK_ADDRESS_CLAMP`, and `CLK_ADDRESS_NONE`. These are described briefly in the following bullet list:

- `CLK_ADDRESS_CLAMP_TO_EDGE`: It clamps the pixel coordinate using the `clamp (coord, 0, size - 1)` function.
- `CLK_ADDRESS_CLAMP`: It clamps the pixel coordinate using the `clamp (coord, -1, size)` function.

- `CLK_ADDRESS_NONE`: It returns the `coord`.
- `CLK_ADDRESS_MIRRORED_REPEAT` and `CLK_ADDRESS_REPEAT`: These addressing modes can be used only with normalized coordinates. The following diagram describes the difference between the two addressing modes visually. The `CLK_ADDRESS_MIRRORED_REPEAT` addressing mode flips the image coordinate at every junction of normalized coordinate 1.0. The `CLK_ADDRESS_REPEAT` addressing mode wraps the coordinates to a valid range by repeating the image at every junction of normalized coordinates.

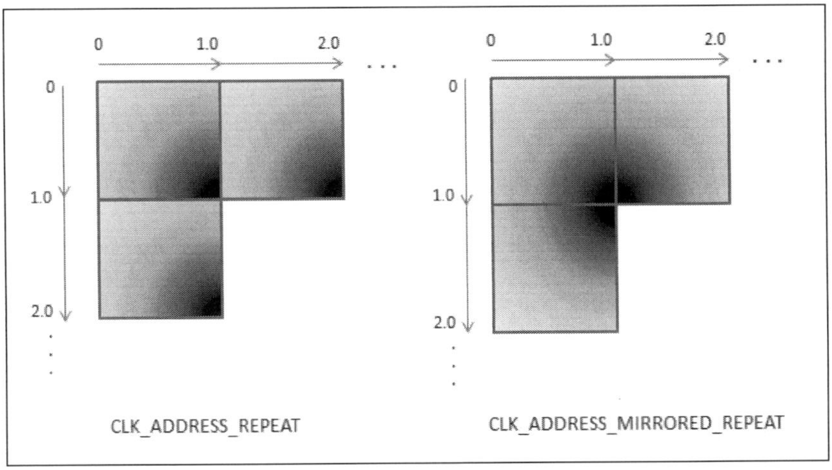

Difference between Address Repeat and Address Mirrored Repeat.

Filter mode can be one of the following:

- `CLK_FILTER_NEAREST`: It calculates the pixel coordinate, which is nearest in terms of the normalized values. The nearest distance is calculated by using the Manhattan distance formula.
- `CLK_FILTER_LINEAR`: It returns the weighted average of the four texture elements that are closest to the specified texture coordinates.

The samplers can also be created at the host side using the `clCreateSampler` function:

```
cl_sampler clCreateSampler (cl_context context,
  cl_bool normalized_coords,
  cl_addressing_mode addressing_mode,
  cl_filter_mode filter_mode,
  cl_int *errcode_ret)
```

The `normalized_coords`, `addressing_mode`, and `filter_mode` addressing modes can take the values as discussed earlier.

To understand the different types of addressing modes and filtering modes, one should try the example code `image_sampler` with different combinations of samplers in this chapter.

Reading and writing buffers

Till now we discussed how to create an image. The OpenCL provides APIs to transfer image data to device image buffer before the kernel is launched. Similarly, there is a function which transfers the image computed data back to the host memory. The `clEnqueueWriteImage` function copies the data from host to device memory as follows:

```
cl_int clEnqueueWriteImage (cl_command_queue command_queue,
  cl_mem image,
  cl_bool blocking_write,
  const size_t *origin,
  const size_t *region,
  size_t row_pitch,
  size_t slice_pitch,
  const void * ptr,
  cl_uint num_events_in_wait_list,
  const cl_event *event_wait_list,
  cl_event *event)
```

The `clEnqueueReadImage` function copies the data back from device to host memory as follows:

```
cl_int clEnqueueReadImage (cl_command_queue command_queue,
  cl_mem image,
  cl_bool blocking_read,
  const size_t *origin,
  const size_t *region,
  size_t row_pitch,
  size_t slice_pitch,
  void *ptr,
  cl_uint num_events_in_wait_list,
  const cl_event *event_wait_list,
  cl_event *event)
```

The following bullet list describes the objects mentioned in the preceding code:

- `command_queue`: The write command will be queued in this OpenCL queue. One should make sure that the `cl_mem` object buffer and the `command_queue` object are created using the same context.
- `image`: This is a valid `cl_mem` image object created using the `clCreateImage` function.
- `blocking_write/blocking_read`: This indicates whether the read or write operation is blocking or non-blocking. If set to `CL_TRUE` function does not return until the status of the event associated with enqueued read or write command has reached `CL_COMPLETE`.
- `origin`: This is a three tuple index for the start offset for the read or write operation. `origin` is an array of three elements, `origin[0]`, `origin[1]`, and `origin[2]`. For 3D images all the three tuples must be specified. For 2D images only two tuples is specified, the third one is set to 0. Similarly, for 1D images and 1D image buffer objects only the first tuple is specified, the second and third are set to 0. If the image is a 2D array, then the first two tuples `origin[0]`, `origin[1]` specify the pixel offset, the third tuple origin[2] specifies the image index. In the case of 1D image array types, the first tuple origin[0] specifies the pixel offset and origin[1] specifies the image array index.
- `region`: It is also a three element array and defines the `region[0]` as width, `region[1]` as height, and `region[2]` as depth in pixels for the 1D, 2D, or 3D rectangle. For a 2D image array `region[0]` specifies the width and `region[1]` specifies the height in pixels of the 2D rectangle, and `region[2]` specifies the number of images, if the image_type is a 2D image array. Similarly for 1D image the `region[0]` specifies the width in pixels of the 1D rectangle and `region[1]` specifies the number of images, if the `image_type` is a 1D image array. If image is a 2D image then `region[2]` must be 1. If image is a 1D image or 1D image buffer object, `region[1]` and `region[2]` should be set to 1. If image is 1D image array object then `region[2]` must be 1.

> Note that both region and origin define the pixel offsets and not byte offsets. The byte offset is calculated internally using the channel data type and the channel order which was specified while creating the image object.

- `row_pitch`: It defines the length of each row in bytes. If set to 0 then the `row_pitch` object is calculated as `size` of each element in bytes * width. `width` is specified as the first tuple element in region.

- `slice_pitch`: This specifies the size of the 2D slice in a 3D image or 2D image array object in bytes. This is set to zero if the image is a 1D or 2D image. This can also be used to specify the size of 1D or 2D image in a 1D image array or 2D image array. The `row_pitch` and `slice_pitch` object are shown in the diagram "1D 2D and 3D image formats".
- `ptr`: It is the pointer to the image array, which will be the source for `clEnqueueWriteImage` and a destination for `clEnqueueReadImage`.

The parameters `num_events_in_wait_list`, `event_wait_list`, and `event` have their usual meaning as any other `clEnqueue*` functions.

If the `cl_mem` object is created using `CL_MEM_USE_HOST_PTR`, the read and write operation must ensure that the `host_ptr` buffer specified when creating the image object contains the latest bits. That means all the operations associated with the image object are completed. One way to make sure that the `host_ptr` is latest is to specify the events in `event_wait_list` which is associated with the image.

Copying and filling images

The write and read functions help to copy the data buffer from the host to the device memory or vice versa. There is another function which helps in copying the data from one OpenCL image buffer object to another. This is specified as `src_image` and `dst_image` in the following function:

```
cl_int clEnqueueCopyImage (cl_command_queue command_queue,
  cl_mem src_image,
  cl_mem dst_image,
  const size_t *src_origin,
  const size_t *dst_origin,
  const size_t *region,
  cl_uint num_events_in_wait_list,
  const cl_event *event_wait_list,
  cl_event *event)
```

The `src_origin` and `dst_origin` parameter have the usual meaning as specified for the `origin` parameter for the read and write routines in the previous section.

The `region` parameter also has the same meaning as specified in the previous section.

This function can be used to do one of the following tasks:

- Copy a 1D image object to a 1D image object, 2D image object, or 2D slice of a 3D image object and vice-versa
- Copy a 1D image object to a scan line of a specific image index of a 1D or 2D image array object and vice versa

- Copy a 2D image object to a 2D image object or to a 2D slice of a 3D image object
- Copy a 2D image object to a specific image index of a 2D image array object and vice versa
- Copy a 3D image object to a 3D image object

The `clEnqueueCopyImage` function will copy data between two image objects. `clEnqueueCopyImageToBuffer` and `clEnqueueCopyBufferToImage` are the two APIs which allow to copy data from an image object to a buffer object or vice versa. Their function prototypes are as follows:

```
cl_int clEnqueueCopyImageToBuffer (cl_command_queue command_queue,
  cl_mem src_image,
  cl_mem dst_buffer,
  const size_t *src_origin,
  const size_t *region,
  size_t dst_offset,
  cl_uint num_events_in_wait_list,
  const cl_event *event_wait_list,
  cl_event *event);
cl_int clEnqueueCopyBufferToImage (cl_command_queue command_queue,
  cl_mem src_buffer,
  cl_mem dst_image,
  size_t src_offset,
  const size_t *dst_origin,
  const size_t *region,
  cl_uint num_events_in_wait_list,
  const cl_event *event_wait_list,
  cl_event *event);
```

The other function `clEnqueueFillImage`, helps an OpenCL developer to fill an image with a particular color value.

```
cl_int clEnqueueFillImage (cl_command_queue command_queue,
  cl_mem image,
  const void *fill_color,
  const size_t *origin,
  const size_t *region,
  cl_uint num_events_in_wait_list,
  const cl_event *event_wait_list,
  cl_event *event)
```

The `fill_color` parameter will be converted to the appropriate image channel format associated with the image when it was specified while creating the image object. All the pixel elements in the image will be filled with this value.

Mapping image objects

As discussed in the mapping of buffer objects in the previous chapter, images can also be mapped to a host pointer. Images computed at the device may sometimes needs to be available at the host address space, say for writing the image back to the file system. The `clEnqueueMapImage` function will map the image from the device memory to the host address space. This is also a task which is enqueued on the device `command_queue`.

```
void * clEnqueueMapImage (cl_command_queue command_queue,
  cl_mem image,
  cl_bool blocking_map,
  cl_map_flags map_flags,
  const size_t *origin,
  const size_t *region,
  size_t *image_row_pitch,
  size_t *image_slice_pitch,
  cl_uint num_events_in_wait_list,
  const cl_event *event_wait_list,
  cl_event *event,
  cl_int *errcode_ret)
```

The `clEnqueueMapImage` function enqueue a command to map a region of the device buffer in the image object to host accessible buffer. Note that the return type of this function is `void *`.

- `image`: It is the valid image `cl_mem` object
- `blocking_map`: This is set to true or false for a blocking or a non-blocking call respectively
- `map_flags`: It has the same definition as discussed in the previous chapter

The `origin`, `region`, `image_row_pitch`, and `image_slice_pitch` functions, all have the same definition as discussed in the previous section where we discussed the read and write functions.

Querying image objects

Similar to all OpenCL objects, image objects can also be queried using the `clGetImageInfo` function. In the previous chapter, we discussed the `clGetMemObjectInfo` function, which was used to query the OpenCL `cl_mem` object. This API can be used to determine if the `cl_mem` object is of type `CL_MEM_OBJECT_BUFFER` or one of the image types specified by `cl_image_desc.image_type` argument while creating the image object.

Once you know that the `cl_mem` object is for an OpenCL image object, you can retrieve information about the image using the `clGetImageInfo` function.

```
cl_int clGetImageInfo (cl_mem image,
  cl_image_info param_name,
  size_t param_value_size,
  void *param_value,
  size_t *param_value_size_ret)
```

The different `param_name` values which can be given are as follows:

- `CL_IMAGE_FORMAT`: It gives the image format descriptor when the image was created
- `CL_IMAGE_ELEMENT_SIZE`: It gives the size of a pixel element in the image
- `CL_IMAGE_ROW_PITCH`: It gives the size of a row in bytes
- `CL_IMAGE_SLICE_PITCH`: It gives the size of a 2D slice in the 2D image array or in a 3D image
- `CL_IMAGE_WIDTH`: It gives the pixel width of the image
- `CL_IMAGE_HEIGHT`: It gives the pixel height of the image
- `CL_IMAGE_DEPTH`: It gives the pixel depth of the image
- `CL_IMAGE_ARRAY_SIZE`: It gives the number of images in a 1D or a 2D array image
- `CL_IMAGE_BUFFER`: It gives the cl_mem buffer object associated with the image

The following code snippet helps you to get information about the image width and height using the `param_name` values, `CL_IMAGE_WIDTH` and `CL_IMAGE_HEIGHT`

```
size_t image_width;
size_t image_height;
size_t size_returned;
cl_context context = . . .;
cl_mem clImage = . . .;
clStatus= clGetImageInfo (context,
  CL_IMAGE_WIDTH,
  sizeof(size_t),
  & image_width,
  & size_returned);
clStatus= clGetImageInfo (context,
  CL_IMAGE_HEIGHT,
  sizeof(size_t),
  & image_height,
  & size_returned);
```

Image histogram computation

In the previous chapter, we computed the RGB histogram of an input image on an OpenCL buffer object. In this chapter, we will discuss the same with input as an OpenCL image object. The input image is read into a contiguous buffer and an image object is created using the `clCreateImage` function. At the kernel side the pixel values can be sampled using `read_image` OpenCL built-in. The next diagram illustrates how an image is read and processed in the example code. The input image from the file system is read into a contiguous buffer, row wise as shown by step 1 in the diagram. The input image can be of any format BMP, PNG, or JPEG. The raw image pixel buffer is then used to create an OpenCL image object using the `clCreateImage` function. The CL_MEM_USE_HOST_PTR flag is passed. This is shown as step 2 in the diagram. Finally each kernel instance executes on the image buffer as shown by step 3.

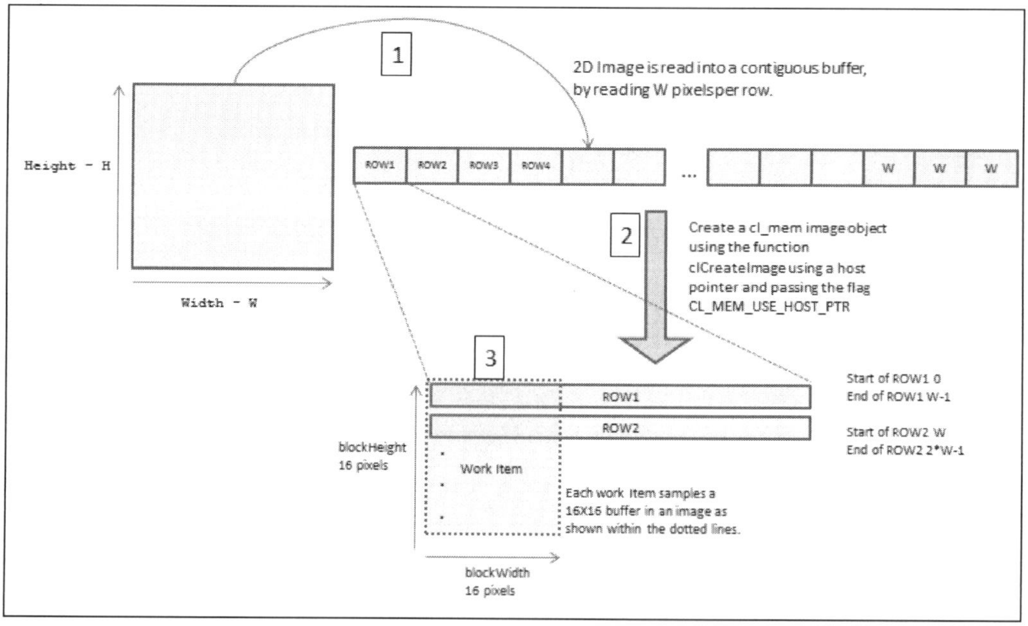

Take a look at the following **histogram_image_kernel** OpenCL kernel. This kernel processes 16 X 16 size image pixels. Let's consider an image of size (1024, 1024), then the NDRange of this kernel is globally (64,64), and the local work group dimensions are (4,4). We are using (4,4) because we want to keep our local memory usage within the permissible limit. The permissible limit for local device memory can be obtained using the `clGetDeviceInfo` function with `param_name`, `CL_DEVICE_LOCAL_MEM_SIZE`. The `histogram_kernel` uses a local memory of size:

```
3*BIN_SIZE*groupSize* sizeof(cl_uchar);
```

For a `groupSize` object of 16 and `BIN_SIZE` of 256 a total of 12288 bytes (12 K) of local memory is used. For almost all of AMD graphics devices, 32 K of local memory can be allocated. The OpenCL kernel code should ensure that it uses the local memory within this permissible limit otherwise it may result in adverse performance degradation. Each work item processes a 16 X 16 block of an image that is 256 elements. So for a 1024 X 1024 image, a total of (64, 64) work items are spawned. With each work group size of (4,4) there are a total of 16 X 16 work groups. The following diagram shows work groups and work item processing on an image:

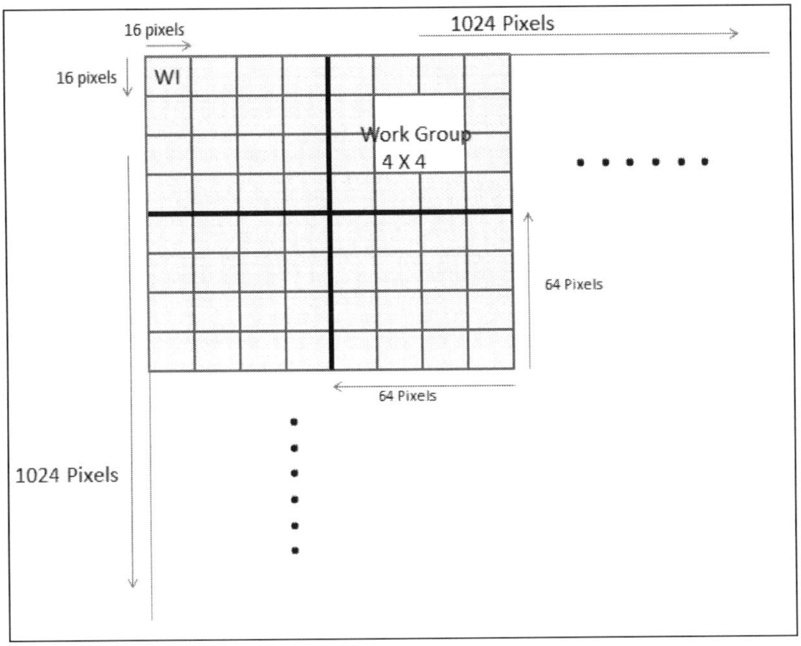

The execution model of histogram_image_kernel

The OpenCL device kernel code is as follows. The `histogram_image_kernel` computes the histogram of a 16 X 16 block in an image:

```
#define BIN_SIZE 256
#pragma OPENCL EXTENSION cl_khr_byte_addressable_store : enable
  __kernel
void histogram_image_kernel(__read_only image2d_t image,
  __local uchar* sharedArray,
  __global uint* binResultR,
  __global uint* binResultG,
  __global uint* binResultB,
    uint  blockWidth,
    uint  blockHeight)
{
```

```
size_t localIdX = get_local_id(0);
size_t localIdY = get_local_id(1);
size_t localSizeX = get_local_size(0);
size_t localSizeY = get_local_size(1);
size_t globalIdX = get_global_id(0);
size_t globalIdY = get_global_id(1);
size_t groupIdX = get_group_id(0);
size_t groupIdY = get_group_id(1);
size_t totalGroupSize = get_local_size(0) *
  get_local_size(1);
size_t groupSizeX = get_global_size(0)/get_local_size(0);
__local uchar* sharedArrayR = sharedArray;
__local uchar* sharedArrayG = sharedArray +
  totalGroupSize * BIN_SIZE;
__local uchar* sharedArrayB = sharedArray +
  2 * totalGroupSize * BIN_SIZE;
sampler_t smplr = CLK_ADDRESS_REPEAT | CLK_FILTER_NEAREST;
uint sharedArrayOffset = localIdY * localSizeX + localIdX;
/* initialize shared array to zero */
for(int i = 0; i < BIN_SIZE; ++i)
{
    sharedArrayR[sharedArrayOffset * BIN_SIZE + i] = 0;
    sharedArrayG[sharedArrayOffset * BIN_SIZE + i] = 0;
    sharedArrayB[sharedArrayOffset * BIN_SIZE + i] = 0;
}

/* calculate the histograms */
int xCoord = globalIdX*blockWidth;
int yCoord = globalIdY*blockHeight;
for(int i = 0; i < blockHeight; ++i)
{
   for(int j = 0; j < blockWidth; ++j)
   {
       int pixelCoordX  = xCoord+j;
       int pixelCoordY  = yCoord+i;
       uint4 pixelValue = read_imageui(image, smplr,
                  (int2)(pixelCoordX, pixelCoordY));
       uint valueR = pixelValue.x;
       uint valueG = pixelValue.y;
       uint valueB = pixelValue.z;
       sharedArrayR[sharedArrayOffset * BIN_SIZE + valueR]++;
       sharedArrayG[sharedArrayOffset * BIN_SIZE + valueG]++;
       sharedArrayB[sharedArrayOffset * BIN_SIZE + valueB]++;
   }
```

```
    }
    barrier(CLK_LOCAL_MEM_FENCE);

    uint numOfElements = BIN_SIZE/totalGroupSize;
    uint offsetforWI = (localIdY*localSizeX + localIdX)
      *numOfElements;
    for(int i = 0; i < numOfElements; ++i)    {
       int binCountR = 0;
       int binCountG = 0;
       int binCountB = 0;
       for(int k = 0; k < totalGroupSize; ++k)
       {
           int localOffset = k*BIN_SIZE + offsetforWI;
           binCountR += sharedArrayR[localOffset + i];
           binCountG += sharedArrayG[localOffset + i];
           binCountB += sharedArrayB[localOffset + i];
       }
       uint WGBinOffset = groupIdY * groupSizeX + groupIdX;
       binResultR[WGBinOffset * BIN_SIZE + offsetforWI + i] =
         binCountR;
       binResultG[WGBinOffset * BIN_SIZE + offsetforWI + i] =
         binCountG;
       binResultB[WGBinOffset * BIN_SIZE + offsetforWI + i] =
         binCountB;
    }
}
```

In the first for loop of the kernel, each work item will set its share of 256 elements in `sharedArrayR`, `sharedArrayG`, and `sharedArrayB` memory to zero. Then the kernel computes the image histogram pixel wise. Note here that the image is read using the `read_imageui` function. This function takes as input a `sampler_t` object, the pixel coordinates, and the image itself from where the pixel values are to be read. Since the image is a 4-channel `CL_RGBA` format, the return value of the `read_imageui` function is a unit4 vector, which contains the RGB values of a pixel.

In the last step in the kernel the local histogram computed by each work item is added element wise to get the number of red pixels with 0,1, 2, and so on in that work group. Each work item would compute the `numOfElements` histogram values. In the end, we will have 256 elements per work group. This is filled in the global memory, which is transferred back to the host. At the host, we add each work group histogram values to get the final 256-histogram values for the entire image.

Summary

In this chapter we discussed the OpenCL `cl_mem` image objects. We also understood why image objects are required, and how they can be used to represent pixels of different formats or data types. We also solved the image histogram problem using the OpenCL image objects. The same problem was discussed using OpenCL buffers in the previous chapter. Sampling of an image pixel is an important topic and one should try the image_sampler example program to understand that completely.

In this and the previous chapter we discussed we discussed the two important forms of `cl_mem` data objects. We created a program and kernel object in our histogram example in order to execute our kernels. In the next chapter we will understand the creation of program and kernel objects in detail. These kernel objects are the execution entities, which can run on any OpenCL capable device.

5
OpenCL Program and Kernel Objects

In the last two chapters we discussed about the OpenCL memory objects in the form of buffer and image objects. In the previously discussed examples of saxpy and histogram in first and the third chapter respectively; we implemented a parallel OpenCL C kernel, which is executed on a device. A program object and a kernel object were created before execution of the kernel. These kernel and program object are the important execution entities in the OpenCL framework. In this chapter we shall concentrate on the set up steps required to create a program object and execute a kernel. Once you have expertise in this then you can concentrate on the problem, which you want to solve using OpenCL. The following topics will be discussed in this chapter:

- Creating program objects
- Program build options
- Querying program objects
- Offline and online compilation
- Creating kernel objects
- Setting kernel arguments
- Executing the kernels
- Querying kernel objects
- Source versus binary program creation
- Querying kernel objects

Creating program objects

An OpenCL application can execute a function in parallel on a device using the kernel objects. There may be more than one kernel functions, which run in parallel in an application based on the hardware you have. An application can create multiple program objects each for a different context. Each of these program objects can have more than one kernel object. Each kernel in a program source string is identified by a `__kernel` qualifier. Let us first create a `cl_program` object.

Creating and building program objects

The OpenCL kernel programs needs to be built and linked at runtime. In OpenCL a program object can be created using the functions, `clCreateProgramWithSource` or `clCreateProgramWithBinary`. A program object is created once for a context in execution. Input to these functions is a source text string in ASCII or in binary format respectively. The program object is created for the devices associated with the OpenCL context. The `clCreateProgramWithSource` function declaration is as follows:

```
cl_program
clCreateProgramWithSource (cl_context context,
  cl_uint count,
  const char **strings,
  const size_t *lengths,
  cl_int *errcode_ret)
```

The following bullet list explains the preceding function prototype in detail:

- `context`: It is an OpenCL context for the underlying platform.
- `count`: It specifies the number of pointers to be held in strings argument.
- `strings`: It is an array of count pointers. Each pointer is a `char` string which holds the OpenCL C source code.
- `lengths`: It specifies the length of each `strings` pointer. The value of `lengths[i]` specifies the length of the `strings[i]`, that is there is a one to one correspondence between `lengths` array and the `strings` array. If `lengths` is set to `NULL` then, `strings` is also considered `NULL` terminated. If `lengths[i] = 0` then `strings[i] = NULL`.
- `errorcode_ret`: It holds the error code returned by the OpenCL implementation, after the API completes its execution. If it is `NULL` this parameter is ignored. A valid non-zero program object is created with `clCreateProgramWithSource` and `errcode_ret` is set to `CL_SUCCESS`. Otherwise an error code is set in `errcode_ret`. An important point to note is that this program object is a per context object and not per device object. It is when you build the program using the `clBuildProgram` function, and then only the program binary is created for the devices specified.

Sometimes loading and building the program object will result in some delay during runtime. Take a look at the following CodeXL screenshot:

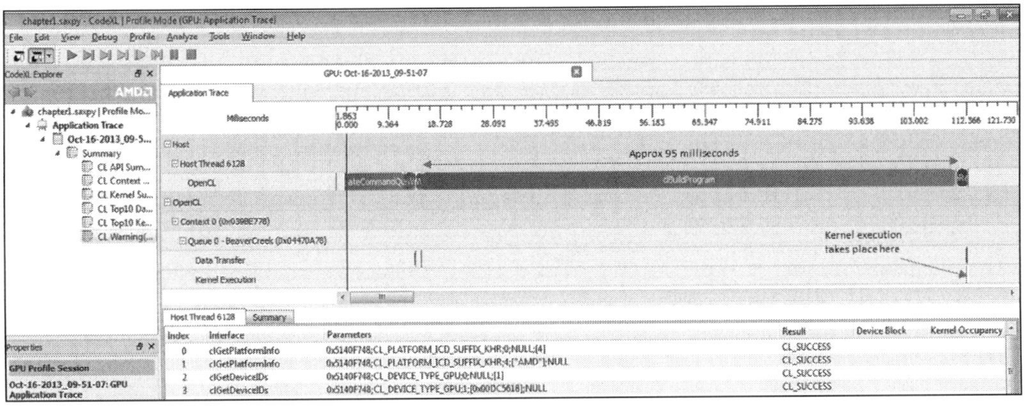

CodeXL snapshot showing the duration of clBuildProgram

Alternatively a program object can also be created using binary source files. Since the program is already compiled, loading them would be a faster option. Take a look at the following CodeXL screenshot, which shows the benefit of loading the binary using `clCreateProgramWithBinary` and then building the program object. The `clBuildProgram` function takes only 1.69 milliseconds for a binary program, whereas for the source program it takes approximately 95 milliseconds, which is a huge gap.

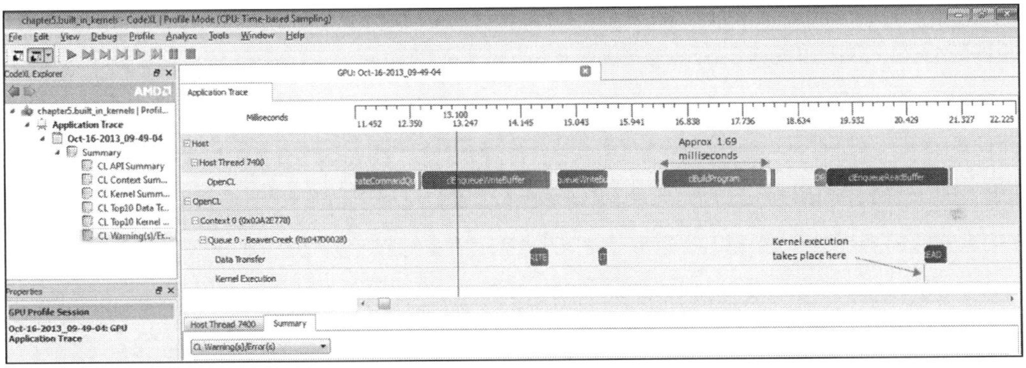

CodeXL snapshot showing the duration of clBuildProgram for a binary kernel

Note that the preceding two screenshots are from AMD CodeXL OpenCL debugging and profiler utility. CodeXL works only for AMD OpenCL runtimes.

Binaries can be used to protect intellectual property. An application during installation time may only need the program binaries. In this way there is no need for storing the kernel source files on the disk. The important thing to note here is that each binary is device specific. Some implementations instead of storing many binaries for each device can store the binary in an intermediate representation, which can be common representation across all devices. The format of binary file is OpenCL implementation specific and OpenCL vendors are free to choose any format of representation. OpenCL standard does not specify any format for binary representation. The other important point to note is that once you create a program using binary source files you need to again build the program object using the `clBuildProgram` API. This is because the `clBuildProgram` function acts like a linking step. The OpenCL implementation during build step can resolve some of the proprietary implementations. Once a program is successfully built, one can get a binary file using the `clGetProgramInfo` function with the `param_name`, `CL_PROGRAM_BINARIES`. Till now we have mentioned three new APIs `clBuildProgram`, `clCreateProgramWithBinary`, and `clGetProgramInfo`. Let us discuss each of these APIs in detail and also aid the discussion with an example code.

Programs created with `clCreateProgramWithBinary`, should provide a valid binary file created for any of the devices in context:

```
cl_program
clCreateProgramWithBinary (cl_context context,
  cl_uint num_devices,
  const cl_device_id *device_list,
  const size_t *lengths,
  const unsigned char **binaries,
  cl_int *binary_status,
  cl_int *errcode_ret)
```

The following bullet list explains the parameters of `clCreateProgramWithBinary` function in detail:

- `context`: It is an OpenCL context for the underlying platform.
- `num_devices`: It specifies the size of the `device_list` pointer.
- `device_list`: This is an array of `num_devices` devices that are present in the OpenCL context. The `device_list` array should not be `NULL`. Binaries are loaded for every device in the `device_list` array.
- `lengths`: It is the size of each pointer holding the number of bytes in binaries.
- `binaries`: This is an array of pointers to the program binaries. The program object is created for these pointer objects. The `binaries[i]` pointer of length `lengths[i]` will be loaded for device `device_list[i]`.The `binaries[i]` pointer cannot be a `NULL` pointer and `lengths[i]` cannot be zero.

- `binary_status`: The `binary_status[i]` pointer stores the status of load of `binaries[i]`.
- `errcode_ret`: It holds the error code for the completion status of this API.

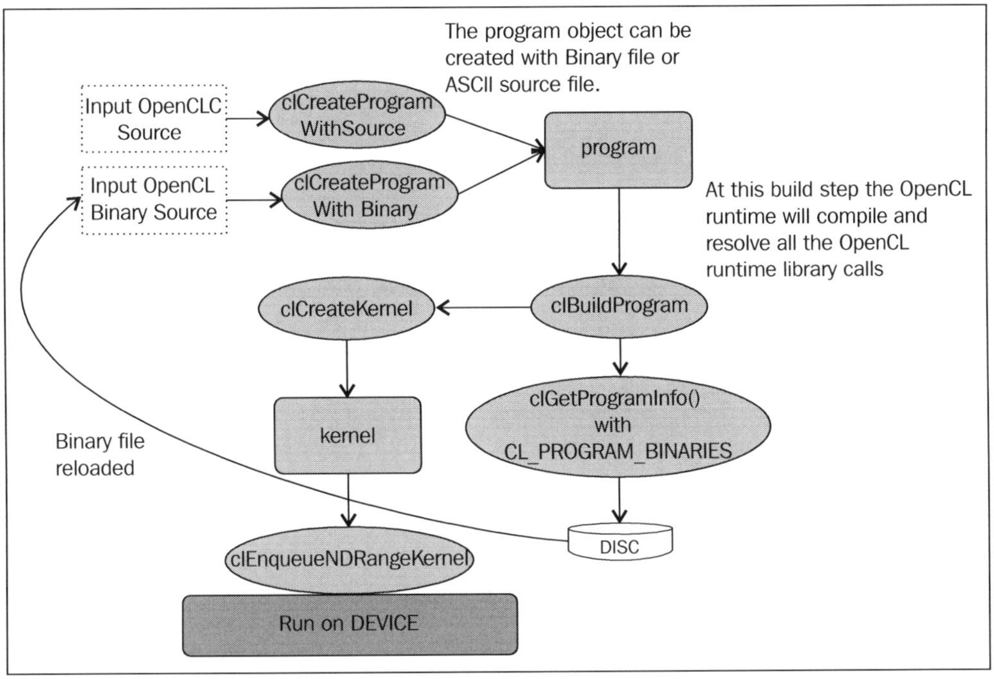

Flowchart showing creation of program object using binary and ASCII source files

Once a new program object is created for a context either using the binary or an OpenCL C source file, the next step is to build the program. The `clBuildProgram` function builds an OpenCL program. This build step involves the source code compilation if program was created using the `clCreateProgramWithSource` function and then linking the compiled binaries. If the program is created using `clCreateProgramWithBinary` then only the link step is performed.

```
cl_int
clBuildProgram (cl_program program,
  cl_uint num_devices,
  const cl_device_id *device_list,
  const char *options,
  void (CL_CALLBACK *pfn_notify)(cl_program program,
    void *user_data),
  void *user_data)
```

The following bullets list explains the functioning of the objects used in the preceding code:

- `program`: A valid program object.
- `num_devices`: It specifies the size of the `device_list` pointer.
- `device_list`: This is an array of `num_devices` devices that are present in the OpenCL context. The program object is built for all the devices mentioned in this list. If it is `NULL` then an executable program is created for the devices list while creating the program object.
- `options`: The OpenCL runtime compiler invoked in this call can be given some compile time options. The `options` string is a `NULL` terminated string of compiler options.
- `pfn_notify`: This is a pointer to callback function, which is called when the OpenCL implementation completes the build procedure.
- `user_data`: This is the data which is passed by the OpenCL implementation to the callback routine.

The question which might arise to any reader is that, what if there is a compilation error? On a build failure the OpenCL implementation returns `CL_BUILD_PROGRAM_FAILURE` for the call to `clBuildProgram`. OpenCL specification provides a function to look for the compilation error.

```
cl_int
clGetProgramBuildInfo (cl_program program,
  cl_device_id device,
  cl_program_build_info param_name,
  size_t param_value_size,
  void *param_value,
  size_t *param_value_size_ret)
```

If the call to the previous `clBuildProgram` was not successful, an application can use `clGetProgramBuildInfo` to get the build error log per device associated with the program object.

- `program`: This program object is queried here to get error and warning logs.
- `device`: Every device in the OpenCL implementation may throw different errors. For example there may be a device which supports double precision data representation and the other does not. So the OpenCL developer needs to query the error logs for different devices separately.
- `param_name`: As shown in the next table, different values for `cl_program_build_info` can be given.
- `param_value_size`: It is the size in bytes of the `param_value` pointer.

- `param_value`: This is the pointer to memory where the result of this function will be returned.
- `param_value_size_ret`: On return from the function the actual size of the error log is stored. In any case the value of this will not exceed `param_value_size`.

The following table is the list of `cl_program_build_info` enumerations, which can be used to query the program build status:

cl_program_build_info	Description
`CL_PROGRAM_BUILD_STATUS`	Returns the status for the last `clBuildProgram` operation for the device and the program. It can be either of the following: • `CL_BUILD_NONE`: No build performed • `CL_BUILD_ERROR`: Build error • `CL_BUILD_SUCCESS`: Successful build • `CL_BUILD_IN_PROGRESS`: Build is still running
`CL_PROGRAM_BUILD_OPTIONS`	Returns the build, link, or compile options specified as arguments to `clBuildProgram`, `clLinkProgram`, or `clCompileProgram`, which was for the last operation on program for device.
`CL_PROGRAM_BUILD_LOG`	Returns the log for the last build, compile, or link operation.
`CL_PROGRAM_BINARY_TYPE`	Return the type of the binary associated with the program object. The returned values cab be one of the following: • `CL_PROGRAM_BINARY_TYPE_COMPILED_OBJECT` for compiled binary • `CL_PROGRAM_BINARY_TYPE_LIBRARY` for a library based binary when created with clLinkProgram • `CL_PROGRAM_BINARY_TYPE_NONE` for no associated binary program

The following MACRO example gives the details of how to query for the compilation error logs for a program and the associated device. This is defined in the `include/ocl_macros.h` file in our examples code distribution. First call to `clGetProgramBuildInfo` is used to determine the size of the build error log, once the size is determined; an equivalent size buffer is allocated using the `malloc` function. The subsequent call to the `clGetProgramBuildInfo` function is used to retrieve the actual build error.

```
#define LOG_OCL_COMPILER_ERROR(PROGRAM, DEVICE)\
{\
    cl_int logStatus;\
    char * buildLog = NULL;\
    size_t buildLogSize = 0;\
    logStatus = clGetProgramBuildInfo(PROGRAM,\
      DEVICE,\
      CL_PROGRAM_BUILD_LOG,\
      buildLogSize,\
      buildLog,\
      &buildLogSize);\
    if(logStatus != CL_SUCCESS)\
    {\
        std::cout << "Error # "<< logStatus\
            <<":: clGetProgramBuildInfo<CL_PROGRAM_BUILD_LOG>
              failed.";\
        exit(1);\
    }\
\
    buildLog = (char*)malloc(buildLogSize);\
    if(buildLog == NULL)\
    {\
        std::cout << "Failed to allocate host memory.
          (buildLog)\n";\
        return -1;\
    }\
    memset(buildLog, 0, buildLogSize);\
    logStatus = clGetProgramBuildInfo(PROGRAM,\
      DEVICE,\
      CL_PROGRAM_BUILD_LOG,\
      buildLogSize,\
      buildLog,\
      NULL);\
    if(logStatus != CL_SUCCESS)\
    {\
        std::cout << "Error # "<< logStatus\
            <<":: clGetProgramBuildInfo<CL_PROGRAM_BUILD_LOG>
              failed.";\
        exit(1);\
    }\
\
```

```
    std::cout << " \n\t\t\tBUILD LOG\n";\
    std::cout << " ************************************************\n
";\
    std::cout << buildLog << std::endl;\
    std::cout << " ************************************************\n
";\
    free(buildLog);\
}
```

OpenCL program building options

The OpenCL kernels can be specified using some compiler options when the kernel is being built with `clBuildProgram`. These are categorized as pre-processor options, options that control optimization or options for math intrinsic.

Pre-processor options are used by the compiler during the pre-processing stage. `-D` option can be used to enable a specific type of code based on the different vendor.

```
#if defined(ENABLE_ATOMICS)
    atomic_add(ptr, 9);
#else
    *ptr = *ptr + 9;
#endif
```

If the compiler option `-DENABLE_ATOMICS` is given then the `if` part of the code is compiled otherwise the `else` part of the code is compiled. This is particularly useful when a vendor provides support for an OpenCL extension, which might be useful from programmers perspective, but he will have to provide an alternate code when the extension is not supported on other vendors.

Math intrinsic options control the behavior of the floating point math. Some floating point options are `-cl-single-precision-constant` (treats all constants as single precision constants). In most of the C compilers a floating point constant such as, `3.14` is treated as a double precision constant, this might result in a significant performance loss as all floating point operations using constants will be up scaled to double precision and then the result is computed. A programmer has to explicitly specify `3.14f` for treating it as an single precision floating point constant. In order to avoid the explicit mention of the `f` after every constant, programmer can use this option.

`-cl-denorms-are-zero` (treats all denormals as zero). A denormal number is a floating point number whose biased exponent is zero. If the result of any floating point operation results is a denormal float then the results are truncated to 0.

Besides these options there are some optimization control options. They are as follows:

- `-cl-opt-disable`: It disables all optimizations.
- `-cl-mad-enable`: It allows `a * b + c` to be replaced by a `mad()` operation. Note that `mad` are different from **fused multiply add (fma)** operation, the latter being more precise.

Some options are also provided to control the warnings thrown by the compiler for example, `-w` and `-werror`.

Querying program objects

Like any other OpenCL objects, every program object can be queried during runtime to gather information related to the compiled kernels. There are different types of query names given by `cl_program_info`. This is tabulated later. The input to the function is retrieved using the call to `clGetProgramInfo` with `CL_PROGRAM_BINARIES` as the `param_name` which returns a binary and can be stored into a file for future loading. The `clGetProgramInfo` function is defined as follows:

```
cl_int
clGetProgramInfo (cl_program program,
  cl_program_info param_name,
  size_t param_value_size,
  void *param_value,
  size_t *param_value_size_ret)
```

The following bullets list explains the functioning of the objects used in the preceding code:

- `program`: It is a valid program object. This program object is queried to get the program object information.
- `param_name`: The following tabulated list of the `cl_program_info` enumerations, which can be used to retrieve information about the program object.
- `param_value_size`: It is the size in bytes of the `param_value` pointer.
- `param_value`: This is the pointer to memory where the result of this function will be returned.
- `param_value_size_ret`: On return from the function the actual size of the data in bytes is stored. If the `param_value` pointer is not `NULL`, the value of this will not exceed `param_value_size`.

The following table is the list of the cl_program_info enumerations, which can be used to query the program object:

cl_program_info	Description
CL_PROGRAM_REFERENCE_COUNT	Returns the reference count of the program object.
CL_PROGRAM_CONTEXT	Returns the context associated when the program object is created using the function, clCreateProgramWithBinary or clCreateProgramWithSource.
CL_PROGRAM_NUM_DEVICES	Returns the number of devices specified when creating this program object.
CL_PROGRAM_DEVICES	Returns the list of devices specified when creating this program object.
CL_PROGRAM_SOURCE	Returns the OpenCL C source associated with the program. The size of the source code in bytes is specified by param_value_size_ret.
CL_PROGRAM_BINARY_SIZES	This will return an array of size in bytes for the program binaries for each device associated with the program.
CL_PROGRAM_BINARIES	The program binaries for each device associated with the program is returned. The output buffer param_value must be pre-allocated as per the size in bytes returned by a call to CL_PROGRAM_BINARY_SIZES.
CL_PROGRAM_NUM_KERNELS	A program may be associated with many kernels. The number of kernels associated with this program object is returned.
CL_PROGRAM_KERNEL_NAMES	Programs source code may be associated with one or more OpenCL kernels. To retrieve the names of the kernel this function is used. These kernel names can then be used to create a cl_kernel object using the clCreateKernel function. The returned kernel names are semi-colon separated.

Till now we discussed few functions, clCreateProgramWithSource, clCreateProgramWithSource, clBuildProgram, clGetProgramInfo, and clGetProgramBuildInfo. Now let's explain all these functions with two different examples. We will refer back to our first example that is, saxpy discussed in *Chapter 1, Hello OpenCL*. In this chapter we will discuss two different examples. In the first example create_binary we will create binary for the CPU and GPU device types. In the second example we will use the binary created in the first example to solve our saxpy problem.

Creating binary files

To create a binary file out of the input source string, one should follow the following sequence of operations. First read the file and create a `cl_program` object for an OpenCL context in execution using the `clCreateProgramWithSource` API. Build this program object using the `clBuildProgram` function, as follows:

```
cl_program program;
cl_int     clStatus = CL_SUCCESS;
cl_device_id  *device_list = NULL;
program  = clCreateProgramWithSource(context, 1,
  (const char **)&kernelCode, NULL, &clStatus);
//Build the program
clStatus = clGetContextInfo(context,CL_CONTEXT_NUM_DEVICES,
  sizeof(num_devices),&num_devices,NULL);
device_list = new cl_device_id[num_devices];
clStatus = clGetContextInfo(context,CL_CONTEXT_DEVICES,
  num_devices*sizeof(cl_device_id),
  device_list,NULL);
clStatus = clBuildProgram(program, num_devices,
  device_list, NULL, NULL, NULL);
```

Note that we have used `clGetContextInfo` for getting the number of devices and the list of devices. Ideally it would have been good if we had used the `clGetProgramInfo` API. Since we had used the same context to create the program object, and we are sure that the OpenCL implementation will provide the same set of `device_list` as it would have provided if we had used `clGetProgramInfo`. But in large programs it would be good to get the number of devices `num_device` using the `clGetProgramInfo` API with `param_name`, `CL_PROGRAM_NUM_DEVICES` and the `device_list` with `param_name` as `CL_PROGRAM_DEVICES`. This is what we have done in our next code snippet.

After we have built the program for a set of devices, it's time to get the code binary size using `CL_PROGRAM_BINARY_SIZE` and then the actual built binary using `CL_PROGRAM_BINARIES`. See the following code snippet:

```
//Get back the number of devices associated with the program object
clStatus = clGetProgramInfo(program, CL_PROGRAM_NUM_DEVICES,
  sizeof(cl_uint), &num_devices,
  &bytes_read);
```

```
size_t *binarySize = new size_t[num_devices];//Create size array
clStatus = clGetProgramInfo(program, CL_PROGRAM_DEVICES,
  sizeof(cl_device_id) * num_devices,
  device_list, &bytes_read);
//Load the size of each binary associated with the corresponding
device
clStatus = clGetProgramInfo(program, CL_PROGRAM_BINARY_SIZES,
  sizeof(size_t)*num_devices,
  binarySize, &bytes_read);
char** programBin = new char* [num_devices];
//Create the binary array
for(cl_uint i = 0; i < num_devices; i++)
    programBin[i] = new char[binarySize[i]];
//Read the Binary
clStatus = clGetProgramInfo(program, CL_PROGRAM_BINARIES,
  sizeof(unsigned char *) * num_devices,
  programBin, &bytes_read);
```

Finally after getting the binary buffer, we need to write it to a file for storing it in the disk and for future loading. Try to build and run the sample code and see the output binary file. There are some advantages of using the binary as a representation for the kernel. One is to save on compilation time for the OpenCL kernels. The other advantage is that the OpenCL developer may not want to deliver his proprietary kernel code in the form of a readable code. Instead he will store and distribute the binary. OpenCL SPIR extension also provides a standard intermediate representation for making the OpenCL kernel binaries portable across different vendors. We will discuss this in a later section.

As an exercise, try to link two different program objects using the `clLinkProgram` function. Once a new program object is created then try to store the binary of that kernel as shown earlier. You can additionally try to implement the code for creating binary files for multiple kernels.

Offline and online compilation

We have discussed the creation of binary object. An OpenCL kernel can be created at runtime, this is referred to as online compilation. In the previous section we have seen how a kernel binary can be created. We can store this kernel binary in the form of a library and an application can load it on demand from the disk. This is referred to as offline compilation. The following diagrams show the difference between the two compilation modes.

For offline compilation the application developer shall create the binary and distribute the binary with his application as shown in the following diagram:

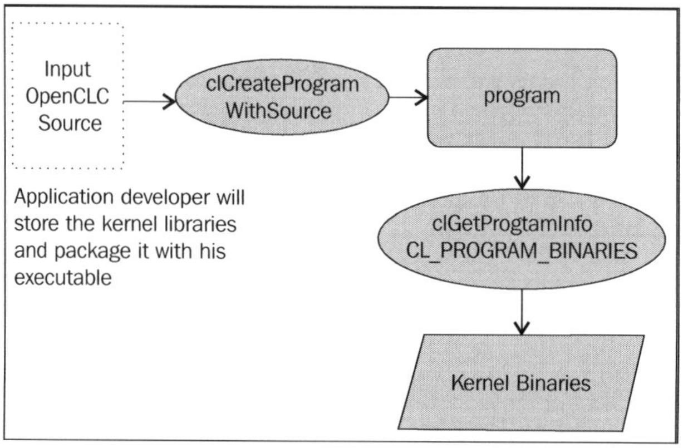

Offline Program Compilation and storing

In offline compilation mode the application will load the created kernel binary and execute the kernel. Note that even if the program is created using the `clCreateProgramWithBinary` function, `clBuildprogram` is necessary as the OpenCL runtimes library calls and built-ins are resolved at this step. The following diagram shows the offline compilation mode.

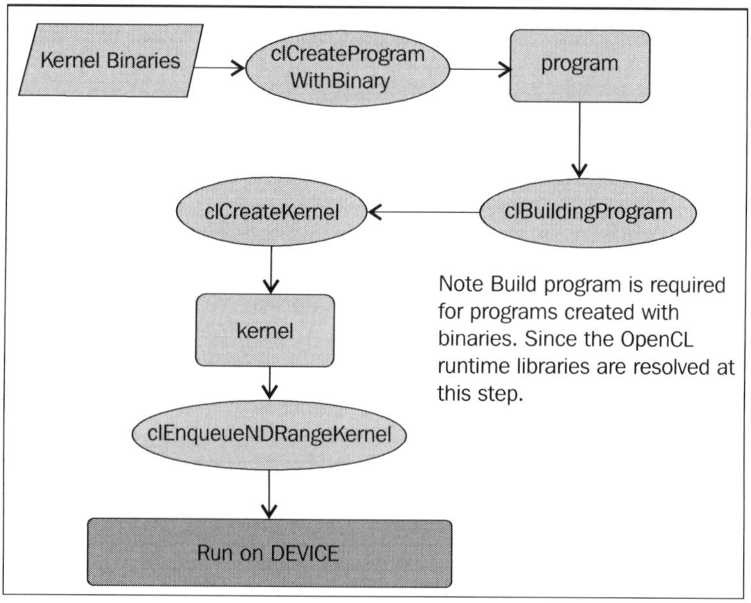

Offline Compilation

In online compilation mode the program is created with the `clCreateProgramWithSource` function. The `clBuildProgram` function step will compile and resolve the OpenCL runtime library calls. This is a little slower since compilation times may be high in an OpenCL implementation.

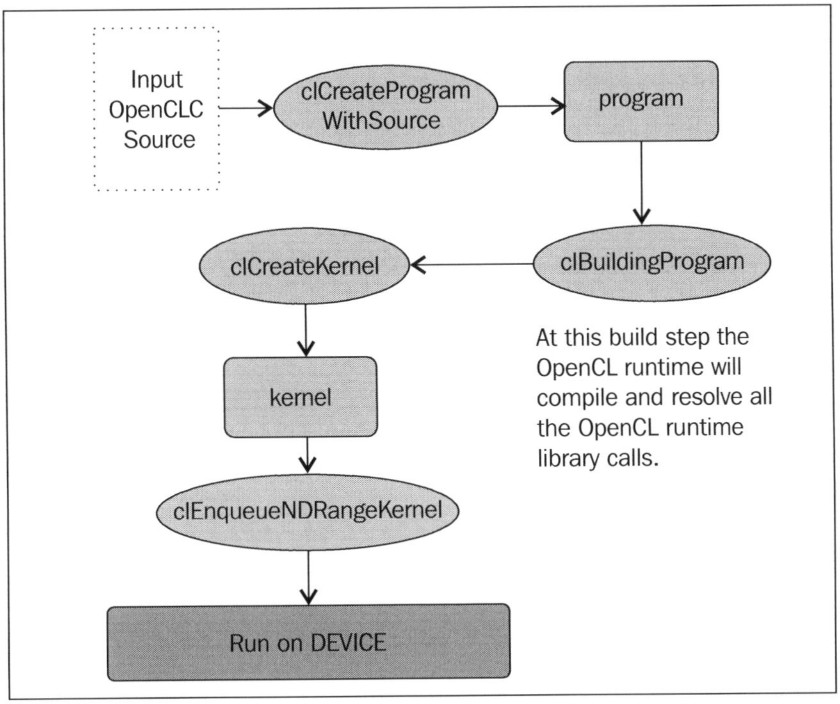

Online Compilation

SAXPY using the binary file

In the previous section we discussed creating a binary file which will be loaded by some other host program. Let us now discuss another example wherein we will use the same binary file, which is created in the previous example and run the `saxpy_kernel` function. We shall first read and load the binary file and create a program object using the `clCreateProgramWithBinary` API.

```
//Open the file for reading
fopen("saxpy_kernel_binary_gpu.clbin", "rb");
fseek(fp,0L,SEEK_END);
size_t fileSize = ftell(fp);
```

```
rewind(fp);
unsigned char * saxpy_kernel = new unsigned char [fileSize];
fread(saxpy_kernel,fileSize,1,fp);
// Create a program from the kernel source
cl_int binary_status;
cl_program program = clCreateProgramWithBinary(context, 1,
  &device_list[0], &fileSize,
  (const unsigned char **)&saxpy_kernel,
  &binary_status, &clStatus);

// Build the program
clStatus = clBuildProgram(program, 1, device_list, NULL, NULL, NULL);
```

Next we shall create a `cl_kernel` object with function `clCreateKernel` for the kernel `saxpy_kernel`, then set the arguments using the `clSetKernelArg` function. The details of these two functions are given after this code snippet.

```
// Create the OpenCL kernel
cl_kernel kernel = clCreateKernel(program, "saxpy_kernel", &clStatus);

// Set the arguments of the kernel
clStatus = clSetKernelArg(kernel, 0, sizeof(float), (void *)&alpha);
clStatus = clSetKernelArg(kernel, 1, sizeof(cl_mem), (void *)&A_clmem);
clStatus = clSetKernelArg(kernel, 2, sizeof(cl_mem), (void *)&B_clmem);
clStatus = clSetKernelArg(kernel, 3, sizeof(cl_mem), (void *)&C_clmem);

// Execute the OpenCL kernel on the list
size_t global_size = VECTOR_SIZE; // Process the entire lists
size_t local_size = 64;           // Process one item at a time
clStatus = clEnqueueNDRangeKernel(command_queue, kernel,
  1, NULL,
  &global_size,
  &local_size,
  0, NULL, NULL);
```

SPIR – Standard Portable Intermediate Representation

One of the drawbacks with OpenCL is that by default an application can distribute there OpenCL program in one of the following two ways:

- In the form of a high level OpenCL C program
- Or in the form of a low-level binary which is compiled for the specific device

We have seen both with samples, about how to use them. But each of these has the drawback of the source code being available to as the distribution. And the later one has the drawback of the binary not being portable across different vendors' OpenCL devices. In order to avoid the two drawbacks, *Khronos* group came up with the SPIR specification. SPIR is an extension of OpenCL, where the vendors can provide a SPIR compliant binary consumer and a producer. Have a look at the following diagram:

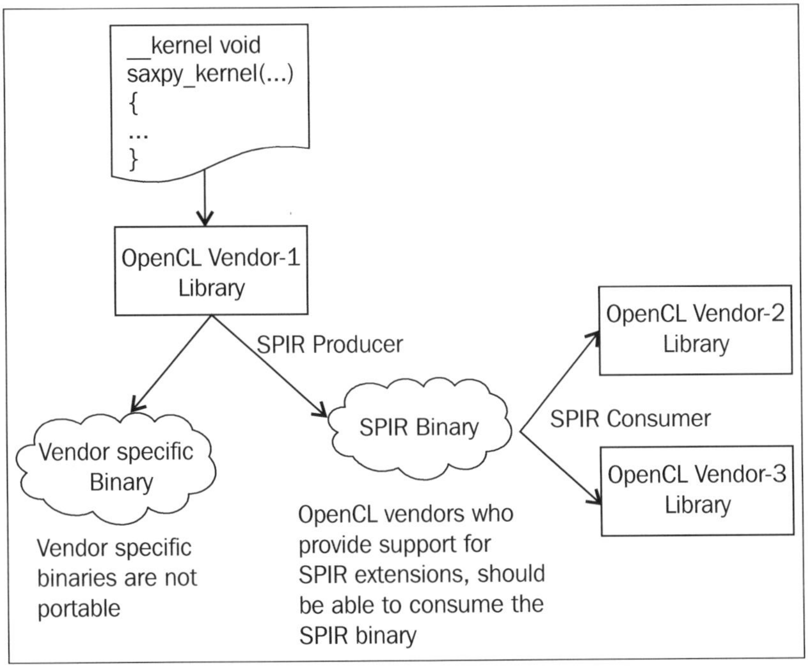

SPIR Producer and Consumer

OpenCL vendor 1 or application developers can produce a SPIR compliant binary and distribute their proprietary algorithms in this intermediate representation. OpenCL vendor 2 and 3 can consume these binaries. Thus SPIR provides benefits by allowing code integrity and making the OpenCL applications portable across different vendors. SPIR is a mapping of the OpenCL C program to the LLVM IR; and it adopts two notations, which are part of the LLVM IR. One is the binary bit code representation and the other is the assembly language notation provided by LLVM. For more details take a look at the SPIR specification.

Creating kernel objects

In this section we will discuss details about the kernel objects, and how kernel objects can be created using the program objects. Every program is a collection of kernels, you can consider a program object as a library of kernels. As shown in the following figure a `program` is associated with `kernel1` and `kernel2`. The `program` is built with inputs as two devices `device1` and `device2`. A kernel when enqueued on the command queue, the OpenCL runtime generates the binary for execution on the device. Note that each kernel can be executed on different devices. It is at the runtime the binaries are generated.

A kernel object can be created from a well formed OpenCL C program, which is built as discussed in the previous section. A kernel object is an encapsulation for a parallel executable entity. The kernel object is used to pass arguments using the `clSetKernelArg` API, before running the kernel using the `clEnqueueNDRangeKernel` API. Have a look at the following diagram:

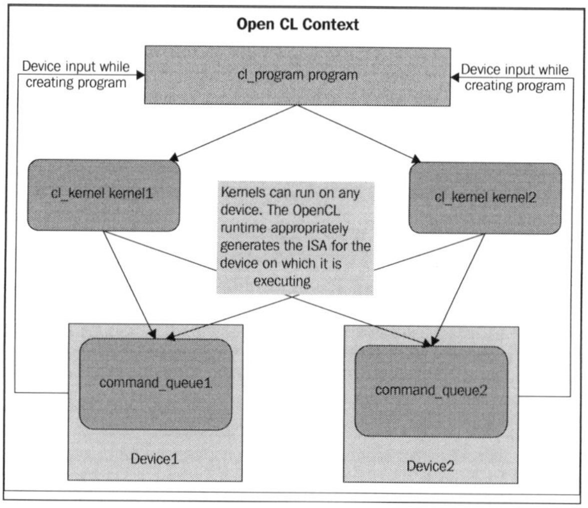

Kernels and Program

In the OpenCL programs the `cl_kernel` objects are created using the `clCreateKernel` function. Each kernel in an OpenCL C code is identified by the `__kernel` function keyword.

```
cl_kernel
clCreateKernel (cl_program program,
  const char *kernel_name,
  cl_int *errcode_ret);
```

The following bullets list explains the functioning of the objects used in the preceding code:

- `program`: It is a valid program object. This program object is used to create a kernel object
- `kernel_name`: It provides function name in the OpenCL C code declared with the `__kernel` qualifier
- `errcode_ret`: It returns an error code if the kernel was not created successfully

There is another mechanism with which kernels can be created. The `clCreateKernelsInProgram` function creates all the kernel objects associated with the program.

```
cl_int
clCreateKernelsInProgram (cl_program program,
  cl_uint num_kernels,
  cl_kernel *kernels,
  cl_uint *num_kernels_ret)
```

- `program`: A program object which is successfully built
- `num_kernels`: It is the size of memory pointed to by kernels
- `kernels`: It is the buffer where all the kernel objects will be returned
- `num_kernels_ret`: It is the actual number of kernel objects returned

Setting kernel arguments

Before executing the kernel, the arguments must be set for the kernel using the `clSetKernelArg` function, as follows:

```
cl_int
clSetKernelArg (cl_kernel kernel,
                cl_uint arg_index,
                size_t arg_size,
                const void *arg_value)
```

The following bullets list explains the functioning of the objects used in the preceding code:

- `kernel`: It is a kernel object for which you want to set the arguments
- `arg_index`: The index of the argument starting from 0 to the last argument
- `arg_size`: It specifies the size of `arg_value`
- `arg_value`: It is the pointer to the data that shall be passed to the device for the argument `arg_index`.

For memory objects, the `arg_value` is the address associated with the buffer or image object. The `arg_value` can be `NULL` also. If the associated kernel argument is a `__global` or `__constant` memory qualifier then this argument will be `NULL` while the kernel is executed. Otherwise if the argument is a `__local` address space qualifier the `arg_value` has to be `NULL`. The `__local` address space qualifier specifies a local memory in the device. This memory need not be allocated on the host, hence it is `NULL`. The size of the local memory is defined by the `arg_size` value.

Let's take our example in the `saxpy_kernel`:

```
// Set the arguments of the kernel
    clStatus = clSetKernelArg(kernel, 0,
      sizeof(float), (void *)&alpha);
    clStatus = clSetKernelArg(kernel, 1,
      sizeof(cl_mem), (void *)&A_clmem);
    clStatus = clSetKernelArg(kernel, 2,
      sizeof(cl_mem), (void *)&B_clmem);
    clStatus = clSetKernelArg(kernel, 3,
      sizeof(cl_mem), (void *)&C_clmem);
```

The `saxpy_kernel` takes four arguments. The first argument is a constant float value which is passed to the kernel. The next three arguments are memory buffers. For creating local memory buffers in the kernel one must pass the size of the buffer required in bytes to the `arg_size` argument and set the `arg_value` argument to `NULL`. The parameter received in the kernel code is a local memory buffer, which is specified with a `__local` qualifier. Similarly `arg_value` is set to pointer to sample objects for arguments of type `sampler_t`.

Let's take a sample kernel prototype which describes most of the preceding explanation:

```
__kernel
void example_kernel(int i,
  float f,
  __local float l_Array,
  __global float g_Array,
  read_only image2d_t srcImg,
  sampler_t sampler)
```

The following code snippet sets the arguments of the `kernel`, which is the `cl_kernel` object for `example_kernel`:

```
// Set the arguments of the kernel
kernel = clCreateKernel(program, "example_kernel", NULL);
clStatus = clSetKernelArg(kernel, 0, sizeof(int),
  (void *)&host_int);
clStatus = clSetKernelArg(kernel, 1, sizeof(float),
  (void *)&host_float);
clStatus = clSetKernelArg(kernel, 2, 1024, NULL);
clStatus = clSetKernelArg(kernel, 3, sizeof(cl_mem),
  (void *)&host_clmem);
clStatus = clSetKernelArg(kernel, 4, sizeof(cl_mem),
  (void *)&host_img_clmem);
clStatus = clSetKernelArg(kernel, 5, sizeof(cl_sampler),
  (void *)&host_sampler);
```

Executing the kernels

The created `cl_kernel` object can now be run on the device associated with it using the `clEnqueueNDRangeKernel` API. This shall enqueue the command for kernel execution on the `command_queue`. The queue shall then run this command if there are no commands waiting to be executed or else complete the execution of all the commands and then execute this kernel on the device associated with the `command_queue` command.

```
cl_int
clEnqueueNDRangeKernel (cl_command_queue command_queue,
  cl_kernel kernel,
  cl_uint work_dim,
  const size_t *global_work_offset,
  const size_t *global_work_size,
  const size_t *local_work_size,
  cl_uint num_events_in_wait_list,
  const cl_event *event_wait_list,
  cl_event *event)
```

The following bullets list explains the functioning of the objects used in the preceding code:

- `command_queue`: It is a command queue for the device where the command is enqueued.
- `kernel`: It is a valid OpenCL kernel object.

- `work_dim`: It is the dimension for the NDRange. The value it can take is `1`, `2`, or `3`. The value of `work_dim` specifies the size of the `global_work_offset`, `global_work_size`, and `local_work_size` arrays.
- `global_work_offset`: This is an array of `work_dim` unsigned values that gives the offset used to calculate the global ID of a work item.
- `global_work_size`: This is an array of the `work_dim` unsigned values that gives the global size of the NDRange. These values specify the number of work items, which will constitute the NDRange in each dimension.
- `local_work_size`: This is also an array of the `work_dim` unsigned values that gives the number of work items in a work group. A detailed explanation of this is given in *Chapter 2, OpenCL Architecture*.

The `num_events_in_wait_list`, `event_wait_list`, and `event` objects will have their usual meanings as explained for each of the `clEnqueue*` routines.

There is one other way with which a kernel can be executed. If `clEnqueueNDRange` is available for data parallel workloads then `clEnqueueTask` is available for task parallel workloads.

```
cl_int clEnqueueTask (cl_command_queue command_queue,
  cl_kernel kernel,
  cl_uint num_events_in_wait_list,
  const cl_event *event_wait_list,
  cl_event *event)
```

The `clEnqueueTask` function enqueues a task on `command_queue` to execute the kernel on the device associated with the `command_queue` command. Note that there is no dimension information provided and neither global nor local size are provided. That means this function executes only a single work item for the kernel. This is equivalent to call `clEnqueueNDRange with dim=1`, `global_work_offset = NULL`, `local_work_size[0] = 1`, and `global_work_size[0] = 1`.

Querying kernel objects

Similarly to get the information about the program object, OpenCL provides an API to receive information about the `cl_kernel` object created. One can use this API to receive information about the kernel function name, number of arguments, the associated program, context, and so on.

```
cl_int
clGetKernelInfo (cl_kernel kernel,
  cl_kernel_info param_name,
  size_t param_value_size,
  void *param_value,
  size_t *param_value_size_ret)
```

The following bullets list explains the functioning of the objects used in the preceding code:

- `kernel`: This is a valid `cl_kernel` object for which information is being queried.
- `param_name`: The following tabulated list of `cl_kernel_info` enumerations can be used to retrieve information about the kernel object.
- `param_value_size`: size in bytes of the `param_value` pointer.
- `param_value`: This is the pointer to memory where the result of this function will be returned.
- `param_value_size_ret`: On return from the function the actual size of the data in bytes is stored. If the `param_value` pointer is not `NULL` the value of this will not exceed `param_value_size`.

The following table is the list of `cl_kernel_info` enumerations that can be used to query the kernel object:

cl_kernel_info	Description
CL_KERNEL_FUNCTION_NAME	Returns the name of the `kernel` function.
CL_KERNEL_NUM_ARGS	Returns the kernel function's number of arguments.
CL_KERNEL_REFERENCE_COUNT	Returns the reference count of the `kernel` object.
CL_KERNEL_CONTEXT	Returns the `context` associated with the kernel object. This context is the context which was passed during the creation of program object using `clCreateProgramWithBinary` or `clCreateProgramWithSource`.
CL_KERNEL_PROGRAM	Returns the associated `program` object associated for the kernel.
CL_KERNEL_ATTRIBUTES	Returns any attributes specified using the `__attribute__` qualifier with the kernel function declaration in the program source.

Querying kernel argument

OpenCL provides functions to query information regarding the kernel arguments also, which can be stored in the kernel binary using the `-cl-kernel-arg-info` option. This allows the compiler to store the argument information for the kernel. It gives information about the type of the argument, the name of the argument, it's address and the access qualifiers. The `clGetKernelArgInfo` function returns this information. The kernel argument information is only available for the program's created with the `clCreateProgramWithSource` function as follows:

```
cl_int
clGetKernelArgInfo (cl_kernel kernel,
  cl_uint arg_indx,
  cl_kernel_arg_info param_name,
  size_t param_value_size,
  void *param_value,
  size_t *param_value_size_ret)
```

The following bullets list explains the functioning of the objects used in the preceding code:

- `kernel`: It is a valid `cl_kernel` object for which information is being queried.
- `arg_indx`: It is the index of the argument for which information is queried. It takes values from *0* to *n-1* for an *n* argument kernel. The total number of arguments for the kernel can be obtained using the `clGetKernelInfo` function with `param_name` as `CL_KERNEL_NUM_ARGS`.
- `param_name`: It is the list of `cl_kernel_arg_info` for which information can be queried. The `param_value_size`, `param_value`, and `param_value_size` objects have the same meaning as for any `clGet*Info` function.

The following table is the list of `cl_kernel_arg_info` enumerations, which can be used to query the details about the arguments to a kernel object:

cl_kernel_arg_info	Description
`CL_KERNEL_ARG_ADDRESS_QUALIFIER`	Returns the address space qualifier for the `arg_indx` argument. It can be one of the following: • `CL_KERNEL_ARG_ADDRESS_GLOBAL` • `CL_KERNEL_ARG_ADDRESS_CONSTANT` • `CL_KERNEL_ARG_ADDRESS_LOCAL` • `CL_KERNEL_ARG_ADDRESS_PRIVATE`
`CL_KERNEL_ARG_ACCESS_QUALIFIER`	Returns the access qualifier for the argument arg_indx. It can be one of the following: • `CL_KERNEL_ARG_ACCESS_READ_ONLY` • `CL_KERNEL_ARG_ACCESS_READ_WRITE` • `CL_KERNEL_ARG_ACCESS_WRITE_ONLY` • `CL_KERNEL_ARG_ACCESS_NONE`
`CL_KERNEL_ARG_TYPE_NAME`	Returns the argument type name for the `arg_indx` argument.

cl_kernel_arg_info	Description
CL_KERNEL_ARG_TYPE_QUALIFIER	Returns the type qualifier for the arg_indx argument. It can be a combination of the following: • CL_KERNEL_ARG_TYPE_CONST • CL_KERNEL_ARG_TYPE_VOLATILE • CL_KERNEL_ARG_TYPE_RESTRICT • CL_KERNEL_ARG_TYPE_NONE
CL_KERNEL_ARG_NAME	Returns the name argument arg_indx.

Another function which allows the user to query the kernel object for a particular device is clGetKernelWorkGroupInfo. The CL_KERNEL_WORK_GROUP_SIZE query can be used to determine the maximum work group size that can be used on the device. Optimal performance can be achieved if the work group size is selected to be a multiple of CL_KERNEL_PREFERRED_WORK_GROUP_SIZE_MULTIPLE. This value is useful as the OpenCL platforms dispatch the work items in warps or wave front. AMD GPUs dispatch work items in wave fronts. The size of a wave front is 64 in AMD GPUs. If the work group size is not a multiple of 64 then it would result in wastage of hardware resource. For example, Let's take 100 as the work group size. For a 64 preferred work group size, the hardware will schedule the 100 work items in chinks of 64 and 36 work items. This results in the wastage of *64 -36 = 28* processing elements not being utilized.

```
cl_int
clGetKernelWorkGroupInfo (cl_kernel kernel,
  cl_device_id device,
  cl_kernel_work_group_info param_name,
  size_t param_value_size,
  void *param_value,
  size_t *param_value_size_ret)
```

The following bullets list explains the functioning of the objects used in the preceding code:

- kernel: It is a valid cl_kernel object for which information is being queried.
- device: The information is queried for the combination of device associated with the kernel.
- param_name: It specifies the list of information which can be queried. This is tabulated below.

The param_value_size, param_value, and param_value_size values have the same meaning as for any get*Info function.

The following table is the list of `cl_kernel_work_group_info` enumerations, which can be used to query the kernel object to get the kernel work group related information.

cl_kernel_work_group_info	Description
`CL_KERNEL_GLOBAL_WORK_SIZE`	This is used to query the maximum global size that can be used to execute a `kernel`.
`CL_KERNEL_WORK_GROUP_SIZE`	This returns the maximum work group size, which can be used to execute the `kernel` on the `device`.
`CL_KERNEL_COMPILE_` and `WORK_GROUP_SIZE`	This returns the work group size specified using the kernel attribute qualifier: `__attribute__((reqd_work_group_size(X, Y, Z)))`.
`CL_KERNEL_LOCAL_MEM_SIZE`	This returns the local memory used in bytes by the kernel.
`CL_KERNEL_PREFERRED_WORK_GROUP_SIZE_MULTIPLE`	This returns the performance hint to the application such that multiple of this value will result in optimal performance.
`CL_KERNEL_PRIVATE_MEM_SIZE`	Returns the minimum amount of private memory in bytes used by each of the work items in the kernel.

Releasing program and kernel objects

Every program object needs to be released from the OpenCL implementation space. This is achieved by using the following code:

```
cl_int
clReleaseProgram(cl_program program)
```

Here, `program` is a valid program object.

The call to `clReleaseProgram` function will decrement a reference count, and if the count reaches 0, then the program object is released. To query the reference count associated with the program object, one can use `clGetProgramInfo` with the `param_name` as `CL_PROGRAM_REFERENCE_COUNT`. For increasing the reference count of the program object one can use the OpenCL function, `clRetainProgram`.

```
cl_int
clRetainProgram(cl_program program)
```

Similar to program objects kernel objects can also be released using `clReleaseKernel`. The kernel reference count can be determined using `clGetKernelInfo` with `param_name` as `CL_KERNEL_REFERENCE_COUNT`. The reference count can be increased using `clRetainKernel`.

Built-in kernels

Some custom devices contain specific unique functionality that are now integrated more closely into the OpenCL framework. The OpenCL 1.2 specification allows devices with special capabilities to expose a standard kernel implementation to perform specific tasks. Kernels can be called to use specialized or non-programmable aspects of underlying hardware. Some of these examples include video encoding/decoding and digital signal processors. The `clCreateProgramWithBuiltInKernel` function returns a `cl_program` object for the kernel names specified.

```
cl_program
clCreateProgramWithBuiltInKernels (cl_context context,
  cl_uint num_devices,
  const cl_device_id *device_list,
  const char *kernel_names,
  cl_int *errcode_ret)
```

The following bullets list explains the parameters passed to the function `clCreateProgramWithBuiltInKernels`:

- `context`: It is a valid OpenCL context
- `num_devices`: It is the number of devices listed in `device_list`
- `device_list`: This is an array of `num_devices` device's for which you want to get the list of kernel names
- `kernel_names`: It is a return value and contains the list of semicolon separated built-in kernel names

Summary

In this chapter we discussed the creation of the OpenCL program objects and the kernel objects. Kernel objects were created from the program objects. We also looked at how a program object can be used to look at the build errors. Additionally we took an example of creating a binary file from the program for a device and reload the binary file to perform our saxpy operation. We also discussed how SPIR will allow application developers to distribute there proprietary software and yet be portable.

In the next chapter we will discuss the OpenCL events and synchronization mechanisms. Events and synchronization are important topics for any parallel programming. Event handles are needed to keep track of the various tasks enqueued on to the command queue. We will also discuss the various synchronization models.

6
Events and Synchronization

The previous chapter was all about the OpenCL program and kernel creation, and enqueing the kernels in an NDRange. We also discussed different types of tasks, which will be queued on to a device command queue. Every application will need to keep track of these tasks and synchronize the data view for a computational task. The OpenCL standard provides this synchronizing entity in the form of `cl_event` objects.

A simple Wikipedia definition defines Events as an action that is usually initiated outside the scope of a program and the status of these events is handled by a piece of code inside the program. There may be multiple sources for events. A typical source of event handle is the OpenCL `clEnqueue*` routines. An OpenCL runtime libraries changes the state of all events enqueued to the command queue. It keeps track of all the operations, which a host program initiates on to the various OpenCL devices. OpenCL Events are used mainly to synchronize the execution of tasks, and also to determine/interpret the state of the task in execution.

In this chapter we shall discuss about the following topics:

- Coarse-grained events
- Fine-grained events
- Various synchronization models
- Querying events and event profiling

For "coarse grained" synchronization, OpenCL provides functions such as, `clFlush`, and `clFinish`. When the need arises for "finer grained" synchronization, the OpenCL specification provides a `cl_event` object, which is used to determine the status of a task enqueued on a command queue. The `cl_event` object helps to identify the status of unique commands in a queue and thus enable a host level monitoring of each event. An OpenCL developer may want to wait for the completion of event associated with any of the `clEnqueue*` functions unless they are explicitly specified to wait by setting the `blocking_[read|write]` variable to `CL_TRUE`.

If set to CL_FALSE these functions immediately return before the enqueued task is completed. Have a look at the following diagram. Execution of the kernel **A** is dependent on two write events of buffers **A** and **B** to complete. Similarly kernel **B** can be executed only when write of buffer **C** is completed and the execution of kernel **A** is also completed:

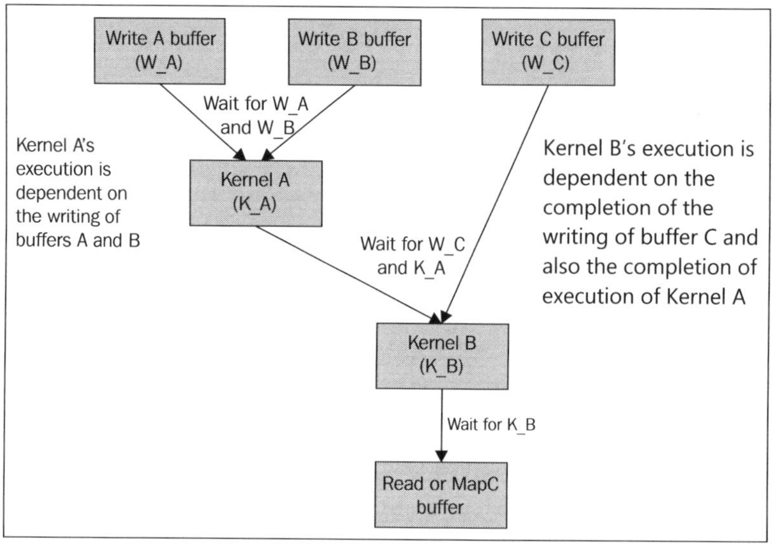

Diagram showing dependency of task execution

All the OpenCL clEnqueue* functions provide a mechanism to submit the dependency list when enqueing a task on the device command queue.

You can make sure that queue has dequeued all the commands and every command is completed by calling clFinish. The clFinish function will block the host program until the entire queue has completed. If you want to monitor the execution of the task enqueued by the clEnqueue* functions, they have an optional cl_event parameter that can be passed. The clEnqueue* functions will return a handle to cl_event, which can be queried for its status using the clGetEventInfo function. An OpenCL program can also wait for a list of events to finish with clWaitForEvents. This is also a host blocking call but the developer has a control on the events on which he wants to wait for instead of the all the events in the command_queue queue. And if you don't want to stop the host execution then use clEnqueueBarrierWithWaitList and clEnqueueMarkerWithWaitList. We will discuss about all this later in this chapter.

OpenCL events and monitoring these events

An event is a `cl_event` object that forms a medium of communication between the application and the OpenCL implementation. These event objects help in monitoring the OpenCL operations and commands. This monitoring can be of data transfer between the host and the devices and vice versa or either for the execution of the NDRange kernel. In OpenCL, an event is an object that specifies the state of a command queued into the OpenCL command queue. In OpenCL, events can be queried to notify the host that a command has completed its execution on the device. Besides this it can also be used for command synchronization. During command synchronization, a command which is queued for execution will wait on a list of events to complete before executing itself. In all the previous chapters you might have seen the last few parameters common across all the APIs starting with signature `clEnqueue*`.

```
clEnqueue*( ***, cl_uint num_events_in_wait_list,
  const cl_event *event_wait_list,
  cl_event *event);
```

For example, `clEnqueue{Read|Write|Map}Buffer` and `clEnqueueNDRangeKernel` all have to wait for `event_wait_list` events before finally executing itself. These event wait lists can be used to wait on one or more than one command. The `num_events_in_wait_list` and `event_wait_list` parameters specifies the number of events to wait for. On return of this function the last parameter event shall contain the handle to the `cl_event` object for the task being enqueued. This handle can be used to keep track of the execution of the command which is being queued. Every event is associated with a context. The contexts associated with events in `event_wait_list` and the context of the `command_queue` all should be same.

In OpenCL we can use events in three main ways which are follows:

- **Host notification**: An event can notify the host that a command has completed its execution on a device
- **Command synchronization**: An event can force commands to delay their execution until another event's occurrence has taken place
- **Profiling**: An event can monitor how much time a command takes to execute

OpenCL event synchronization models

In OpenCL, the command queues are used to submit work to a device and each work or task can be associated with an event object. The queuing of the command takes place in-order or as the program flow occurs. But when the commands are dequeued the tasks can execute in-order or out-of-order. In ordered execution one does not need an explicit synchronization that means the next command is executed only when the previous one has completed its execution. But in the case of out-of-order execution, there is a need for synchronization. The OpenCL provides this framework for synchronization. Synchronization is needed in the case of multiple command queues also. The user might want to divide his work load across multiple devices, and the running dynamics of each device may be different. So it becomes necessary to do synchronization. Let us discuss some models for queuing commands in OpenCL.

No synchronization needed

This is the simplest form of OpenCL programming. This is the ideal situation when the algorithm is very simple and no interaction between the various OpenCL devices is needed.

Single device in-order usage

This is the simplest form of task queuing mechanism, which uses an in-order queue associated with a device in context. All commands execute on single device and all the memory operations occur in a single memory pool.

The following code snippet explains the scenario:

```
cl_uint num_devices;
cl_device_id devices;
err = clGetDeviceIDs(NULL, CL_DEVICE_TYPE_CPU,
  1, &devices, &num_devices);
context = clCreateContext(0, 1, devices, NULL, NULL, &err);
cl_command_queue queue_cpu;
queue_cpu = clCreateCommandQueue(context, devices[0],
  0 /* IN-ORDER */, &err);
/* ... enqueue the tasks for the selected device here ... */
```

Here we created an in-order OpenCL command queue for the CPU device. In this case the device executes commands after the previous one finishes, and all the memory transactions are synchronized and consistently viewed. Hence there may be no need for fine-grained synchronization of events. The `clFlush` and `clFinish` objects should suffice. We will discuss about these functions in a later section.

Synchronization needed

This is bit more complex model and the complexity grows with multiple devices needing synchronization. This model is the default choice when the OpenCL developer wants to distribute his work load across multiple devices. Synchronization will also be needed when an out-of-order queue is used. In the following sections we will discuss the three different scenarios, where an OpenCL developer will need synchronization.

Single device and out-of-order queue

In this case we use an out-of-order queue, which is also associated with a single device in a context, same as the previous. All the memory operations occur in a single memory pool. All the commands will execute in a single device, but the order in which the commands get dequeued will have no guarantee for an ordered execution. The following code snippet shows how to create an out-of-order queue:

```
cl_uint num_devices;
cl_device_id devices;
err = clGetDeviceIDs(NULL, CL_DEVICE_TYPE_CPU, 1, &devices,
  &num_devices);
context = clCreateContext(0, 1, devices, NULL, NULL, &err);
cl_command_queue queue_cpu;
queue_cpu = clCreateCommandQueue(context, devices[0],
  CL_QUEUE_OUT_OF_ORDER_EXEC_MODE_ENABLE, &err);
/* ... enqueue the tasks for the selected device here ... */
```

The device starts executing as soon as it can and the memory transactions may overlap. The device may have capability to execute multiple tasks simultaneously, which results in better hardware utilization. This results in a need for an explicit synchronization of the algorithm when out-of-order execution is used.

Multiple devices and different OpenCL contexts

Here the commands execute on separate devices associated with a queue and each device has a separate memory pool. This model is useful if there are multiple devices in the platform and one wants to divide and run separate algorithms in different devices. The following code snippet shows creation of different command queues for the CPU and GPU devices separately:

```
cl_uint num_devices;
cl_device_id devices[2];
err = clGetDeviceIDs(NULL, CL_DEVICE_TYPE_CPU,
  1, /*Get one CPU device*/
  &devices[0], &num_devices);
```

```
err = clGetDeviceIDs(NULL, CL_DEVICE_TYPE_GPU,
  1, /*Get one GPU device*/
  &devices[1], &num_devices);
context_cpu = clCreateContext(0, 1, &devices[0],
  NULL, NULL, &err);
context_gpu = clCreateContext(0, 1, &devices[1],
  NULL, NULL, &err);
cl_command_queue queue_cpu, queue_gpu;
queue_cpu = clCreateCommandQueue(context_cpu, devices[0],
  0 /* IN-ORDER */, &err);
queue_gpu = clCreateCommandQueue(context_gpu, devices[1],
  0 /* IN-ORDER */, &err);
```

In this model the command queues cannot synchronize between the contexts.

Multiple devices and single OpenCL context

Multiple devices in the platform belong to the same context and each device has an associated queue and will modify or read data from a combined memory pool.

```
cl_uint num_devices;
cl_device_id devices[2];
err = clGetDeviceIDs(NULL, CL_DEVICE_TYPE_CPU, 1,
  &devices[0], &num_devices);
err = clGetDeviceIDs(NULL, CL_DEVICE_TYPE_GPU, 1,
  &devices[1], &num_devices);
context = clCreateContext(0, 2, devices, NULL, NULL, &err);
cl_command_queue queue_cpu, queue_gpu;
queue_cpu = clCreateCommandQueue(context, devices[0],
  0 /* IN-ORDER */, &err);!
queue_gpu = clCreateCommandQueue(context, devices[1],
  0 /* IN-ORDER */, &err);!
```

This is a true multi device model, and will need programming expertise to divide the workload across the different devices. Once each device completes its execution the associated event handle is set to `CL_COMPLETE`. The host program is expected to explicitly track the status of each task queued on each device. This is called as coarse-grained synchronization and OpenCL provides different functions for achieving this synchronization.

In this section we have discussed the various queuing synchronization models possible in OpenCL. Now we should be able to look into the various synchronization mechanisms which the OpenCL specification provides. It's true that basic synchronization can be done with simple OpenCL commands such as, `clFinish` and `clFlush`, but complex algorithms where you want to get the maximum out of the underlying hardware, will need functions for various event handling mechanisms and querying the event status. In the next few sections we will precisely explain each of these OpenCL functions.

Coarse-grained synchronization

There are two APIs which enable coarse-grained synchronization, they are `clFlush` and `clFinish`. The reason why we call coarse grained is that both lack control over the individual tasks queued on the command queue. These two functions have control only at the queue level.

```
cl_int clFlush (cl_command_queue command_queue);
```

This function ensures that all the commands, which are queued on the `command_queue` object will be submitted to the corresponding device. This does not guarantee that all the commands in the `command_queue` will be completed after `clFlush` returns.

First question which would arise is that what would happen if there is any blocking command queued to the device. Blocking commands do an implicit flush of the command_queue and on return from the blocking commands it will result in an implicit finish for the `command_queue`. This means that these functions will not return until this command gets completed. All the `clEnqueueRead*` and `clEnqueueWrite*` commands with their corresponding parameters `blocking_read` and `blocking_write` when set to `CL_TRUE` are referred to as blocking commands. The `clReleaseCommandQueue` function also performs an implicit flush of the command queue. Besides this the buffer mapping functions such as, `clEnqueueMapBuffer` and `clEnqueueMapImage` with `blocking_map` as `CL_TRUE` and the `clWaitForEvents` function all do an implicit flush of the command_queue.

There is another function `clFinish`, which helps in coarse-grained synchronization.

```
cl_int clFinish (cl_command_queue command_queue)
```

This function is a blocking function, that means `clFinish` will not return until all the previously enqueued commands in the `command_queue` are issued and reached its state of completion. This is a coarse-grained synchronization point. This function also guarantees that all the commands queued in the queue have reached the state `CL_COMPLETE`. If there is an error code associated with a command event handle then that indicates that the task was abnormally terminated.

The two APIs return `CL_SUCCESS` if the function calls were executed successfully, if not then either `CL_INVALID_COMMAND_QUEUE`, `CL_OUT_OF_RESOURCES`, or `CL_OUT_OF_HOST_MEMORY` is returned.

There is another function, `clEnqueueBarrierWithWaitList`, which queues a synchronization point.

```
cl_int
  clEnqueueBarrierWithWaitList (cl_command_queue command_queue,
    cl_uint num_events_in_wait_list,
      const cl_event *event_wait_list,
        cl_event *event)
```

The barrier command will be queued in the `command_queue` OpenCL queue.

The `clEnqueueBarrierWithWaitList` function is a non-blocking call and can achieve the same result as the `clFinish` function. Here the application developer needs to wait for the `event` to reach `CL_COMPLETE`. This function has two uses. First, it will wait for `num_events_in_wait_list` events in `event_wait_list` to reach `CL_COMPLETE`. Only then the status of the `event` handle is set to `CL_COMPLETE`. The second use is that if `num_events_in_wait_list` and `event_wait_list` are set to `0` and `NULL` respectively, then the event associated with this function will reach the state of `CL_COMPLETE` only if all the previously enqueued commands are completed. Any other command which is enqueued after this barrier command will not continue its execution until this barrier has reached a state of `CL_COMPLETE`. You might question what is the difference between `clEnqueueBarrierWithWaitList()` and `clFinish()`?

If you are using `clFinish` in your code then every kernel invocation using `clEnqueueBarrierWithWaitList` will have no impact on your code, because `clFinish` will wait for all the previously queued commands to complete. You can use `clEnqueueBarrierWithWaitList` when the queue is an out-of-order queue. Consider the following sequence of OpenCL function calls:

```
clEnqueueNDRangeKernel(queue, pre_compute_kernel, *** );
clEnqueueNDRangeKernel(queue, compute_kernel, *** );
```

Here the `pre_compute_kernel` must be completed first before the `compute_kernel` task is run. How would you synchronize this scenario when your queue is an out-of-order queue? You will think of the following quick solution:

```
clEnqueueNDRangeKernel(queue, pre_compute_kernel, *** );
clFinish(queue);
clEnqueueNDRangeKernel(queue, compute_kernel, *** );
```

But the moment you write `clFinish` in your code it will result in the host execution to block till all the previously issued commands complete execution. You can avoid this by using the following function:

```
clEnqueueNDRangeKernel(queue, pre_compute_kernel, *** );
clEnqueueBarrierWithWaitList (queue, *** );
clEnqueueNDRangeKernel(queue, compute_kernel, *** );
```

This will return the control back to the host and the host can continue with processing other useful code rather than waiting for the `clFinish` function to complete.

Event-based or fine-grained synchronization

OpenCL has an event-based synchronization mechanism. These event handles identify the unique commands in the queue and can be used for synchronizing algorithm execution. It can also be used for profiling the queued task. We will discuss more about profiling in a later section. OpenCL event is an object which holds the state of the task. An OpenCL event state is defined as one of the following stages based on the life time of the task:

- `CL_QUEUED`: The command is enqueued into the `command_queue` queue, but it has not yet been submitted to the device. This state is the first state for all events except for the user events.
- `CL_SUBMITTED`: This state means that the host has submitted this command to the host. All user events reach this state before running.
- `CL_RUNNING`: When the command is dequeued on the device the event reaches the state of `CL_RUNNING`. The device has started to execute this command. If this event is waiting for other events to complete then all those events should reach the state of `CL_COMPLETE`, then only this event shall reach a state of `CL_RUNNING`.
- `CL_COMPLETE`: This state is reached when the command has successfully completed its execution on the device.

If the application does not need to monitor the commands execution status and wants to ignore all other events, then the clEnqueue* functions use the following code:

```
clEnqueue*( ***, cl_uint num_events_in_wait_list,
  const cl_event *event_wait_list,
    cl_event *event);
clEnqueue*( ***, 0, NULL, NULL);
```

The application developer can set the `num_events_in_wait_list` queue to `0`, `event_wait_list` and `event` to `NULL`. This call will not generate any event for the application to monitor. Note that `num_events_in_wait_list` must be `0` if `event_wait_list` is `NULL`.

In OpenCL 1.1 there was an API as follows:

```
cl_int clEnqueueBarrier ( cl_command_queue command_queue )
```

This API was replaced with `clEnqueueBarrierWithWaitList` discussed earlier. You can perform the same operation as `clEnqueueBarrier` by passing parameters as discussed earlier.

Another function, `clEnqueueMarkerWithWaitList` helps in synchronizing. Unlike the `clEnqueueBarrierWithWaitList` function, it does not stop the execution of subsequent tasks enqueued in the command queue. It can be used to catch the status of execution of all the commands enqueued before this.

```
cl_int
clEnqueueMarkerWithWaitList (cl_command_queue command_queue,
  cl_uint num_events_in_wait_list,
    const cl_event *event_wait_list,
      cl_event *event)
```

Let's take an example and explain an use case of this function as follows:

```
cl_event write_event[2];
clEnqueueWriteBuffer(queue, clmem_A, ***, &write_event[0] );
clEnqueueWriteBuffer(queue, clmem_B, ***, &write_event[1] );
clEnqueueMarkerWithWaitList (queue, 2, write_event, &marker);
clEnqueueNDRangeKernel(queue, kernel_1, *** );
clWaitForEvents(1, &marker);
clEnqueueNDRangeKernel(queue, kernel_2, *** );
```

The `kernel_2` instance's execution is dependent on writing of two buffers `clmem_A` and `clmem_B` to the device. During the data transfer step, which might involve the data transfer through a DMA engine, the OpenCL device is not doing any computational work. So you can spawn another independent kernel `kernel_1`, so that both the data transfer and kernel execution can take place simultaneously. After the launch of `kernel_1` the developer can wait on the `marker` event to reach `CL_COMPLETE`. Once completed only then it can go ahead and spawn the second kernel, `kernel_2`. This could not have been achieved using `clEnqueueBarrierWithWaitList`, since it would not have launched any task after the barrier in the preceding highlighted code.

The `clEnqueueMarkerWithWaitList` function can also be used to simulate `clEnqueueMarker`, which is deprecated in OpenCL 1.2, by passing `0` to `num_events_in_wait_list` and `NULL` to `event_wait_list` and `event`. A marker command is enqueued on to the `command_queue` queue. This marker command shall wait for all events in `event_wait_list` to complete before it sets the state of `event` to `CL_COMPLETE`. If `event_wait_list` is `NULL` then all the events prior to itself will be waiting for completion. Both the functions `clEnqueueMarkerWithWaitList` and `clEnqueueBarrierWithWaitList` are OpenCL runtime mechanisms, which can be used to track the task queuing in an out-of-order queue. In an in-order queue these may not be that important.

Barrier and Marker functions are asynchronous in nature, but the same operations can be performed using another function called `clWaitForEvents`. This function is synchronous in nature.

The code for this function is as follows:

```
cl_int clWaitForEvents (cl_uint num_events,
  const cl_event *event_list);
```

This function waits on the host thread for commands identified by event objects in `event_list` to complete. The `num_events` object is the number of events specified in `event_list`. A command is considered complete if its execution status is `CL_COMPLETE`. The events specified in `event_list` act as synchronization points.

Getting information about cl_event

Let's understand the `cl_event` object in more detail. Every object in OpenCL has a mechanism to get information about itself. A user can query its associated context, its command queue, its status of execution or the type of the command it is associated with. Similar to `clGetContextInfo`, `clGetDevicenfo`, and so on. The function is defined as follows:

```
cl_int clGetEventInfo (cl_event event,
  cl_event_info param_name,
    size_t param_value_size,
      void *param_value,
        size_t *param_value_size_ret);
```

This function returns the information as requested in `param_name` for the `event` object. The following bullet list describes the objects used in the preceding code:

- `event`: It specifies the `cl_event` object being queried.
- `param_name`: It specifies the information to query and is of type `cl_event_info`. The following table lists out the different enumerations of `cl_event_info`, which can be queried and returned in `param_value`.

The `param_value`, `param_value_size`, and `param_value_size_ret` objects have the same meaning as for any `clGet*Info` function.

Let's take an example wherein you want to do a busy wait on an event to complete, as shown in the following code:

```
cl_event x_event;
cl_int   x_event_status;
/*... Task created here and associated with x_event...*/
while ( clGetEventInfo(x_event, CL_EVENT_COMMAND_EXECUTION_STATUS,
  sizeof(int), &x_event_status, NULL) != CL_COMPLETE)
{
  // spin here for fast completion detection.
}
```

The following table shows the different `cl_event_info` parameter names, which can be queried using `clGetEventInfo`:

cl_event_info	Description
CL_EVENT_COMMAND_QUEUE	Returns the `command-queue` associated with the `event` and is of type `cl_command_queue`.
CL_EVENT_CONTEXT	Returns the OpenCL context associated with event and is of type `cl_context`.
CL_EVENT_COMMAND_TYPE	Returns the `cl_command_type` value type for the command associated with `event`, and is of type `cl_command_type`. The value returned in `param_value` can be one of the list of OpenCL enqueue commands.
CL_EVENT_COMMAND_EXECUTION_STATUS	The event status is returned. It can be one of `CL_SUBMITTED`, `CL_RUNNING`, `CL_QUEUED`, or `CL_COMPLETED`. This is of type `cl_int`. Note that an error code which is a negative integer can also be returned. This may be because of an erroneous execution or abnormal termination of the command.
CL_EVENT_REFERENCE_COUNT	Return the event reference count.

The type of OpenCL commands associated with the `CL_EVENT_COMMAND_TYPE` object is the enumeration of `cl_command_type` given as follows:

- CL_COMMAND_NDRANGE_KERNEL
- CL_COMMAND_TASK
- CL_COMMAND_NATIVE_KERNEL
- CL_COMMAND_READ_BUFFER
- CL_COMMAND_WRITE_BUFFER
- CL_COMMAND_COPY_BUFFER
- CL_COMMAND_READ_IMAGE
- CL_COMMAND_WRITE_IMAGE
- CL_COMMAND_COPY_IMAGE
- CL_COMMAND_COPY_BUFFER_TO_IMAGE
- CL_COMMAND_COPY_IMAGE_TO_BUFFER
- CL_COMMAND_MAP_BUFFER
- CL_COMMAND_MAP_IMAGE
- CL_COMMAND_UNMAP_MEM_OBJECT
- CL_COMMAND_MARKER
- CL_COMMAND_ACQUIRE_GL_OBJECTS
- CL_COMMAND_RELEASE_GL_OBJECTS
- CL_COMMAND_READ_BUFFER_RECT
- CL_COMMAND_WRITE_BUFFER_RECT
- CL_COMMAND_COPY_BUFFER_RECT
- CL_COMMAND_USER
- CL_COMMAND_BARRIER
- CL_COMMAND_MIGRATE_MEM_OBJECTS
- CL_COMMAND_FILL_BUFFER
- CL_COMMAND_FILL_IMAGE

The `CL_COMMAND_USER` command is an user created event. Till now what we had discussed is the OpenCL generated event handle. In the next section we will take a look at how to create user events.

Like every other OpenCL objects, `cl_event` is also an object and needs to be explicitly freed. An OpenCL object can be released or retained. Every OpenCL object is associated with a reference count. This event reference count can be retrieved for the event objects by calling the `clGetEventInfo` function with `CL_EVENT_REFERENCE_COUNT` as the `param_name`. The `clRetainEvent` function increments the event reference count.

```
cl_int clRetainEvent (cl_event event)
```

Similarly the following function decrements the event reference count and allows for the event object to be deleted. Once the reference count decrements to zero the `event` object is deleted:

```
cl_int clReleaseEvent (cl_event event)
```

User-created events

All the events which we have discussed till now are all command queue created events. Applications may want to create user defined events, and use it to track the progress of different workloads given to different devices in an OpenCL context. The function for performing the same is as follows:

```
cl_event clCreateUserEvent (cl_context context,
  cl_int *errcode_ret)
```

The preceding function creates an user event object. Note that the user event created is per context. This means that each device in a context can wait on a user event to complete before the device command queue can execute next task. User-created events are useful for an application developer, in such a way that the developer can wait on this event in-order to reach a point of computation in his algorithm. An OpenCL algorithm may consist of many kernel tasks and data transfer operations. All user-created events reach a state of `CL_SUBMIITTED` first. They do not reach a state of `CL_QUEUED` since no task is queued to a `command_queue` queue. The `clCreateUserEvent` function sets `errcode_ret` to `CL_SUCCESS` if the user event object is created successfully.

How can one change the status of the user created event? OpenCL provides the `clSetUserEventStatus` function for this purpose, which is given as follows:

```
cl_int clSetUserEventStatus (cl_event event,
  cl_int execution_status)
```

This function sets the state of a user event object to either of CL_QUEUED, CL_SUBMITTED, CL_RUNNING, or CL_COMPLETE. An OpenCL application developer must ensure that the events in event_wait_list argument of clEnqueue*** must reach a state of CL_COMPLETE. If any event is a user event then the application developer should set the state of that event to CL_COMPLETE. Have a look at the following example, which is adapted from the OpenCL specification and shows what is the undefined behavior:

```
user_event = clCreateUserEvent(context, NULL);
clEnqueueWriteBuffer(queue, buf1, CL_FALSE, ***,
  1, &user_event, NULL);
clEnqueueWriteBuffer(queue, buf2, CL_FALSE, ***);
clReleaseMemObject(buf2);
clSetUserEventStatus(user_event, CL_COMPLETE);
```

Consider that the queue is an in-order queue, that is the second write will occur only after the first one is completed. The first write is enqueued and is waiting on the user_event to complete. The second write also gets enqueued. Immediately after that the clReleaseMemObject function will release the OpenCL buffer object. And finally the user_event is set to CL_COMPLETE. This will trigger the first write to complete, and then when the second write starts its execution, but the buffer object was already released. This will cause an undefined behavior.

Event profiling

Profiling is an important tool, which must be used for tuning any high performance application. OpenCL provides this mechanism by making the cl_event objects to hold the timing information. This timing information can be captured using the clGetEventProfilingInfo function. The command_queue queue should be created with CL_QUEUE_PROFILING_ENABLE flag set as properties argument in clCreateCommandQueue.

If the queue is enabled for profiling then the following function returns profiling information for the enqueued task associated with the event object:

```
cl_int clGetEventProfilingInfo (cl_event event,
  cl_profiling_info param_name,
    size_t param_value_size,
      void *param_value,
        size_t *param_value_size_ret)
```

All the timestamps CL_PROFILING_COMMAND_[QUEUED|SUBMIT|START|END] can be obtained using this function. The returned value is a 64 bit cl_ulong value, which specifies the device time counter in nanoseconds. You can determine the time of when the command got enqueued | submitted | started | ends in a command queue by the host. The following code snippet calculates the start and end time of an OpenCL event:

```
double get_event_exec_time(cl_event event)
{
  cl_ulong start_time, end_time;
  /*Get start device counter for the event*/
  clGetEventProfilingInfo (event,
    CL_PROFILING_COMMAND_START,
    sizeof(cl_ulong),
    &start_time,
    NULL);
  /*Get end device counter for the event*/
  clGetEventProfilingInfo (event,
    CL_PROFILING_COMMAND_END,
    sizeof(cl_ulong),
    &end_time,
    NULL);
  /*Convert the counter values to milli seconds*/
  double total_time = (end_time - start_time) * 1e-6;
  return total_time;
}
```

The counter values are returned in a cl_ulong variable. The resolution of the counter values are in nanoseconds. We multiply it with 1e-6 to get the time in milliseconds.

Have a look at the example code profiling_saxpy given with the code distribution. In this example code we will modify the saxpy example to get the timing information of each of the tasks enqueued on the device.

Memory fences

OpenCL C specification provides for runtime barriers in a work item and across a single work group. Barriers may only synchronize threads in the same workgroup. There is no way to synchronize between different work groups. For synchronizing outside of the work group the kernel should complete its execution. There are two types of memory fences:

- `CLK_LOCAL_MEM_FENCE`: This ensures correct ordering of operations on local memory. It is used as follows:

  ```
  barrier(CLK_LOCAL_MEM_FENCE);
  ```

  The barrier function will either flush any variables stored in local memory or queue a memory fence to ensure correct ordering of memory operations to local memory.

- `CLK_GLOBAL_MEM_FENCE`: This ensures correct ordering of operations on global memory. It is used as follows:

  ```
  barrier(CLK_GLOBAL_MEM_FENCE);
  ```

To help you understand, in short you should use `CLK_LOCAL_MEM_FENCE` when reading and writing to the `__local` memory space, and `CLK_GLOBAL_MEM_FENCE` when reading and writing to the `__global` memory space.

Sometimes both can be used together as shown in the following code. This will help in debugging, or the algorithm uses both the global and local memory:

```
barrier(CLK_LOCAL_MEM_FENCE | CLK_GLOBAL_MEM_FENCE);
```

Summary

In this chapter we have learned about the various synchronization models, which can be used by an OpenCL programmer. We discussed everything about the OpenCL `cl_event` objects. These events can be `clEnqueue*` generated or user-created events. These synchronization models may be fine-grained or coarse-grained. An OpenCL developer can make use of these in his application.

In previous chapters we have seen all the OpenCL objects, and its creation and deletion. We discussed about the host side objects in the form of contexts, queues, programs, kernels, buffers, and events. In the next chapter we will see the device side kernel code, and the OpenCL C language specification in detail.

7
OpenCL C Programming

To support cross platform compatibility across a large combination of OpenCL devices, every OpenCL device should be compliant to a standard. OpenCL C language specification is based out of the C99 standard (ISO/IEC 9899:1999). Besides this there are certain restrictions, which are applicable to all the OpenCL C kernels. A compliant C kernel code is compiled by the OpenCL runtime compiler using the `clBuildProgram` function. In this chapter we will discuss the specifications and restrictions for writing an OpenCL compliant C kernel code. The following bullet list states the topics which will be discussed in this chapter:

- Built-in data types
- Conversions and type casting
- Address space qualifiers
- Function qualifiers
- Built-in functions

Built-in data types

OpenCL specification provides its own set of data types, whether vector or scalar. This is important since it will enable the kernel code to be portable across various OpenCL devices and different device compilers. In the following sections we will discuss the different data types, which are defined in the OpenCL specification.

Basic data types and vector types

OpenCL C standard categorizes a list of data types referred to as "basic data types". This is tabulated in the following table. Associated with each basic data type is a vector data type, which can be used by a C programmer. Most of the OpenCL devices do support **Instruction Set Architecture (ISA)**, which take inputs as vector data types. For example, the AMD FMA4 ISA extension supports **Fused Multiply Add (FMA)** operation on 256 bit vector data. So if these vector data types are used while writing code it is more likely that the vector data type are processed by codes, which uses vector instructions at runtime and is converted to a vector instruction binary at runtime. The basic data types have an associated application data type, which a programmer can use. The following table describes the various basic and vector data types, which can be used within the OpenCL C kernel code and there corresponding application data types.

The following table depicts the Basic and vector data types the contents of the first, column are referred to as the basic data type in this chapter. We exclude `half` data type for discussion in the subsequent sections:

Basic data types	Application data types	Vector data types	Application vector data types
`bool`	`n/a`	`n/a`	`n/a`
`char`	`cl_char`	`charn`	`cl_charn`
`unsigned char, uchar`	`cl_uchar`	`ucharn`	`cl_ucharn`
`short`	`cl_short`	`shortn`	`cl_shortn`
`unsigned short, ushort`	`cl_ushort`	`ushortn`	`cl_ushortn`
`int`	`cl_int`	`intn`	`cl_intn`
`unsigned int, uint`	`cl_uint`	`uintn`	`cl_uintn`
`long`	`cl_long`	`longn`	`cl_longn`
`unsigned long, ulong`	`cl_ulong`	`ulongn`	`cl_ulongn`
`float`	`cl_float`	`floatn`	`cl_floatn`
`double`	`cl_double`	`doublen`	`cl_doublen`
`half*`	`cl_half`	`halfn`	`cl_halfn`

Let's explain the difference between the application data type (column 2 and 4) and the OpenCL C data type (column 1 and 3) with an example. The following is a sample OpenCL C kernel code:

```
__kernel void opencl_kernel(int i_value, float f_value)
{
...
}
```

The application may want to launch the opencl_kernel as shown above. For this the application code will pass the kernel arguments as follows:

```
cl_int i_value;
cl_float f_value;
/*....Create the opencl_kernel for the OpenCL kernel showed above....*/
clSetKernelArg(opencl_kernel, 0, sizeof(cl_int), (void *) &i_value);
clSetKernelArg(opencl_kernel, 0, sizeof(cl_float), (void *) &f_value);
```

OpenCL application developers should use the `cl_*` data types as it will make the code portable across different host compilers, and also make sure that the size of these data types are same as the application data type across different OpenCL devices.

For all vector data types the supported value for n are 2, 3, 4, 8, and 16. They form a vector of `n` element data type. The built-in vector data types have a corresponding vector data type for an application programmer to use. As far as possible the application programmer should use these data types. Note that `size_t` does not have any vector data type. This is because `size_t` is a data type, which is dependent on the bit depth of the compiled target architecture. For example for 32 bit applications `sizeof(size_t)` is 4 bytes and for 64 bit applications it is 8 bytes.

The half data type

All floating point data types like float and double are IEEE 754-2008 compliant. The `half` data type must also be compliant to this standard data representation. This data type is a floating point value of length 16 bits, comprising of 1 sign bit, 5 exponent bits with values ranging from: 15 to 16, and 10 mantissa bits, with exponent bias constant as 15. They are all similar in definition of a 32 bit single precision floating point values with 1 sign bit, 8 exponent bits, and 23 mantissa bits with exponent bias constant as 127. The application programmer is responsible to choose for choosing the appropriate data type to represent dynamic range of the values taken by the data object. `half` is not supported as computing data type as a `float` data type that means there is no dedicated hardware to compute the `half` precision data types. Though some vendors may provide this feature, as of OpenCL 1.2 `half` data type can only be used to declare a pointer to a buffer of half values.

The following `half` data type diagram shows the size of the data type and some values represented by half precision data types:

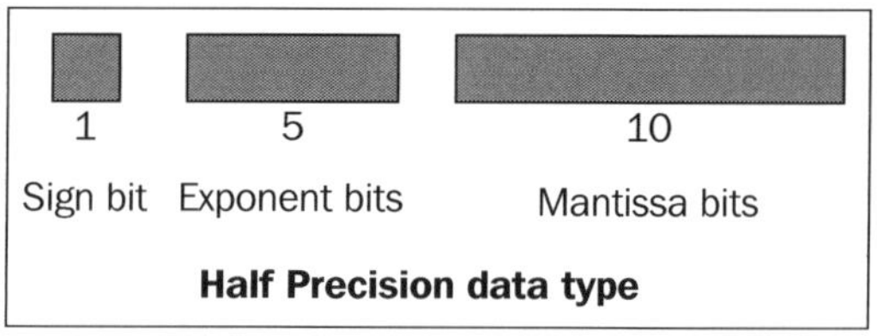

Some examples of half precision data types:

- `0 01111 0000000000 = 1.0`
- `0 10000 1000000000 = 2.0 + 2-1 = 2.5`
- `1 10001 1000000001 = -4.0 + 2-1 + 2-10 = -4.0 - 0.5 - 0.0009765625 = -4.500976525`

Other data types

Besides the data types discussed till now there are some other data types, which depend on the value of `CL_DEVICE_ADDRESS_BITS`. This value can be obtained using the OpenCL function, `clGetDeviceInfo` and passing the `param_name` value as `CL_DEVICE_ADDRESS_BITS`. Based on the value of `CL_DEVICE_ADDRESS_BITS` returned, if its 32 or 64, the size of the following data types will be respectively 32 and 64 bits in size. This is similar to the size of `size_t` being 32 bits in a 32 bit application, and 64 bits in a 64 bit application. The following table describes these special data types:

Data type	Description
`size_t`	This is an unsigned integer type and is the return type of the `sizeof()` operator.
`ptrdiff_t`	This is a signed integer type which is a result of subtracting two pointers.
`intptr_t` and `uintptr_t`	A signed and unsigned integer type which can be used to convert any pointer to this type and then can be converted back to a void pointer.

Another data type `void` comprises an empty set of value.

Reserved data types

There is a list of data types which are reserved for OpenCL implementations, which may be used by OpenCL vendors as extensions or may be provided by the OpenCL specifications in the future. These reserved data types are listed in the OpenCL 1.2 specification in table 6.4 section 6.1.4:

Example in the table given in section built-in data types all other values of *n* are reserved other than 2,3,4,8, and 16; which are already defined in the OpenCL specification.

Alignment of data types

Every built-in and vector data type in OpenCL as given in table of section built-in data types are aligned to the size of the data type itself. Example a `float` variable will be aligned on a 4 byte boundary, a `float4` variable will be aligned to a 16 byte boundary. In the case of data types which are not the size equal to a power of 2, then such data types must be aligned to a size of the next power of 2 bytes. An example is a `float3` or `int3` vector data type. 3 component vector data types shall be aligned to `4* sizeof (component)` bytes. Let's take an example of `4*sizeof (component)` boundary and explain the data type alignment.

The OpenCL compiler while compiling the kernel code is responsible for aligning the local data items to the appropriate alignment as required by the data type. Let us consider the following example:

```
typedef struct
{
    cl_float8 x;
    cl_float3 y;
} OpenCLStruct;
```

Here the size of `OpenCLStruct` at the host compiler side is 48 or 64 bytes depending upon the compiler options you use. But the size of `OpenCLStruct` at the OpenCL device compiler will be 64 bytes. Assume that you create an array of elements with type as `OpenCLStruct`. The first element is aligned to their respective sizes that is, `float8` is aligned to 32 bytes boundary, and `float3` is aligned to 16 bytes boundary (3 component vector data type will be aligned to a `4 * sizeof (component)` boundary). So the OpenCLStruct will be aligned to 48 byte boundary. Now when we access the second element in the array `float8` parameter will not be aligned to 32 byte boundary. So for compliance the OpenCL device compiler must add a filler of 16 bytes after `float3` element which is also of 16 bytes. This makes the size of `OpenCLStruct` as 64 bytes. So subsequent data access of `float8` variables will be 32 byte aligned. Here the OpenCL device compiler refers to the device compiler when we call the `clBuildProgram` function to build a `cl_program` object.

Now the question will arise if you create a buffer at the host side, and then try to pass on the buffer to the device using the `cl_mem` object, how will the difference be handled? Take a look at the following code snippet:

```
#if defined( _MSC_VER)
    typedef struct
    {
        cl_float8 __declspec(align(32)) y;
        cl_float3 __declspec(align(16)) x;
    } OpenCLStruct;
#elif defined( __GNUC__ )
    typedef struct
    {
        cl_float8 __attribute__ (aligned(32)) y;
        cl_float3 __attribute__ (aligned(16)) x;
    } OpenCLStruct;
#else
    #warning align data here
    typedef struct
    {
       float8 x; //Needs 32 byte alignment
       float3 y; //Needs 16 byte alignment
    } OpenCLStruct;
#endif
```

The application programmer is responsible for aligning the respective data types to their respective boundaries. The code snippet shows for both the GCC and MS Visual Studio compilers. Now the reads and writes to the `OpenCLStruct` function buffer will result in the same behavior and data alignment for the host compiler and the OpenCL device compiler. If the kernel argument is a pointer argument then the OpenCL compiler will assume that the pointer is appropriately aligned as required by the data type.

Vector data types

One can create vectors using vector literals. Vector literals can be formed using a list of scalars or vectors or a mixture of a scalar and a vector. The following is an example of creating a vector data type:

```
int4 i4 = (int4)(1, 2, 3, 4); or
int4 i4 = {1, 2, 3, 4};
```

The operands are assigned vector lane wise to their respective positions in the resultant vector. The vector lanes are similar to contiguous array elements as they appear in memory. The elements are assigned in lane wise in the same order as they appear. An example of this is as follows:

```
float f = 4.0f;
float3 f3 = (float3)(1.0f, 2.0f, 3.0f);
float4 f4 = (float4)(f3, f);
//f4.x = 1.0f,
//f4.y = 2.0f,
//f4.z = 3.0f,
//f4.w = 4.0f
```

In the preceding code which is highlighted, `f3` forms the first three entries for the `float4 f4` variable, and finally followed by a scalar `f` value.

If the literal is of the form of a single scalar then the scalar value is replicated across all the lanes in a vector. All vector components are stored in a contiguous array.

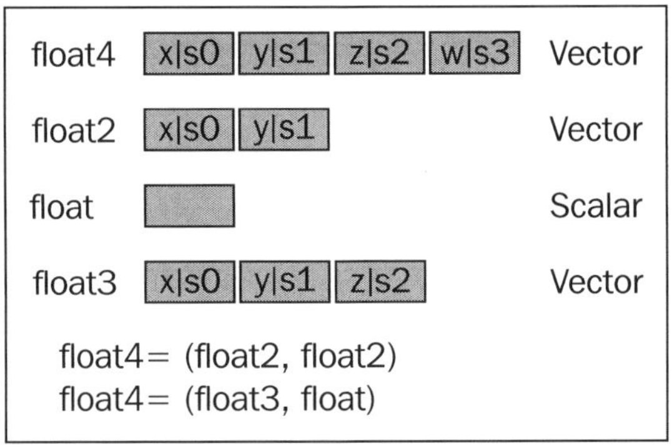

Vector assignments which are not allowed are as follows:

```
float4 f = (float4)(2.0f, 1.0f); // compiler error
```

Vector components

The components of a vector of size 2, 3, and 4 can be accessed using, `[x,y]`, `[x,y,z]`, and `[x,y,z,w]` respectively. That is the first element of a four component vector `v` can be accessed using `v.x`, the second element using `v.y`, the third element using `v.z`, and the fourth element using `v.w`. Accessing beyond the vector size results in a compile time error for the OpenCL C runtime compiler. Example in a 2 component vector `v` you cannot access `v.z`. OpenCL provides mechanisms to select multiple components. You can also select multiple components shown as follows:

```
float4 pos       = (float4)(4.0f, 3.0f, 2.0f, 1.0f);
float4 reverse   = pos.wzyx; //reverse = (1.0f, 2.0f, 3.0f, 4.0f)
float4 duplicate = pos.xxyy; //duplicate =
  //(4.0f, 4.0f, 3.0f, 3.0f)
```

The lanes in vector data types can also be accessed using numeric index to refer to the appropriate element in the vector. A 16 component vector data type can be indexed using `[s|S]0`, `[s|S]1`, `[s|S]2`, `[s|S]3`, `[s|S]4`, `[s|S]5`, `[s|S]6`, `[s|S]7`, `[s|S]8`, `[s|S]9`, `[s|S][a|A]`, `[s|S][b|B]`, `[s|S][c|C]`, `[s|S][d|D]`, `[s|S][e|E]` and, `[s|S][f|F]`. For example the 13th element in the 16 component vector `v` can be accessed using `v.sc`, `v.Sc`, `v.Sc`, or `v.SC`.

Vector sub components can be accessed using `.lo`, `.hi`, `.even`, `.odd`.

The `.lo` suffix refers to the lower half of the vector.

The `.hi` suffix refers to the upper half of the vector.

The `.even` and `.odd` suffixes can be used for interleaving the data. The `.even` suffix refers to the even elements in the vector. The `.odd` suffix refers to the odd elements of the vector lane.

It is illegal to take the address of the vector sub components.

- Allowed component group notations:

```
float4 pos = (float4)(4.0f, 3.0f, 2.0f, 1.0f);
pos.yw = (float2)(5.0f, 6.0f);// pos = (4.0f, 5.0f, 2.0f, 6.0f)
pos.wx = (float2)(8.0f, 9.0f);// pos = (9.0f, 5.0f, 2.0f, 8.0f)
pos.xyz = (float3)(5.0f, 6.0f, 9.0f);
                              // pos = (5.0f, 6.0f, 9.0f, 8.0f)
float4 a, b, c, d;
float16 x;
x = (float16)(a, b, c, d);
x = (float16)(a.yyzz, b.xzwy, c.xyz, d.xyz, a.yzw);
float4 f, a;
a.xyzw = f.s0123; // valid
```

- Illegal component group notations:

```
float4 pos = (float4)(1.0f, 2.0f, 3.0f, 4.0f);
pos.xx = (float2)(3.0f, 4.0f);// illegal - 'x' used twice
pos.xy = (float4)(1.0f, 2.0f, 3.0f, 4.0f); // float4 cannot be
assigned to 2 components
a = f.x12w; // illegal use of numeric indices with .xyzw
// illegal - component a.xxxxxxx is not a valid vector type
x = (float16)(a.xxxxxxx, b.xyz, c.xyz, d.xyz);

float *f = &vf.x; // is illegal
```

Aliasing rules

OpenCL C standard is based on the strict aliasing rules of the C99 standard. What is meant by strict aliasing rule? Consider the following example:

```
cl_int data;
cl_int *pToIntData = &data;
cl_short *pToShortData = (cl_short *)pToIntData;
//Now one can access the sub data as follows
cl_short hi = pToShortData[1];
cl_short lo = pToShortData[0];
```

In the preceding example `pToShortData` is an alias to `pToIntData`. According to C99 standard an alias cannot be created for the type other than the original. Though the preceding code will compile just fine and may result in a correct behavior since you are only reading from the aliased pointer, but when you write to an aliased pointer, compiler will result in a "strict aliasing rule broken" warning and will result in an undefined behavior. The GCC compiler will throw a warning at higher optimization levels. Similarly aliasing a vector type pointer to a different data type pointer is illegal, though it may be correct since built-in vector types are similar to a contiguous array type.

Conversions and type casts

All programming languages support converting a numerical data type to another numerical data type. There is also a need to reinterpret a data type in some other form, for example, if one wants to extract only the exponent component from a floating point data type, how can one do that? We will discuss the implicit and explicit type conversions, followed by reinterpreting the data types.

Implicit conversion

Implicit conversion refers to the conversion of a data in one type to another type, which is equivalent to the original data type. This conversion is allowed for basic data types, which is described in the table earlier. For example, the integer value 1 will be converted to an equivalent floating point value `1.0f`. The corresponding hex representation is `0x3F800000`. When you convert a `float` value to an `int`, the compiler will usually throw a warning. To avoid that you explicitly cast the scalar data types. Example:

```
float f = 2.0f;
int i = (int) f;
```

Explicit cast of vector data types is not allowed. But the casting of basic data types from scalar to vector data type is allowed:

```
int4 i;
uint4 u = (uint4) i; // not allowed
```

Note that the implicit conversion of the corresponding vector data types is not allowed.

Type casting will result in converting the input data to the destination data type. The "round to zero" rounding modes will be used for converting to built-in integer vector types. The default rounding mode round-to-nearest will be used for conversions to floating-point vector types. This is in accordance with IEEE-754 floating point standard. When casting a `bool` to a vector integer data type, if the `bool` value is `true` then all the bits are set to 1. If `false` they are all cleared to 0.

Explicit conversion

Explicit conversions are allowed in OpenCL using the intrinsics of the form:

```
convert_destType(sourceType)
```

This conversion is possible between any basic data type and their corresponding vector types described in basic data types table earlier in this chapter except for `bool` and `half`.

Example for the same is as follows:

```
uchar4 u4 = {'0', 'b', 'c', 'd'};
//u4.x = 48, u4.y = 98, u4.z = 99, u4.w = 100 - ASCII values
int4   i4 = convert_int4(u);
i4 = i4 + (int4)200;
//i4.x = 248, i4.y = 298, i4.z = 299, i4.w = 300
u4 = convert_char4_sat(i4);
//u4.x = 248, u4.y = 255, u4.z = 255, u4.w = 255
```

Here 4 unsigned char vector `uchar4 u4` is converted to 4 signed integer vector `int4`. These `u4` vector values are converted to integer vector values and stored in `i4` using the OpenCL built-in `convert_int4`. A upper case adding 200 to each element in the vector `i4`, and then converting it back to unsigned char vector using the `convert_uchar4_sat` function, will result in the saturation of the values to the maximum possible value which the destination type can take.

Rounding modes can also be specified for the input operand. There are 4 different rounding modes, `rte` (Round to nearest even), `rtp` (Round toward positive infinity), `rtz` (Round toward zero), and `rtn` (Round toward negative infinity). If the rounding mode is not specified the default rounding mode of `rtz` is considered when the destination is an integer. For floating point destination types the rounding mode is **rte**—Round to nearest even. The `convert*` function prototype when converting to a destination type is as follows:

Scalar convert function:

```
destType convert_destType[_sat][roundingMode] (sourceType val);
```

Vector convert function:

```
destTypen convert_destTypen[_sat][roundingMode] (sourceTypen
  valn);
```

In the case of vector data types the destination and source operands must have the same number of elements. If the source and destination types are same then the conversion will have no effect. The saturation to floating point formats may not be used for example, `_sat` modifier is not used when converting to floating point formats.

Some examples of explicit conversions:

Saturation conversions when converting from signed integer to unsigned integer format:

First example is as follows:

```
int4 i4;
uint4 u = convert_uint4_sat( i4 );
//Here the negative values are clamped to 0
```

Second example is as follows:

```
float4 f;
// values are implementation defined for
// f > INT_MAX, f < INT_MIN or NaN
int4 i = convert_int4( f );
// values > INT_MAX clamp to INT_MAX, values < INT_MIN clamp
// to INT_MIN. NaN should produce 0.
// The _rtz rounding mode is used to produce the integer values.
int4 i2 = convert_int4_sat( f );
// similar to convert_int4, except that floating-point values
// are rounded to the nearest integer instead of truncated
int4 i3 = convert_int4_rte( f );
// similar to convert_int4_sat, except that floating-point values
// are rounded to the nearest integer instead of truncated
int4 i4 = convert_int4_sat_rte( f );
```

Third example is as follows:

```
int4 i;
// convert ints to floats using the default rounding mode.
float4 f = convert_float4( i );
// convert ints to floats. integer values that cannot
// be exactly represented as floats should round up to the
// next representable float.
float4 f = convert_float4_rtp( i );
```

The arithmetic conversions occur based on the rank of the arithmetic type. A compile-time error will occur if any type with a higher rank is being converted to the type of the lower rank element. Following given are the rules of rank in the order of highest to lowest rank:

- All vector types shall be considered to have higher conversion ranks than scalars.
- The rank of a floating-point type is greater than the rank of another floating point type, if the first floating point type can exactly represent all numeric values in the second floating point type. (For this purpose, the encoding of the floating-point value is used, rather than the subset of the encoding usable by the device.).
- The rank of any floating point type is greater than the rank of any integer type.
- The rank of an integer type is greater than the rank of an integer type with less precision.
- The rank of an unsigned integer type is greater than the rank of a signed integer type with the same precision.
- The rank of the `bool` type is less than the rank of any other type.
- The rank of an enumerated type shall equal the rank of the compatible integer type.
- For all types, `T1`, `T2`, and `T3`, if `T1` has greater rank than `T2`, and `T2` has greater rank than `T3`, then `T1` has greater rank than `T3`.

Let's take an example and discuss the preceding rules:

```
int a;
short4 b;
short4 c = b + a;
```

Assuming `a` and `b` are initialized, here `b` is of lower rank than that of `a` since the size of `short` is 2 bytes, and `int` is of size 4 bytes (point 4 above). Hence this will be a compile time error and the arithmetic operation specified by `b + a` cannot be performed.

```
float  a;
float4 b;
float4 c = b + a;
```

Here `b` is of higher rank than that of `a` since `a` is a scalar component (point 1 above). And the rank of destination operand is equal to that of `b` or higher than `a` (point 8 above). Hence this operation will work for an OpenCL device compiler.

Reinterpreting data types

C programmers need a mechanism to take a look at the contents of the bit representation of a data type and perform an operation on them. For example a programmer will need to look at the sign bit, or mantissa bit or the exponent bit in a floating point representation. One of the mechanisms to achieve this is using unions is follows:

```
union{
   float f;
   uint u;
} u;
u.f = 1.0f;
//then u.u will 0x3f800000
```

Here both `uint` and `float` are of size 4 bytes. The OpenCL language allows the use of union to programmers to access a member of a union object using a member of a different type.

Pointer aliasing and `memcpy` are other methods to achieve the same. But pointer aliasing is not allowed in OpenCL C, and `memcpy` is not defined in OpenCL C either.

OpenCL C standard provides a mechanism to reinterpret data in another basic data type by using the following function prototype:

Scalar types:

```
type = as_type(src_type);
```

Vector types:

```
typen = as_typen(src_typen);
```

The difference between the `as_*` and `convert_*` routines is shown in the following example:

```
float f = 1.0f;
uint u1 = as_uint(f); //  Contains: 0x3f800000
uint u2 = convert_uint(f); //  Contains: 0x00000001
```

The source and destination sizes for `as_*` routines must be the same. If they differ then it is an error. When "reinterpreted" from one type to another the usual bit representation of the source operand is retained. Note in the `as_*` routines the source data type is reinterpreted into the destination data type. No conversion takes place. Refer to the following for the same:

```
float4 f, g;
int4 is_less = f < g;
```

```
// Legal. f[i] = f[i] < g[i] ? f[i] : 0.0f
f = as_float4(as_int4(f) & is_less);
```

In the preceding example the OpenCL C compiler will perform a lane wise "less than" operation, and the resultant `bool` will set or clear all the corresponding lane bits, depending upon the result of the less than operation. The `is_less` function now contains a mask for the elements `f[i] < g[i]`.

In the last step `f` shall contain the elements, which were less than the corresponding `g` elements.

Operators

C programming language has a big set of operators, which a programmer can use in OpenCL C also. Following is the list of operator categories, which OpenCL C allows for. For more information refer to section 6.3 of OpenCL 1.2 standard specification.

- Arithmetic operators: Arithmetic operators add (+), subtract (-), multiply (*), and divide (/) operate on built-in integer and floating point scalar, and vector data types. The remainder or the modulo operator (%) operates on built-in integer scalar and integer vector data types.
- Arithmetic unary operators: The arithmetic unary operators (+ and -) operate on built-in scalar and vector types.
- Arithmetic post- and pre-increment and decrement operators (++ and --).
- Relational operators
- Equality operators
- Bitwise operators
- Logical operators
- Logical unary operator
- Ternary selection operator
- Shift operators
- sizeof operator
- comma operator
- indirection (*) operator
- unary address (&) operator
- Assignment operator

Operation on half data type

Except for the `sizeof` operator, the `half` data type cannot be used with any of the operators mentioned in the preceding section. This means that doing the following are invalid operations on the `half` data type:

```
half a;
half b[100];
half *p;
a = *p;
```

Now the usual question would arise how can one do operations on `half` data types?

For loading and storing `half` data types `vload_halfn` and `vload_storen` should be used. The prototype of `vload_halfn` is as follows:

```
float vload_half (size_t offset, const __global half *p)
```

The `vload_half` function reads a `half` value from `p + offset` location and returns a `float` value. The `half` value is converted to a `float` value, and the `float` value is returned. Performance wise, `half` cannot be worse than `float`. But there are many devices which do not support `half` computation, but the `half` values are up scaled to a floating point value and computation can be performed on them. There may be a slight overhead but all this can be hardware specific but you can make up that loss by having a far superior transfer time of a `half` data type buffer. Hence **half** data types cannot be passed as kernel arguments.

Address space qualifiers

There are four different address space qualifiers supported by OpenCL. The address space qualifier is used in variable declarations to specify the region of memory to allocate the declared object. The following is the list of address qualifiers:

- `__global or global`
- `__local or local`
- `__constant or constant`
- `__private or private`

A data type object in a kernel program is allocated space in the specified address space qualifier. If no specifier is given then a generic address space is considered. For example all kernel function arguments and local variables will take a `__private` if no address space qualifier is specified. Image memory objects arguments of type `image2d_t`, `image3d_t`, `image2d_array_t`, `image1d_t`, `image1d_buffer_t`, and `image1d_array_t` refer to the `__global` address space. Address space qualifiers for return types are allowed only for pointer types.

The OpenCL memory model specifies the different memory regions. Each of these are categorized into the address space qualifier, discussed as follows:

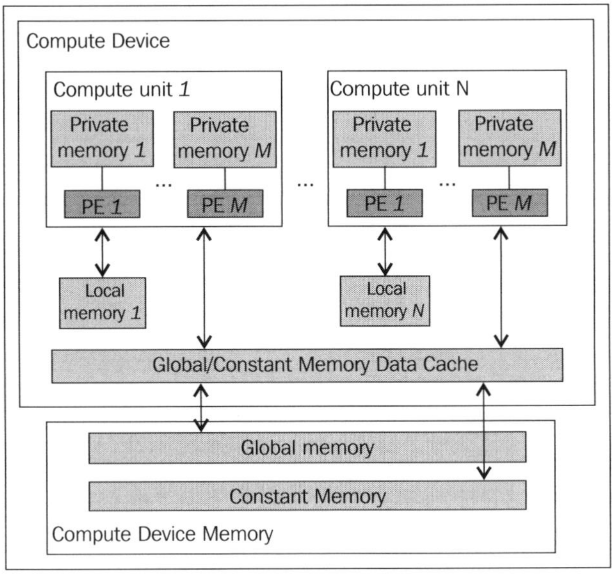

__global/global address space

The `__global` or `global` address space name is used to refer to memory objects (buffer or image objects) allocated from the global memory pool. They can be either pointers to scalar buffers or pointers to vector buffers. All the memory usually gets allocated at the host side, and is passed to the kernel as a `cl_mem` object created using the `clCreateBuffer` function. For image objects the argument is of type `image2d_t`, `image3d_t`, `image2d_array_t`, `image1d_t`, `image1d_buffer_t`, and `image1d_array_t`. These by default refer to the `__global` address space qualifier.

The `const` qualifier can also be added to the `__global` qualifier to specify that the memory object is read only.

__local/local address space

This memory address space specifier is allocated space in local memory of the computing device. It can be shared across all the work items in a work group. The variables or memory objects created with `__local` address space qualifier, have life time only till the execution of the work group executing the kernel. The `clGetDeviceInfo` function can be used with `param_name` as `CL_DEVICE_LOCAL_MEM_SIZE` to determine the total local memory size offered by every compute unit.

__constant/constant address space

The `__constant` or `constant` address space name is used to describe variables allocated in global memory and which are accessed inside a kernel(s) as read-only variables and can be accessed by all the global work item of the kernels during its execution. Pointers to `__constant` variable are allowed inside the kernel and can be passed as an argument to the kernel. String literals are allocated `__constant` address space. All program scope variables get defined in the `__constant` address space. This means that these variables need to be initialized and must be resolved during compile time. Any write operation to a `__constant` variable should be a compile time error.

Now consider a following example where in you do filtering operations on the input buffer `filter_in`, by multiplying with the corresponding elements in the `filter` buffer. Here the buffer `filter` is accessed by every work item, and the `filter` variable is always a constant and is only read from and never written into. From a performance perspective it would be good to specify the filter argument with a `__constant` qualifier rather than global. Some hardware devices have a dedicated constant global buffer, which allows for fast access to itself. The constant buffers can be passed as a kernel argument using the `clSetKernelArg` function, or can also be defined in the global scope in the corresponding OpenCL kernel code. The OpenCL buffer objects which are meant to be "read only" inside the kernel, must be created with the `CL_MEM_READ_ONLY` flag set. Performance wise it will be advantageous to define the `__constant` variable in global program scope in the OpenCL kernel as follows:

```
__kernel void filterKernel (__constant float4 *filter,
                            __constant float4* filter_in,
                            __global float4* filter_out)
{
...
//l_tid -> local work item ID
//g_tid -> global work item ID
filter_out[tid] = filter_in[g_tid] * filter[l_id];
...
}
```

__private/private address space

All the kernel arguments which do not specify any qualifier are by default treated as `__private` address space qualifiers. Similarly all variables inside non-kernel and kernel functions are in the `__private` or `private` address space.

Restrictions

Pointer arguments to kernel functions must be declared with any one of the address specifiers `__global`, `__constant`, or `__local` qualifier. By default unless specified they will be assumed in the `__private` region. The `__constant`, `__local`, or `__global` pointers can only be assigned to a pointer declared with the `__constant`, `__local`, or `__global` qualifiers respectively. Function pointers are not allowed. The functions with `__kernel` function attribute cannot have arguments as pointer to pointer(s).

Image data types, `image2d_t`, `image3d_t`, `image2d_array_t`, `image1d_t`, `image1d_buffer_t`, or `image1d_array_t` can only be passed as function arguments. Only global address space qualifiers can be applied on the image. These cannot be used to declare `unions` or `structs`. Image data types cannot be accessed directly, instead to read the contents one has to use samplers. This is discussed in detail in *Samplers* section of *Chapter 4, OpenCL Images*.

Image access qualifiers

OpenCL specification provides two types of access qualifiers for different types of image memory objects. They can be either `read_only` or `write_only`. In the following example `imageA` is read-only image object, and `imageB` is a write-only image object:

```
__kernel void foo (read_only image2d_t imageA,
                   write_only image2d_t imageB)
```

About function qualifiers and attributes, `__kernel` qualifier declares a function which is defined explicitly to run on an OpenCL device. A `__kernel` qualified function can be invoked inside another kernel function. In such a situation the kernel function just behaves as another function call. There are optional function attributes which can be specified for kernel functions.

The `__kernel` qualified functions cannot return any data type. The return type is always void for those functions.

The keyword `__attribute__` allows you to specify the special attributes for `enums`, `structs`, `unions`, or to the functions or kernels. An attribute specifier can be given in the form of:

```
__attribute__ ((attribute-list))
```

The `attribute-list` attribute is the list of comma separated attributes which will be associated with the object.

Let's consider some of the attributes supported by OpenCL C.

Function attributes

```
__attribute__((vec_type_hint(<type>)))
```

This attribute is a hint to the compiler, such that when the compiler is looking to auto vectorization, then it would vectorize around the <type> specified in the attribute. For example, when the hint <type> is `float4` then the complier would decide to merge work items or possibly even separate one work item. This is an optimization hint to the compiler.

```
__attribute__((work_group_size_hint(X, Y, Z)))
```

This hints to the compiler about the local work group size for the kernel.

```
__attribute__((reqd_work_group_size(X, Y, Z)))
```

This specifies the work group size multiple that must be used to run the kernel.

Data type attributes

The two types of data attributes are aligned and packed. They are described as follows:

- `aligned attribute`: The `aligned` attribute is useful for getting good read and write bandwidths. The `aligned` attribute can be specified to mention the minimum alignment for the specified data type. Note all basic data types and vector types are naturally aligned by the complier to the multiple of their size. In the case of structures shown as follows, 3 `shorts` are of size 6 bytes. When you create an array of `struct S`, then each element is at an aligned address of 8 bytes.:

  ```
  struct S { short f[3]; } __attribute__ ((aligned (8)));
  ```

  All the variables of type `struct S` are aligned to 8 byte boundary. That is `S[0]`, `S[1]` and so all will be at multiples of 8 byte boundaries.

- `packed` attribute: The `packed` attribute, packs the data types within a struct or union, such that memory requirements are reduced. The `packed` attribute can only be specified to C structures and unions.

Variable attribute

`aligned` and `packed` attributes can also be defined for variable declarations. Example:

```
int x __attribute__ ((aligned (16))) = 0;
struct foo { int x[2] __attribute__ ((aligned (8))); };
__attribute__((aligned(128))) struct A {int i;} a;
//a is 128 byte aligned
```

`endian` attribute: Another attribute called `endian` (`endiantype`) can also be specified. The `endiantype` attribute will be either `host` or `device`, if it's `host` then the variable is of type `host` endian, if it's `device` then the data type has `device` endian. If no endian type is specified then the endian type would default to `device` endian.

The kernel attribute specified in the kernel declaration can be retrieved using the `clGetKernelInfo` function using the `param_name` `CL_KERNEL_ATTRIBUTES`.

Storage class specifiers

The `static` and `extern` storage classes are supported. The `auto` and `register` specifiers are not supported inside the OpenCL kernel.

Built-in functions

In OpenCL C you cannot include the standard header files provided by C99 standard such as, `math.h`, `stdio.h`, `stdlib.h`, `errno.h`, and so on. OpenCL C provides a huge set of built in functions, which can be used by the programmer for programming the OpenCL kernels. Using built-in functions wherever possible may result in performance enhancement. Also this will make sure the code is portable across different vendors. We will discuss briefly the group of built-ins and will leave it to the reader to take a look at section 6.12 of OpenCL specification 1.2.

Work item function

While enqueuing a kernel using `clEnqueueNDRangeKernel`, we specify the global and local work sizes. To determine these values during the kernel function execution time or to which index a work item belongs in the NDRange, OpenCL provides some built-in functions. They are as follows:

Function	Description
`uint get_work_dim ()`	Returns the number of dimensions associated with the kernel launch.
`size_t get_global_size (uint dimindx)`	Is used to determine the global number of work items in dimension specified by `dimindx`.
`size_t get_global_id (uint dimindx)`	Returns the global id of the kernel work item for the dimension specified by `dimindx`.
`size_t get_local_size (uint dimindx)`	Is used to determine the local number of work items in a work group for the dimension specified by `dimindx`.
`size_t get_local_id (uint dimindx)`	Returns the local id of the kernel work item in a work group for the dimension specified by `dimindx`.
`size_t get_num_groups (uint dimindx)`	Gives the number of work-groups that are executing with this kernel for the dimension identified by `dimindx`.
`size_t get_group_id (uint dimindx)`	Returns the group ID of the work group in the dimension `dimindx`
`size_t get_global_offset (uint dimindx)`	Returns the offset values specified in the `global_work_offset` argument during the launch of the kernel using the `clEnqueueNDRangeKernel` function.

Synchronization and memory fence functions

OpenCL is used to optimize the performance of data parallel workloads. During the execution of the kernel, the result of processing of data from a work item will be needed in some other work item. Most of the highly parallel OpenCL devices run all the work items in a work group in tandem that is all the work items run the same program counter instruction at the same time (mostly in NVIDIA® and AMD GPUs). In such a case how will a programmer synchronize to share data results across work items? OpenCL C provides the barrier routine to stop the execution of a work item, till to until all the work items in that work group reach the same execution point.

```
void barrier (cl_mem_fence_flags flags)
```

The barrier function can be added to ensure all the work items synchronize at this point. It is a useful function for algorithm developers to optimize their code, using the local memory buffers. `flags` which is of type `cl_mem_fence_flags` can be `CLK_LOCAL_MEM_FENCE`—this ensures correct ordering of operations on local memory. It is used as follows:

```
barrier(CLK_LOCAL_MEM_FENCE);
```

The barrier function will either flush any variables stored in local memory or queue a memory fence to ensure correct ordering of memory operations to local memory.

`CLK_GLOBAL_MEM_FENCE`—this ensures correct ordering of operations on global memory. It is used as follows:

```
barrier(CLK_GLOBAL_MEM_FENCE);
```

For understanding purposes, in short you should use `CLK_LOCAL_MEM_FENCE`, when reading and writing to the `__local` memory space, and `CLK_GLOBAL_MEM_FENCE` when reading and writing to the `__global` memory space.

Other built-ins

OpenCL 1.2 provides another set of OpenCL built-ins. These can be used by within any OpenCL kernel. Vector data load and store functions, image read and write functions, atomic functions, Math, geometric, and relational functions are all discussed in section 6.12 of OpenCL specification 1.2.

Summary

In this chapter we started our discussion with built-in scalar and vector data types, there to their conversion and type casting rules. These data types can be used by the programmer to make his kernel code cross platform and use the underlying hardware for optimization. We discussed the function attributes, data type attributes, and some built-in functions. We strongly encourage you to refer to the OpenCL spec for more details.

In the subsequent chapters we will take up some case studies and learn optimization techniques. Case studies is the most important part of this book as this will enable you to get an in depth knowledge of OpenCL. This will also help you to understand what types of applications can be accelerated using OpenCL.

8

Basic Optimization Techniques with Case Studies

In this chapter we will discuss a few optimization techniques and finally illustrate some of them using a simple example of matrix multiplication. In a step-by-step process we combine multiple optimization strategies one by one to get gradual performance improvement. The main advantages of matrix multiplication over many other simpler algorithms , is that its easy to understand the data parallel work load and it demonstrates well the advantage of private memory, local memory, vectors and the problem of bank conflicts.

We start this chapter with a discussion of various ways to find performance bottleneck. First we discuss event-based timing information collection using `clWaitForEvent` API. Then we mention some available tools for performance detection. After that we jump into case study, starting from sequential implementation for CPU. Then gradually describing naive OpenCL implementation on **Graphics Processor Unit (GPU)**, followed by a series of implementation on GPU each illustrating some optimization techniques like using coalesced read, using vector operation, utilizing local memory, using a combination of local memory and coalesced access, utilizing private memory. Finally, we present some ideas to find the scope of OpenCL optimization in a sequential code, followed by a list of general tips on optimization.

Finding the performance of your program?

In the ongoing process of optimization of an OpenCL program we need to find performance bottlenecks at each step so that we can improve on them. Here are some techniques for this investigation. In a Unix based system the `time` command provides user time, system time, and CPU time of a program-execution in detail. In Windows PowerShell, we use a built-in command called `Measure-Command` that gives total running time of a program. This is also similar to the linux `time` command. To get the execution time of a function or any part of code in `C` we can use either the `clock_t clock (void);` function or the `time_t time (time_t* timer);` and `double difftime (time_t end, time_t beginning);` functions from the standard header `<time.h>` or `<ctime>`. Those including several other techniques are good enough for measuring time of a CPU based program.

In OpenCL optimization, our area of interest is a bit different. As a part of optimization of the entire program, here we focus mainly on the optimization of kernel running on a device. In an OpenCL Kernel code that is running on a device (for example, GPU) we enqueue the kernel in a `command_queue`. Due to the existing pending jobs in that `command_queue` and a few other factors, we don't get a deterministic way to find an exact time difference between kernel submission and start of execution of the submitted kernel. Hence the previous `clock` and `time` based technique fails to find the actual duration of Kernel execution on device. We may also be interested to know exact data transfer time between host and device used by an OpenCL implementation. That means you may want to profile functions like `clEnqueue[Read|Write]Buffer` and `clEnqueue[Map|Unmap]Buffer`. For such enqueued commands, we use an event-based mechanism to get exact start and end time of a kernel execution on a device. All of the `clEnqueue*` commands (such as, `clEnqueueNDRangeKernel`, `clEnqueueReadBuffer`, `clEnqueueWriteBuffer`, `clEnqueueCopyImageToBuffer`) have their last parameter as `cl_event *`. This is an output parameter for the command. If we create a valid `cl_event` object before calling those commands and pass the address of the object to the command, after successful execution this `cl_event` object would contain the event object that identifies the task enqueued. This event has two possible uses, one, to enqueue another command that should wait for this command which is identified by this event, that is, for the purpose of synchronization, two, which is of our current interest is for profiling and query the timing information of the tasks enqueued.

The Time query method is described here with a code snippet. Event objects are used to capture timing information that measures execution time of the enqueued tasks. For this, the application developer should enable the `command_queue` with the `CL_QUEUE_PROFILING_ENABLE` flag set in `properties` argument to `clCreateCommandQueue`.

```
...
cl_event someEvent;
cl_ulong start;//start time
cl_ulong end;//end time
...
clEnqueueNDRangeKernel(commandQueue,
                someKernel,
                2,
                NULL,
                globalThreads,
                localThreads,
                0,
                NULL,
                &someEvent);
...
clWaitForEvents(1, &someEvent);
clGetEventProfilingInfo(someEvent,
        CL_PROFILING_COMMAND_START,x
        sizeof(cl_ulong),
        &start,
        0);
clGetEventProfilingInfo(someEvent,
        CL_PROFILING_COMMAND_END,
        sizeof(cl_ulong),
        &end,
        0);
std::cout << "someKernel time taken is : "
             << (end - start)
             << "nanoseconds" << std::endl;
```

Explaining the code

The preceding code is explained in detail here.

1. Here we measure the duration of execution of a Kernel called `someKernel` on device. This kernel, using `clEnqueueNDRangeKernel` function, is enqueued in `commandQueue`. The `commandQueue` is created with `CL_QUEUE_PROFILING_ENABLE` flag set.
2. Before this `clEnqueueNDRangeKernel` command we have defined a `cl_event` object, `someEvent`. Pointer to this `someEvent` is passed as last parameter of `clEnqueueNDRangeKernel`.
3. Then we call `clWaitForEvent` whose first parameter is number of events (here one) and second parameter is pointer to first element of the event array to wait for (here only one event). This waits for the command identified by the event to complete.
4. Then we make two successive calls to `clGetEventProfilingInfo` to get start and end time in the previously declared start and end respectively. Second parameter of this command is of type `cl_profiling_info` which is an enumerated type that can take any of the four values, which is `CL_PROFILING_COMMAND_QUEUED`, `CL_PROFILING_COMMAND_SUBMIT`, `CL_PROFILING_COMMAND_START`, `CL_PROFILING_COMMAND_END` respectively for enqueue, submit, start and end time of the command identified by the event. In all cases the fourth parameter receives the device's time counter in nanoseconds.

Note that all the above commands return a value of `cl_int` type. This status must be equal to `CL_SUCCESS` to receive a valid data from the command.

Tools for profiling and finding performance bottlenecks

AMD and NVIDIA two major vendors for OpenCL on GPU provide their own profiling and debugging tools for performance profiling, identifying performance bottleneck and kernel debugging. AMD provides a static kernel analyzer for static analysis of OpenCL kernel So that you can see the disassembly of OpenCL kernel. It translates into AMD's **Intermediate Language (IL)** or hardware disassembly (ISA) for multiple driver version and GPU device combinations. NVIDIA had independent OpenCL Visual Profiler and later on released multiple versions of a combined profiler for OpenCL and CUDA together called Compute Visual Profiler. AMD provides an integrated GUI based tool for GPU profiling and debugging as well as CPU Profiling called CodeXL. This tool is also integrated with Visual Studio, and can work in Windows and Linux.

To understand how these tools help, we limit our focus on a single tool and provide a very brief summary on it. We choose CodeXL. This tool is freely downloadable from AMD's website. There are many videos available on YouTube demonstrating how it works.

CodeXL can be used either as a standalone application or as Visual Studio plug-in. It has two modes called Debug and Profile. Profiling can be either CPU Profiling or GPU Profiling, at a run of an application.

In GPU Profiling user can profile an application to analyze application trace that shows a timeline view of occurrence of different important events (like start and end of Kernel or memory transfer) in the entire application and also a list of few top Kernels, Memory transfer, and so on with some relevant information. Another analysis of GPU Profiling is on the Performance Counter. Performance of a kernel depends on a few hardware events (called performance counters) whose counts are dependent on kernel code, hardware configuration in the device, and possibly on some other factors. For example, a branch inside the kernel within a workgroups will waste cycles, since the instructions run in a lock-step manner. Divergent branch (for example, some work item within a wave-front takes `if` part and some other work item in the same workgroup takes `else` part) has worse impact on performance. We can observe the hardware counters for branch indicating the number of branches occurred in the entire lifetime of the kernel and if possible, try to reduce the number of branches by rearranging the indexes of work items so that within a workgroup all the work item either takes the `if` part or takes the `else` part. A few other performance counters presented in CodeXL are the indicator of the amount of local memory used (LDS for GPU) in bytes, number of general purpose vector registers used, and so on.

CodeXL GPU Debugger is an OpenCL and OpenGL application debugger. Debugger enables user to view several statistics of function, view image, and buffer memory, set breakpoint on different OpenCL and OpenGL commands, and so on. It also provides the API function call history displayed in a log of OpenCL, OpenGL, OpenGL extensions, WGL, and glX function calls.

The link `http://developer.amd.com/tools-and-sdks/heterogeneous-computing/codexl/` provides some basic tutorial and download.

Both AMD and NVIDIA provide SDK samples which are optimized OpenCL code for reference.

The following are the web pages with a link to download SDK for NVIDIA and AMD respectively.

- `http://developer.download.nvidia.com/compute/cuda/3_0/sdk/website/OpenCL/website/samples.html`
- `http://developer.amd.com/tools-and-sdks/heterogeneous-computing/amd-accelerated-parallel-processing-app-sdk/downloads/`

NVIDIA also provides CUDA to OpenCL migration guide, to enable the CUDA developer to jump start OpenCL programming.

The following screenshot UI shows the state of an OpenCL Kernel where a breakpoint is hit and at the bottom it lists **Properties** of environment where the program is running, **Watch**, **Call stack**, and **Locals**:

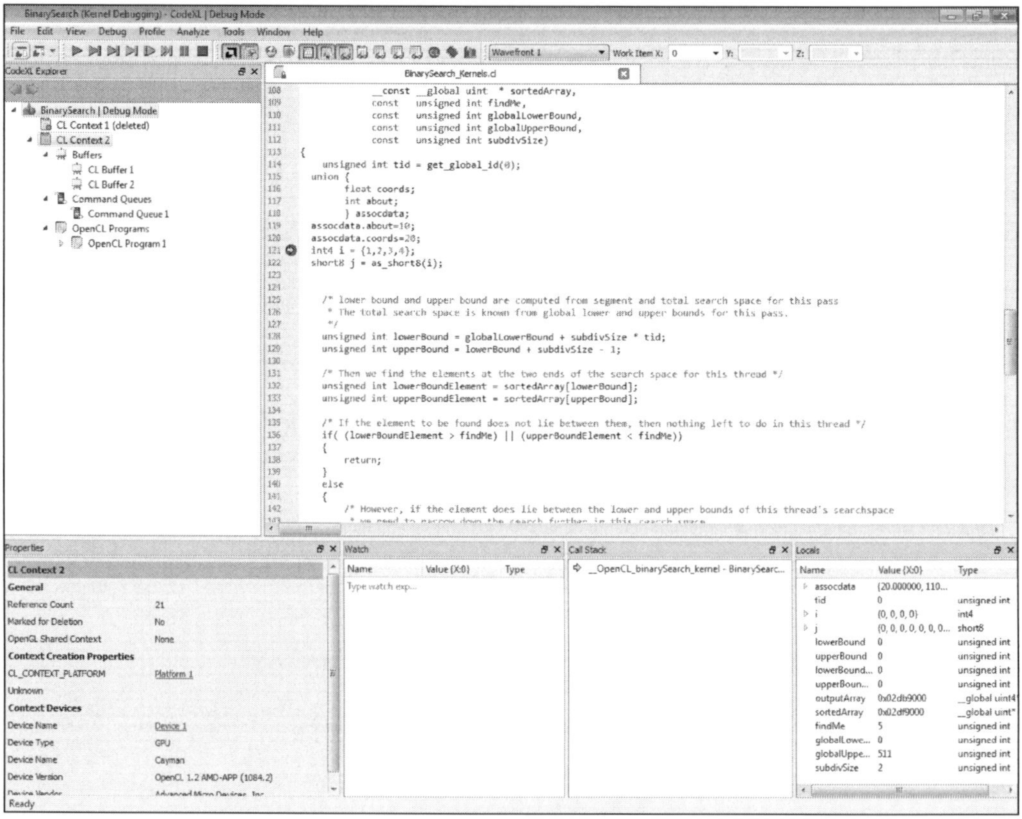

OpenCL Debugger in Visual Studio

The following screenshot displays the Occupancy Analysis in OpenCL Profiler:

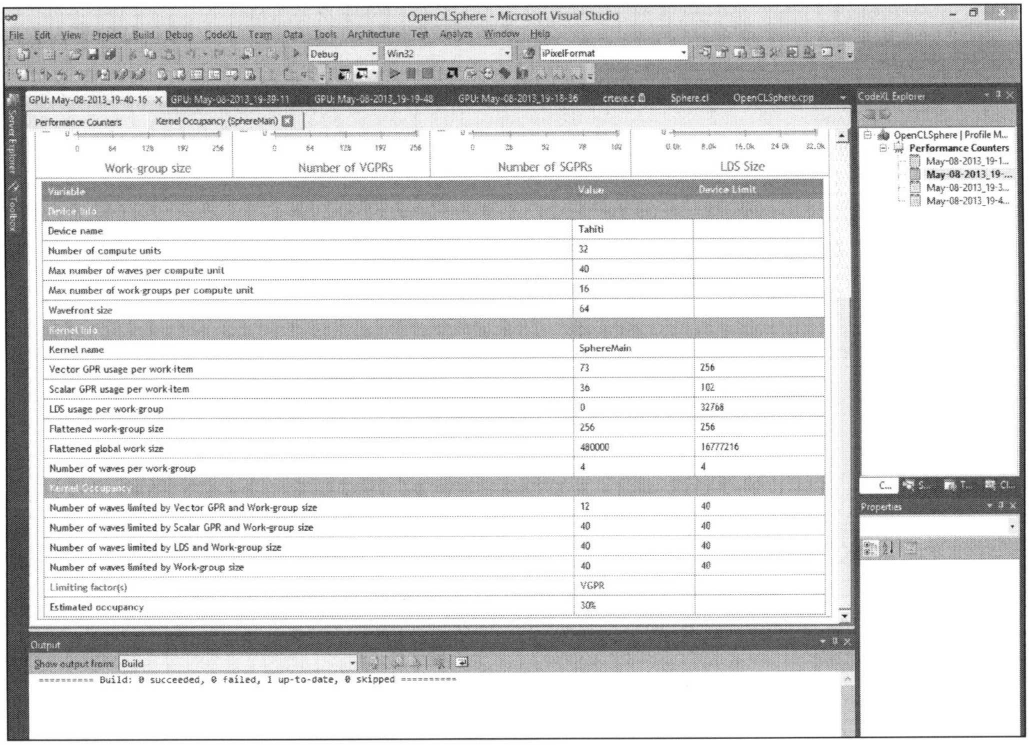

OpenCL Profiler Standalone Version

Case study – matrix multiplication

As we discussed earlier, kernel is just similar to a C function. Each work item will execute this function on the device. We here discuss different optimization strategies and implementations of kernels based on them. In this chapter we present matrix multiplication example to illustrate those optimization strategies with few advantages and disadvantages of them. We need to keep in mind that all the techniques are not applicable to all the problems and also, unfortunately, sometimes they are even in conflict.

Sequential implementation

For the sake of simplicity we take two square matrices called `A` and `B` to multiply (each 1024 by 1024) as input and as a result get a square matrix say `C` of same size (1024 by 1024). To recall, (`iRow`, `iCol`)-th element of matrix `C` is dot product of `iRow`-th row vector of `A` and `iCol`-th column vector of `B`. In other language, i-th element of `iRow` -th row of `A` is multiplied with `i`-th element of `iCol` -th column of `B` for i=1 to N (where N is the dimension of square matrix, here 1024) and all the i products are added to get (`iRow`, `iCol`)-th element of `C`. Illustrated in the following figure.

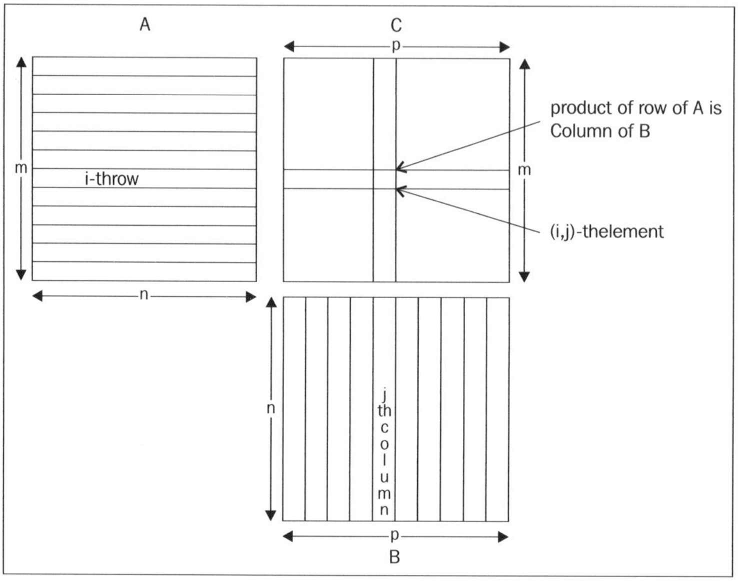

Matrix multiplication algorithm

Sequential implementation is based on nested for loops as shown in the following code:.

```
void MatrixMul_sequential(int dim,
                           float *A,
                           float *B,
                           float *C)
{
  for(int iRow=0; iRow<dim;++iRow)
  {
    for(int iCol=0; iCol<dim;++iCol)
    {
```

```
        float result  = 0.f;
        for(int i=0; i<dim;++i)
        {
          result +=
          A[iRow*dim + i]*B[i*dim + iCol];
        }
        C[iRow*dim + iCol] = result;
      }
    }
  }
```

The function `MatrixMul_sequential` takes four arguments namely, the dimension of matrix and three single dimensional arrays. Size of each array is equal to the square of the dimension, so that each of them holds all the elements of a matrix. `A` and `B` are for input matrices, respectively left and right multiplier. `C` is output matrix, that is,. the product of `A` and `B`.

The two dimensional matrix is represented in a one dimensional array by a row major form. It means the first `dim` elements represent `0` to `dim-1` elements of first row, then `dim` to `2*dim-1` elements represent `1` to `dim` elements of second row, and so on. Hence to get, (`iRow,iCol`)-th element of matrix C we skip all the previous rows and because one row contains `dim` elements we have to skip in total `iRow*dim` elements. Then we get the first element of the `iRow`-th row. Hence (`iRow, iCol`)-th element is obtained by adding the `iCol` offset to first element of the row. So the (`iRow, iCol`)-th element of matrix would have index `(iRow*dim + iCol)` in our single dimensional array representation. We use one dimensional array for two dimensional data because two dimensional array is not allowed in OpenCL.

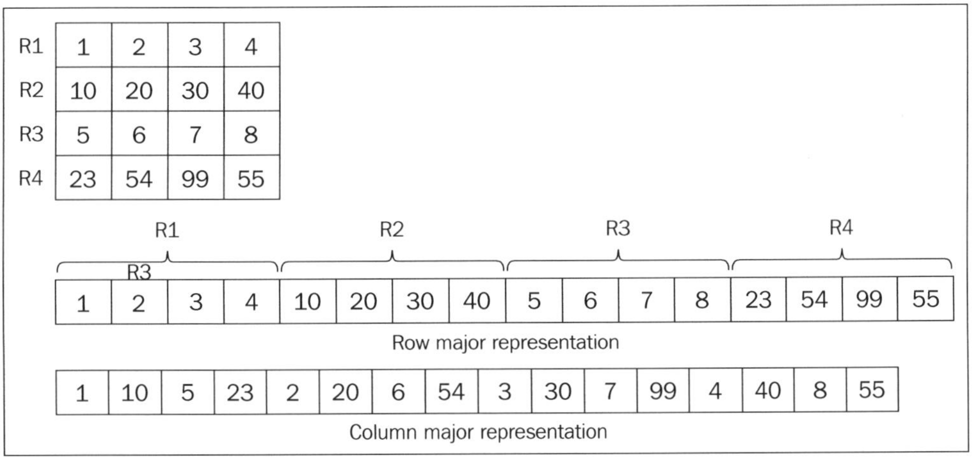

Row major and column major representation

Now the computational scheme is described. Innermost loop, indexed by `i`, computes the dot product, that is, sum of the products of row elements (of `iRow` -th row) and corresponding column elements (`iCol` -th Column) from `A` and `B` respectively and finally the sum is assigned to `(iRow, iCol)`-th element of `C`. Outermost loop, indexed by `iRow`, runs over all the rows of `C` and first inner loop indexed by `iCol` runs over all the column for each row of `C`.

Invoking the `main()` function is easy to write. Allocate memory for `A`, `B`, `C`, and initialize `A` and `B` with random numbers, and `C's` elements with 0.

```
main()
{
  int dim = 1024;
  float *A = (float*)malloc(sizeof(float)*dim*dim);
  float *B = (float*)malloc(sizeof(float)*dim*dim);
  float *C = (float*)malloc(sizeof(float)*dim*dim);
  for(i = 0; i < dim*dim; i++)
  {
    A[i] = (float) (rand() % 10);
    B[i] = (float) (rand() % 10);
    C[i] = 0;
  }
  MatrixMul_sequential(dim,A,B,C);
}
```

OpenCL implementation

With an understanding and background of the preceding implementation we jump to write kernels, to solve the matrix multiplication problem. We here present five variations of the matrix multiplication kernels. Except for the first one, which is a naive implementation of matrix multiplication using kernel, each kernel describes one or more techniques of optimization. To remind again, all the techniques would not give optimized performance in all environments (device hardware architecture, operating system, OpenCL implementation) with all possible data size. But they make us familiar with numerous possible techniques of optimization on GPU, which we can try on other problems with some idea of how they work.

All five kernels take just the same parameter list in same sequence. Instead of `float` which is allocated in host's stack or heap (in our example on heap), kernel takes the global memory pointers for its parameter arrays, for example, `__global float *A`. Since the kernel cannot directly access host memory, so global memory from device is allocated and the array data is copied to those location for kernel's use.

Our NDRange is two dimensional for all the kernels with `global_size` in each dimension as `dim` (1024). Workgroup is also two dimensional and sizes are 256 and 1 respectively in 0-th and 1-st dimension unless otherwise stated.

Simple kernel

For now we will not discuss how to prepare data and invoke kernel. This has been discussed extensively in the section *Creating Kernel Objects* of *Chapter 5, OpenCL Program and Kernel Objects*. We will now jump into our first kernel implementation, which is described in the code that follows:

```
void MatrixMul_kernel_basic(int dim,
                  __global float *A,
                  __global float *B,
                  __global float *C)
{
  //Get the index of the work-item
  int iCol = get_global_id(0);
  int iRow = get_global_id(1);
  float result = 0.0;
  for(int i=0;i< dim;++i)
  {
    result +=
    A[iRow*dim + i]*B[i*dim + iCol];
  }
  C[iRow*dim + iCol] = result;
}
```

Our first kernel, called `MatrixMul_kernel_basic` provides a naive implementation. Each work-item here computes one element of C. Precisely the work-item finds indices based on its global_ids, for example, `get_global_id(1)` and `get_global_id(0)` are respectively row and column indices and then computes the sum of product.

Some performance analysis operation involves the amount of addition or multiplication involved in the task. In matrix multiplication we calculate the number of floating point operations and the amount of global memory read and write operations which we perform. In a single work item, the total number of floating point multiplication here is equal to `dim`, because each iteration of loop does one multiplication. The total number of floating point addition is also `dim` similarly. The total number of global memory fetch is `dim` + `dim` +1 (dim time `A` and dim times `B` within loop and one write operation to `C`). For the entire computation of matrix multiplication the total number of flops is equal to:

`work-items`: total number of work items launched.

```
work-items * (2 * dim)     /*1 for addition and 1 for multiplication*/
```

```
The total global memory fetch is equal to:
```

```
work-items * (2 * dim)
```

```
The total global memory write is equal to:
```

```
work-items
```

Kernel optimization techniques

Our first step to kernel optimization is based on a technique called coalesced memory access. This is illustrated in kernel `MatrixMul_kernel_coallesced_row`. We will first explain coalesced memory access. Take a look at the following diagram. The two work groups have 64 work-items each. The input buffer of size 512 float elements is to be processed by a kernel.

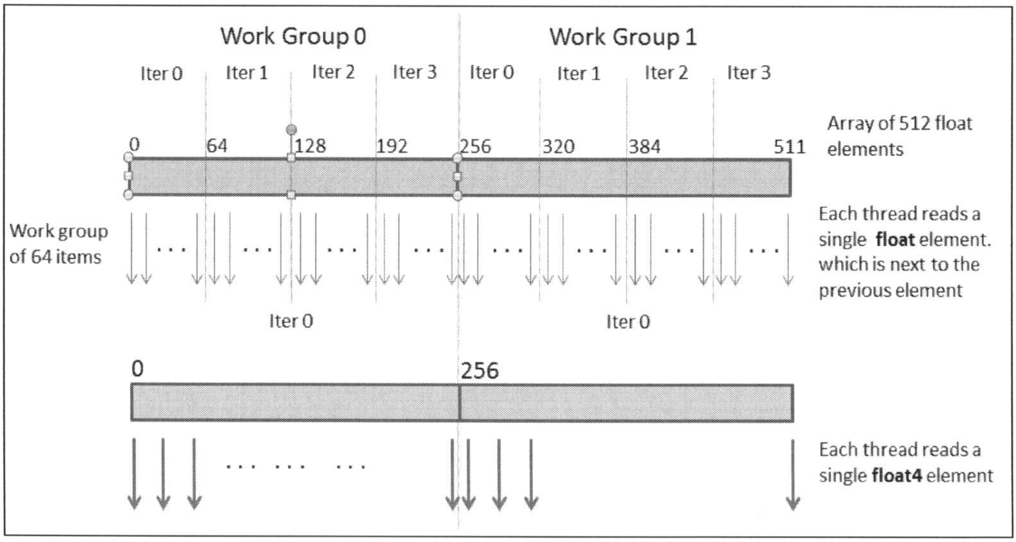

Coalesced read illustration

In the diagram, we have shown two different types of read operations. In the first one, each kernel reads four float elements from the buffer. This is achieved by reading four elements in a loop and is shown with a thin line in the diagram. In the second case, each work-item reads four contiguous elements into a `float4` variable. Both the cases above demonstrate coalesced accesses with respect to a `float` and a `float4` variable respectively.

As far as read is concerned for many types of data parallel workloads, most of the time it will result in coalesced access, easily. But sometimes when it comes to writing back to global memory coalescing is a challenge. The following figure is an example:

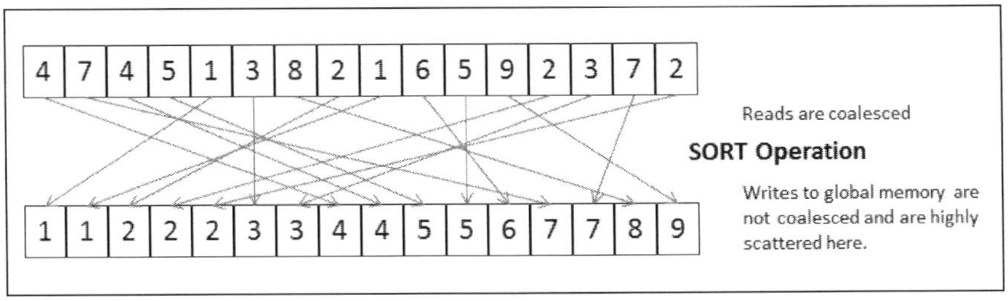

Image showing uncoalesced writes

So coalesced accessing is something like `i`-th work-item should access `(i+k)`-th element of global memory (for some constant k, preferably k=0). In the case of matrix multiplication we coalesce the reads from the A matrix as shown in the following code:

```
void MatrixMul_kernel_coallesced_row(int dim,
                        __global float *A,
                        __global float *B,
                        __global float *C)
{
  //Get the index of the work-item
  int iCol = get_global_id(0);
  int iRow = get_global_id(1);
  int localIdx = get_local_id(0);
  int localSizex = get_local_size(0);
  float result = 0.0f;
  int numElements = dim/localSizex;
  for(int j=0; j<numElements; j++)
  {
    result = 0.0f;
    for(int i=0;i< dim;++i)
    {
      result +=
            A[iRow*dim + i]*B[i*dim + j*localSizex + localIdx];
    }
    C[iRow*dim + j*localSizex + iCol] = result;
  }
}
```

In the matrix multiplication kernel we just showed an example of coalesced global memory access. Some OpenCL devices may not show any gain in performance since all the accesses are from the global memory, and global memory accesses are very time consuming.

Next, we introduce another way of optimization using vectors and vector operations. Since vector operations for such sum of products are far more efficient and private memory access is far faster than global access, we would make out the first attempt for optimization using vectors keeping them in private memory. This is implemented in the kernel `MatrixMul_kernel_basic_vector4`, which computes four elements of `C` per work-item. Here two dimensional NDRange has sizes `dim/4` and `dim` (that is, 256 and 1024) respectively and work-group sizes are 16 in both dimensions.
In `localIdx` and `localIdy`, `global_id(0)`, and `global_id(1)` are stored.

```
#define VECTOR_SIZE 4
void MatrixMul_kernel_basic_vector4(int dim,
                    __global float4 *A,
                    __global float4 *B,
                    __global float *C)
{
  //Get the index of the work-item
  int globalIdx = get_global_id(0);
  int globalIdy = get_global_id(1);
  float result = 0.0;
  float4 Bvector[4];
  float4 Avector, temp;
  float4 resultVector[4] = {0,0,0,0};
  int    noOfVectorsInARow = dim/VECTOR_SIZE;
  for(int i=0; i<noOfVectorsInARow; ++i)
  {
    Avector = A[globalIdy*noOfVectorsInARow + i];
    Bvector[0] = B[dim*i + globalIdx];
    Bvector[1] = B[dim*i + noOfVectorsInARow + globalIdx];
    Bvector[2] = B[dim*i + 2*noOfVectorsInARow + globalIdx];
    Bvector[3] = B[dim*i + 3*noOfVectorsInARow + globalIdx];

    temp = (float4)(Bvector[0].x, Bvector[1].x,
                    Bvector[2].x, Bvector[3].x);
    resultVector[0] += Avector * temp;

    temp = (float4)(Bvector[0].y, Bvector[1].y,
                    Bvector[2].y, Bvector[3].y);
    resultVector[1] += Avector * temp;
```

```
        temp = (float4)(Bvector[0].z, Bvector[1].z,
                        Bvector[2].z, Bvector[3].z);
        resultVector[2] += Avector * temp;

        temp = (float4)(Bvector[0].w, Bvector[1].w,
                        Bvector[2].w, Bvector[3].w);
        resultVector[3] += Avector * temp;

      }
      C[globalIdy*dim + globalIdx*VECTOR_SIZE] = resultVector[0].x +
                                                 resultVector[0].y +
                                                 resultVector[0].z +
                                                 resultVector[0].w;
      C[globalIdy*dim + globalIdx*VECTOR_SIZE + 1] =
                                                 resultVector[1].x +
                                                 resultVector[1].y +
                                                 resultVector[1].z +
                                                 resultVector[1].w;
      C[globalIdy*dim + globalIdx*VECTOR_SIZE + 2] =
                                                 resultVector[2].x +
                                                 resultVector[2].y +
                                                 resultVector[2].z +
                                                 resultVector[2].w;
      C[globalIdy*dim + globalIdx*VECTOR_SIZE + 3] =
                                                 resultVector[3].x +
                                                 resultVector[3].y +
                                                 resultVector[3].z +
                                                 resultVector[3].w;
    }
```

In the kernel `MatrixMul_kernel_basic_vector4` we just saw, the integer `globalIdy*dim` gives the corresponding row's beginning and `globalIdx*VECTOR_SIZE` is the offset part. Since one work-item computes the `VECTOR_SIZE` (here set to four) elements, so work-item with `globalIdx` index would start computation from the element which has the index just next to all the elements computed by all previous work-items. Total number of those elements which are already computed within current row is `globalIdx*VECTOR_SIZE - 1` (since index starts from zero). Hence the first element that the current work-item would compute has the index `globalIdy*dim + globalIdx*VECTOR_SIZE`. Next three elements are obtained by merely adding 1, 2, and 3 respectively to this index. We first define two vector arrays of `float4` of size four where each element of the array holds four floats. This array would ultimately contain 4*4 =16 floats. First, `float4 Bvector[4];`, would hold `B's` element and second, `float4 resultVector[4] = {0,0,0,0};` which is initialized to zero, would hold the final results.

Note the value of `noOfVectorsInARow is equal to dim/VECTOR_SIZE` because by using `float4 Avector` within loop, we are covering four elements in a single iteration of the loop.

The statement `Avector = A[globalIdy * noOfVectorsInARow + i];` fetches four elements from the global memory starting from index `globalIdy * noOfVectorsInARow + i`, for current `i` and loads the values in `Avector`. This `Avector` is now being used to compute the corresponding parts of the sum of four elements of `C`.

First four elements of the global array `B`, with starting index `dim*i + globalIdx` are loaded in `Bvector[0]`. Next successive four element groups are loaded in `Bvector[1]`, `Bvector[2]`, `Bvector[3]`. Using `float4 temp`, we accumulate the sum in the array of `resultVector` and finally when the loop completes all the four elements are computed, we load them in corresponding element of `C`.

The usage of vectors resulted in a gain in performance. You can try this out in your OpenCL device.

Another gain in performance is due to caching the required part of `A` in a private memory (`float4 Avector` is private memory) and reusing it. The private memory is the fastest, but private memory is small, so it may be used up very quickly with variables. When the amount of private variable is so much that it demands more than available amount of private memory, it spills to the global memory which makes the memory access very slow. This reduces the overhead of repeated access to the global memory. Third factor for performance gain is device dependent. When a device has number of compute units say less than or equal to 4, it is advantageous to reduce the number of work-items launched. Here we have done that by a factor of four because each work-item is doing the work of four elements computation as against 1 for each work-item in our previous kernels `MatrixMul_kernel_basic` and `MatrixMul_kernel_coallesced_row`.

Now we discuss few performance penalty factors of this kernel with respect to the previous one. First, extra overhead is due to allocation, initialization, and copy of all private memory elements. But this step overcomes the loss in performance by directly operating on the global memory. Second disadvantage is again device specific. If the number of compute unit is more than the number of work groups launched this may lead to inefficient occupancy which leads to wastage of hardware resources. That factor is aggravated if total number of compute units in the device are not a factor of the total number of work-groups. We have discussed this in the section *Application Scaling* in *Chapter 2, OpenCL Architecture*.

We now further continue in writing next two kernels, namely, `MatrixMul_kernel_localA` and `MatrixMul_kernel_localA_coallesced`. First we discuss the common characteristics between them. In fact, the only difference between these two kernels is in the body of the first loop. In both the kernels, we use the local memory for performance gain. Here again NDrange is two dimensional with dimensions equal to the size of destination Matrix C. Each work item computes one element of `C`. Work groups size is 256 by 1. In this Kernel we pass one extra parameter, the fifth parameter which is a float pointer allocated with the `__local` address space specifier.

```
void MatrixMul_kernel_localA(int dim,
                    __global float *A,
                    __global float *B,
                    __global float *C,
                    __local  float *lA)
{
  //Get the index of the work-item
  int iCol = get_global_id(0);
  int iRow = get_global_id(1);
  int localIdx = get_local_id(0);
  int localSizex = get_local_size(0);
  float result = 0.0f;
  int numElements = dim/localSizex;
  for(int i=0; i<numElements ; i++)
  {
    lA[localIdx*numElements + i] =
        A[iRow*dim + localIdx*numElements + i];
  }
  barrier(CLK_LOCAL_MEM_FENCE);
  for(int i=0;i< dim;++i)
  {
    result += lA[i]*B[i*dim + iCol];
  }
  C[iRow*dim + iCol] = result;
}
```

The statement in the host code that passes this argument is something like `clStatus = clSetKernelArg(kernel, 4, 1024*sizeof(float), NULL);` `4` indicates index of parameter in the parameter-list (this is fifth parameter). Then size of the array is passed. Here the size is `MATRIX_WIDTH*sizeof(float)` and the last argument which is the pointer to local is `NULL`.

Here the entire row of `A` matrix is copied into local memory so that it can be used by all the work-items of same work group. One copy of a row is available for each work-group. As before we do equal partition of task of copying, so each work-item here copies equal amount of the current row of A, since there are 256 work-item per work-group, so for a `MATRIX_WIDTH` equal to 1024 elements each work-item copies `(1024/256) 4` elements.

To make sure the entire row of `A` is available on local memory of a work-group, before proceeding further we apply one work-group level synchronization primitive called `barrier(CLK_LOCAL_MEM_FENCE);`. This ensures that all the work-items in a work-group reached this line before any work-item in that work-group executes the next line. When entire row of `A` is available then we proceed to compute the corresponding element of `C` within next for loop. The main difference between the kernels is that second one uses coalesced memory access for populating row of A.

```
void MatrixMul_kernel_localA_coallesced(int dim,
                          __global float *A,
                          __global float *B,
                          __global float *C,
                          __local  float *lA)
{
  //Get the index of the work-item
  int iCol = get_global_id(0);
  int iRow = get_global_id(1);
  int localIdx = get_local_id(0);
  int localSizex = get_local_size(0);
  float result = 0.0f;
  int numElements = dim/localSizex;
  for(int i=0; i<numElements ; i++)
  {
    lA[i*localSizex + localIdx] = A[iRow*dim + i*localSizex +
      localIdx];
  }
  barrier(CLK_LOCAL_MEM_FENCE);
  for(int i=0;i< dim;++i)
  {
    result += lA[i]*B[i*dim + iCol];
  }
  C[iRow*dim + iCol] = result;
}
```

Main advantage in performance is the use of local memory and the reuse of it for the entire work-group. It is copied once and used 256 times, since 256 work-items are launched per work-group. Since the second kernel `MatrixMul_kernel_localA_coallesced` uses coalesced access that would give some performance gain over first.

Case study – Histogram calculation

In the section *Histogram calculation* in *Chapter 3, Buffers and Image Objects,* we discussed about the naive implementation of histogram computation of an image. We read an input image file and pass the pixel buffer to the OpenCL device to compute the histogram of the image. By now you must have observed that this implementation is not so optimized which involves sequential reads. In this section we will try to optimize this implementation by making use of `atomic_inc` OpenCL C built-in and make use of coalesced reads and writes to the global and local memory. Take a look at the following kernel:

```
#define BIN_SIZE            256
#define ELEMENTS_TO_PROCESS 256
__kernel
void histogram_kernel(__global const uint* data,
                      __global uint* binResultR,
                      __global uint* binResultG,
                      __global uint* binResultB)
{
  __local int sharedArrayR[BIN_SIZE];
  __local int sharedArrayG[BIN_SIZE];
  __local int sharedArrayB[BIN_SIZE];
  __global uchar4 * image_data = data;
  size_t localId   = get_local_id(0);
  size_t globalId  = get_global_id(0);
  size_t groupId   = get_group_id(0);
  size_t groupSize = get_local_size(0);

  /* initialize shared array to zero */
  sharedArrayR[localId] = 0;
  sharedArrayG[localId] = 0;
  sharedArrayB[localId] = 0;

  barrier(CLK_LOCAL_MEM_FENCE);
  int groupOffset = groupId * groupSize * ELEMENTS_TO_PROCESS;
  /* calculate thread-histograms */
  for(int i = 0; i < ELEMENTS_TO_PROCESS; ++i)
  {
    int index = groupOffset + i * groupSize + localId;
    //Coalesced read from global memory
    uchar4 value = image_data[index];
    atomic_inc(&sharedArrayR[value.x]);
    atomic_inc(&sharedArrayG[value.y]);
    atomic_inc(&sharedArrayB[value.w]);
  }

  barrier(CLK_LOCAL_MEM_FENCE);
  //Coalesced write to global memory
  binResultR[groupId * BIN_SIZE + localId] = sharedArrayR[localId];
```

```
    binResultG[groupId * BIN_SIZE + localId] = sharedArrayR[localId];
    binResultB[groupId * BIN_SIZE + localId] = sharedArrayR[localId];

}
```

Note that in this kernel unlike the one which we discussed in *Chapter 3, OpenCL Buffer Objects*, we have not passed the local array size from the host side using the `clSetKernelArg` function. The local arrays can be created inside the kernel also. The `__local` address space specifier makes it clear that this array is accessible across all the work items in the work group. Next, we initialize the shared array to 0. As you can see, each of the accesses to `sharedArrayR`, `sharedArrayG` and `sharedArrayB` are coalesced accesses. And also since the `sharedArray` size is much less compared to the one in the naive implementation, this array is set only once by every work item. This setting to zero of the complete local array is synchronized by adding a barrier inside the kernel.

Following the barrier in the `for` loop we read the pixel values from global memory in a coalesced manner, and use `atomic_inc` OpenCL C built-in to increase the count of the corresponding pixel values. We wait for all work items to process `ELEMENTS_TO_PROCESS` pixel values by adding a barrier instruction, before finally writing it to the global memory `binResultR`, `binResultG` and `binResultB`. There are more advantages in this kernel as compared to the naive implementation. The amount of global memory writes is the same though but the amount of local memory used in the kernel is far less. This enables for a large number of work items to be spawned per work group. In this example we have launched 256 work items as compared to the 16 work items in our naive implementation of *Chapter 3, OpenCL Buffer Objects*.

Now there is one more way that this kernel can be optimized, that is the number of pixels to process per work item is fixed to `ELEMENTS_TO_PROCESS` which is `256` pixels in this case. This also makes the number of work groups to be launched dependent on the number of pixels to process. That is each work group shall process `ELEMENTS_TO_PROCESS * work_group_size` pixels only. So this might sometimes lead to underutilization of the available compute units in the OpenCL device. For example if the number of pixels to be processed is equal 1024*1024, then we shall be launching, `(1024*1024)/(256*256) = 16` work groups. If the number of compute units available in the OpenCL device is say 12, then the OpenCL implementation shall launch in chunks of 12 work groups and four work groups. So to avoid this, the number of pixels to be computed is determined by the host and passed as a parameter to the kernel. Take a look at the kernel code below. Since the last work group will not be processing an exact multiple of work group size pixels, we need to calculate the `elements_to_process` for each work_item in the last work group. The `if` statement inside the for loop takes care of the boundary conditions and makes sure that the global memory is not read outside of the global memory buffer range.

```
#define BIN_SIZE            256
__kernel
void histogram_kernel(__global const uint* data,
                  __global uint* binResultR,
                  __global uint* binResultG,
                  __global uint* binResultB,
                    int elements_to_process,
                    int total_pixels)
{
  __local int sharedArrayR[BIN_SIZE];
  __local int sharedArrayG[BIN_SIZE];
  __local int sharedArrayB[BIN_SIZE];
  __global uchar4 * image_data = data;
  size_t localId = get_local_id(0);
  size_t globalId = get_global_id(0);
  size_t groupId = get_group_id(0);
  size_t groupSize = get_local_size(0);

  /* initialize shared array to zero */
  sharedArrayR[localId] = 0;
  sharedArrayG[localId] = 0;
  sharedArrayB[localId] = 0;

  barrier(CLK_LOCAL_MEM_FENCE);
  int groupOffset = groupId * groupSize * elements_to_process;

  /* For the last work group calculate the number of elements required
*/
  if(groupId == (get_num_groups(0) - 1))
    elements_to_process =
    ((total_pixels - groupOffset) + groupSize - 1) /groupSize;

  /* calculate thread-histograms */
  for(int i = 0; i < elements_to_process; ++i)
  {
    int index = groupOffset + i * get_local_size(0) + localId;
    if(index > total_pixels)              \n"
      break;
    //Coalesced read from global memory
    uchar4 value = image_data[index];      \n"
    atomic_inc(&sharedArrayR[value.x]);
    atomic_inc(&sharedArrayG[value.y]);
    atomic_inc(&sharedArrayB[value.w]);
  }

  barrier(CLK_LOCAL_MEM_FENCE);
```

```
    //Coalesced write to global memory
    binResultR[groupId * BIN_SIZE + localId] =
                                    sharedArrayR[localId];
    binResultG[groupId * BIN_SIZE + localId] =
                                    sharedArrayR[localId];
    binResultB[groupId * BIN_SIZE + localId] =
                                    sharedArrayR[localId];
}
```

We conclude this chapter by summarizing a few general tips for OpenCL optimization. These are neither exhaustive nor universal. Remember "*One size does not fit all*".

Finding the scope of the use of OpenCL

Given an algorithm or even some sequential implementation of it, how do we determine whether OpenCL would really help in performance gain? First, find hotspots in your sequential code. If that hot part can be partitioned into smaller parts which can be executed at least to some extent independently, that is, one smaller computation part can be done without waiting for data of previous computation part? Can we find some part of the algorithm where the same instruction is executed on different data without any mutual dependency? Affirmative answer to the first and second part of questions respectively asserts the existence of task and data parallel components in the algorithm. In either case, taking advantage of OpenCL is probably a good option.

Second consideration is whether the program is memory-bound, I/O bound, or CPU-bound. If the algorithm is dense with conditional statements, a better candidate for OpenCL would be compute bound program with less branches.

General tips

Some of the following strategies are vendor and architecture specific but mostly have a corresponding counterpart in other vendors and architectures.

1. Try to minimize host-device transfer of memory. Also try to hide memory transfer latencies with parallel computation. Host-device transfer has much lower bandwidth than global memory access. (For example, for NVIDIA GTX 280 verses PCI-e it becomes approximately 17 times). So better to store and keep it on the Global memory. Sometimes it is even better to re-compute something in GPU rather than trying to fetch from host.
2. One large transfer is much better than many smaller transfers amounting to same size.

3. Try for coalesced memory access as much as possible, that is, avoid out of sequence and misaligned transactions. This is more OpenCL device architecture and compute capability specific.
4. Use local memory (100 times better latency for GTX 280) for caching, but be careful about overuse to avoid performance penalty due to spilling to global memory. Local memory also helps to avoid non-coalesced global memory access. Entire work-group shares this local so cache ones and use for all work-item in the work-group. Another advantage of local memory is data sharing between work-items within same work-group.
5. Use private memory with same care. No thumb rule exists for local and private memory use. It needs some experiment to find the optimal strategy for your algorithm.
6. Avoid bank conflict as much as possible. In general multiple Read/Write on same memory bank becomes serialized instead of being parallel, resulting in performance penalty. This is more vendor architecture specific. Please refer to the vendor architecture manual for more detailed information, for example AMD_Accelerated_Parallel_Processing_OpenCL_Programming_Guide.pdf downloadable from `developer.amd.com` for AMD GPUs and NVIDIA_OpenCL_ProgrammingGuide.pdf downloadable from cudazone from the NVIDIA website for NVIDIA GPUs.
7. Number of work-groups should be always greater than number of compute units, so that all the compute units are getting at least one work-group, otherwise hardware resources would be under-utilized. Better to have the ratio of number of work-groups to that of number of compute units greater than or equal to two so that if one work-group on a compute-unit is stuck on a barrier, GPU time can be utilized by executing other work-group. Far better is making number of work-group a multiple of number of compute units so that the wavefronts are fully populated. Wavefront is AMD's term means unit of execution that executes in a lock step manner relative to each other. NVIDIA similar concept is termed as warp. More work-group per compute units helps in hiding latency.
8. Number of work-items per work-group should be multiple of wavefront size. It can sometimes be beneficial to add "dummy" work-items so that the work-group becomes a multiple of the unit of execution size even though this means adding extra work.
9. Try to increase the occupancy which is ratio of active wavefront per compute unit to maximum allowed wavefront per compute unit. Occupancy is function of registers, local memory, hardware scheduling, and so on. AMD provides an occupancy analysis chart to see interactively how occupancy varies with different factors.

10. Instruction throughput is defined as number of instructions executed per cycle. For a given architecture, generally the number of cycles needed to be execute each of the instructions is documented by the major vendors. Using that try to use smaller number of cycles to get things done. Avoid automatic conversion from double to float (for example, use `12.3f` rather than 12.3 for float).
11. Use non-blocking command and queue multiple commands in the command queue before it gets flushed to GPU.
12. Avoid branch or divergent branch within a wave-front, since it serializes execution. Sometimes some restructuring of code or index may help. At least minimize the number of instruction within branch. For example, instead of using the following:

    ```
    if(some_cond){ x += y;}else {x -=z;}
    ```

    prefer the following:

    ```
    int tmp = some_cond ? y:-z;
    x+= tmp;
    ```

    Take similar care for the `while` or `for` loops within kernel. Avoid nested if. Also avoid if statements with multiple conditions combined by AND operators like the following:

    ```
    if(condition1 && condition2 && condition3)
    ```

    Because they possibly generate nested if from the statements. Prefer the following:

    ```
    bool singleCond = (condition1 && condition2 && condition3);
    if(singleCond)
    ```

13. For 2D/3D structured data, use texture or image memory, which has hardware accelerated data type conversion and interpolation and optimized 2D/3D caching.
14. Prefer constant memory over global memory if device only needs to read the data, since constant memory is faster than global.
15. Avoid barrier when possible, since it is a costly operation.

Summary

In this chapter we have discussed different optimization techniques. All are illustrated on the same simple problem of matrix multiplication to demonstrate how the same algorithm can be adjusted to accommodate different optimization techniques. We also optimized the histogram computation kernel which was originally discussed in *Chapter 3, OpenCL Buffer Objects*. Based on data size, hardware and software environment different optimization strategies can be applied. The chapter ends with a hint on the kind of application when OpenCL would show real performance improvement and then some general tips or checklist related to optimization. In the next chapter we describe image processing using OpenCL.

9
Image Processing and OpenCL

In the previous chapter we discussed an OpenCL implementation of a very basic algorithm called matrix multiplication. We saw that a matrix multiplication algorithm can be implemented in many different ways, such as by using local, global or private memory. In this chapter we delve into a different subject called image processing, in which we primarily discuss image convolution. Image processing in itself is a very big topic and there are many books which discuss the same. We will briefly deal with image processing in this chapter and explore the data parallel operations in image processing algorithms, and how it can be used with OpenCL. In this chapter, we will also discuss how to perform some filter operations using the convolution operators.

The list of filters we discuss in this case study are as follows:

- Mean filter
- Median filter
- Gaussian filter
- Sobel filter

Image compression is a research topic in itself. One of the most common compression algorithms is the JPEG standard. There are quite a few theoretical data compression techniques, such as Entropy Coding, Huffman decode, and Run Length Encoding. The JPEG decoder in itself is a huge topic. In this chapter, we will discuss a small subset of JPEG compression standard, and how we parallelize the inverse DCT operation using OpenCL.

Since these examples are a bit domain specific, we present a brief introduction to the problem and the algorithm before discussing the actual OpenCL implementation. Readers, who are already familiar with these concepts, may like to skip the sections.

Image representation

We represent an image in a digital computer by a matrix of pixels (picture element). For an image containing only two colors (possibly black and white), the pixel can be a bi-level (Boolean) field with true (1) meaning white, and false (0) meaning black. One of the file formats for representing this kind of image is the **PBM** (**Portable Bit Map**) file format. In this file format, each pixel is represented by one bit. If the image is of size `WIDTH * HEIGHT`, then each row is `WIDTH` bits, packing eight pixels into a byte, with don't care bits to fill out the last byte in the row. There are `HEIGHT` number of such rows.

Now let's consider a gray scale image. The number of distinct gray scale values that can be represented by a pixel depends on the number of **Bits Per Pixel** (**bpp**). For 8 bpp, 256 gray scale values can be represented. In this case, pixel values can vary from `0` to `255`. These pixel values are often referred to as pixel intensity levels. So a pixel may be represented as follows:

```
# define MAX_INTENSITY 255
typedef cl_uchar pixel; //each pixel's valid value is
  0-MAX_INTENSITY
```

An image format which represents the pixel is the **PGM** (**Portable Gray Map**). If the image is of size `WIDTH * HEIGHT`, each row consists of `WIDTH` gray scale values, in order from left to right. Each gray scale value is a number from `0` through `MAX_INTENSITY`, with `0` being black and `MAX_INTENSITY` being white. BMP, also referred to as a bitmap image file, can be used to represent a gray scale image too. The BMP file consists of an image header, followed by the color palate information and the actual pixel colors for each color channel Red, Green, or Blue. The color palate is an array of colors used in the image. Then the actual color information is stored in row descending format, which means first we store all the pixels at height `HEIGHT`, then `HEIGHT-1` and so on. The number of pixels in a row is equal to the `WIDTH`, and the order in which row elements are stored is from element at 0-th width to `WIDTH-1`. Each row may be followed by some padding to make it a multiple of 4 bytes. In our image processing samples we will be using bmp files as input images.

For a color image, each pixel (in order to represent a color) contains three different intensity values—Red, Green, and Blue. Other colors are composed of these three colors only, but in a unique proportion. If each of red, green, and blue's intensity level is **represented** by n-bits, then red may take 2^n values, and similarly green and blue may take 2 superscript n. values each. So a total of $2^n * 2^n * 2^n = 2^{3n}$ possible combinations are possible, which simply means if each of red, green, and blue color (also called channel in this context) is represented using n-bits, we can, in total, represent 23n distinct colors in the image. For example, when n=8, that is each color is given 8-bits, a pixel structure may be as follows:

```
struct pixel{
    cl_uchar red;
    cl_uchar green;
    cl_uchar blue;
};
```

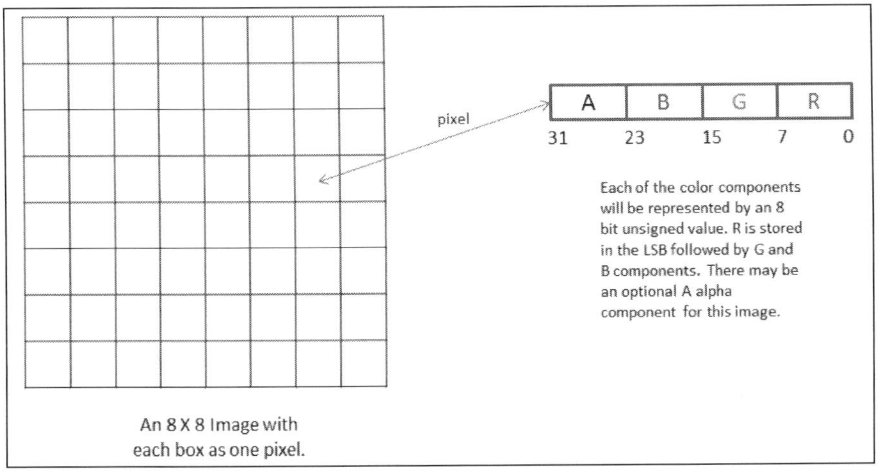
pixel
A
B
G
R
31
23
15
7
0
Each of the color components will be represented by an 8 bit unsigned value. R is stored in the LSB followed by G and B components. There may be an optional A alpha component for this image.
An 8 X 8 Image with each box as one pixel.

If the height and width of the image are respectively `HEIGHT` and `WIDTH`, then a total of `HEIGHT * WIDTH` number of pixels can be represented by a single dimensional array in either the row major form (discussed in *Chapter 8, Basic Optimization Techniques with Case Studies – Compute Bound Problem*), as in the following code, or in the column major form.

```
struct pixel image[HEIGHT * WIDTH];
```

Its two dimensional array representation, as shown in the following code, would be more straightforward:

```
struct pixel image[HEIGHT][WIDTH];
```

PPM (Portable Pixel Map) is one file format which represents this type of image data. In this file format each row consists of `WIDTH` number of pixels, in order from left to right. Each pixel is a triplet of red, green, and blue samples, in that order. Each sample is represented in a binary format by either 1 or 2 bytes. If the `MAX_INTENSITY` is less than `256`, one channel is 1 byte. Otherwise, it is 2 bytes.

Two factors affecting image quality improvement, within perceivable range, are very evident. The first one being, number of bits representing a channel (color), if the number is increased, we can have more combinations, hence more colors can be represented, thus image quality would be improved. The second is, increase in number of pixels per unit area, called pixel density. Both these factors come at the cost of image size.

Implementing image filters

An image filter is a mathematical operation on the original image that transforms it to the filtered image. The goal of the mathematical operation is to perform a mathematical computation for a pixel, based on the values of the neighboring pixels. A precisely defined image filter is a function that transforms each pixel of the original image to pixels of the filtered image. Consider a simple example—what would one do if he or she wants to decrease the brightness of an image?

In an image with gray scale representation, each pixel would contain one integer representing intensity. Deduct some positive integer say `VALUE` from all the pixels and if some integer becomes negative then truncate the result to zero. This is referred to as the mathematical operation which is applied to every pixel in the original image. This function would transform the image into one that is the same as the original image, but with lower brightness. Similarly adding a constant value to all pixels (and if some integer becomes more than `MAX_INTENSITY`, saturating it to `MAX_INTENSITY`) is another function. This would increase the brightness of the image.

We will now discuss the four different types of image filters.

Mean filter

Mean filter also called the blur filter since it blurs the image. For an image of size `WIDTH` by `HEIGHT`, we choose some small window filter operator of size `m by m` (`m` is much smaller than the width or height of the image, in our example we have taken it as 3). This `m` is called as the window size of the applied filter. Now, for each pixel in `(i,j)` th position we consider the small window centered at `(i,j)` th pixel. This window would contain `3 X 3 = 9` pixels shown as follows:

```
(i-1,j-1)    (i-1,j)    (i-1,j+1)
(i,j-1)      (i, j)     (i,j+1)
(i+1,j-1)    (i+1,j)    (i+1,j+1)
```

We now take the mean of all the nine elements and output the `(i,j)` th pixel with the mean value. Impact of this operation is the reduction of difference in pixel intensity within a small region. So the contrast is reduced and the image becomes comparatively blurred in that region. This operation is done for all the pixels (for the pixels at border we can either discard or extrapolate, by taking the value of `(i,j)` th pixel and using it for all the missing neighbors) so the entire image is blurred.

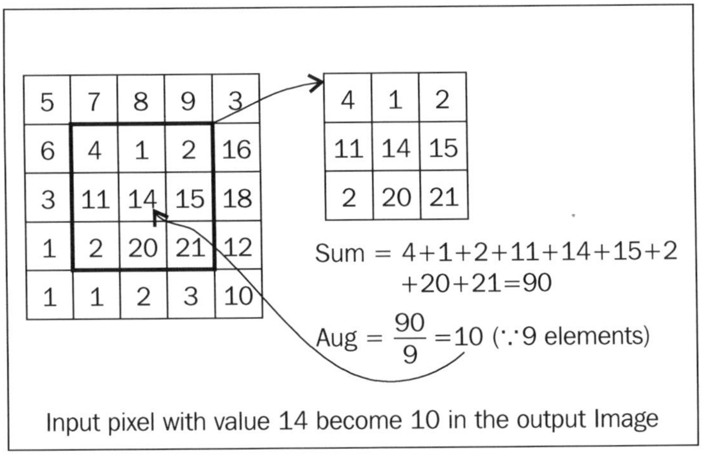

Mean filter operation

Median filter

In this operation, we take the same window as in the mean filter but instead of taking the mean of the nine elements, we take the median and output it in the position of the center pixel. This means, finding the mid value among all the elements in the window with current pixel at center. This filter under certain conditions reduces the salt and pepper noise, but also retains the image edge information intact; hence it is often applied before applying the edge detection algorithm. This filter also provides a slight blurring effect.

Gaussian filter

The Gaussian filter is a low pass filter which removes high frequency values. This also creates a blurring effect. Here, we take the same windows from the original image and the two dimensional Gaussian distribution's coefficient, and convolute them. Convolution is nothing but simply multiplying the corresponding elements of two matrices of size `m X m` and then adding the obtained `m X m` products. The following equation describes the Gaussian distribution formula:

$$G(x, y) = \frac{1}{2\pi\sigma^2} e^{-\frac{x^2+y^2}{2\sigma^2}}$$

Two dimensional Gaussian distribution's coefficients are obtained by approximating the Gaussian distribution. Here in our example we have used the following matrix with a sigma value of 0.85:

```
1.f/16,  2.f/16,  1.f/16,
2.f/16,  4.f/16,  2.f/16,
1.f/16,  2.f/16,  1.f/16,
```

The OpenCL Kernel code is as follows:

```
__constant sampler_t image_sampler = CLK_NORMALIZED_COORDS_FALSE
  | CLK_ADDRESS_CLAMP_TO_EDGE| CLK_FILTER_NEAREST;

__kernel void gaussian_filter_kernel(__read_only image2d_t iimage,
  __write_only image2d_t oimage,__constant float *filter,
  int windowSize)
{
  unsigned int x = get_global_id(0);
  unsigned int y = get_global_id(1);
  int halfWindow = windowSize/2;
  float4 pixelValue;
  float4 computedFilter=0.0f;
  int i, j, ifilter, jfilter;

  for(i=-halfWindow, ifilter=0; i<=halfWindow; i++, ifilter++)
  {
    for(j=-halfWindow, jfilter=0; j<=halfWindow; j++,jfilter++)
    {
      pixelValue = read_imagef(iimage, image_sampler,
        (int2)(x+i, y+j));
      computedFilter +=
      filter[ifilter*windowSize+jfilter]*pixelValue;
    }
  }


  write_imagef(oimage, (int2)(x, y), computedFilter);
}
```

Convolution is described in the following figure:

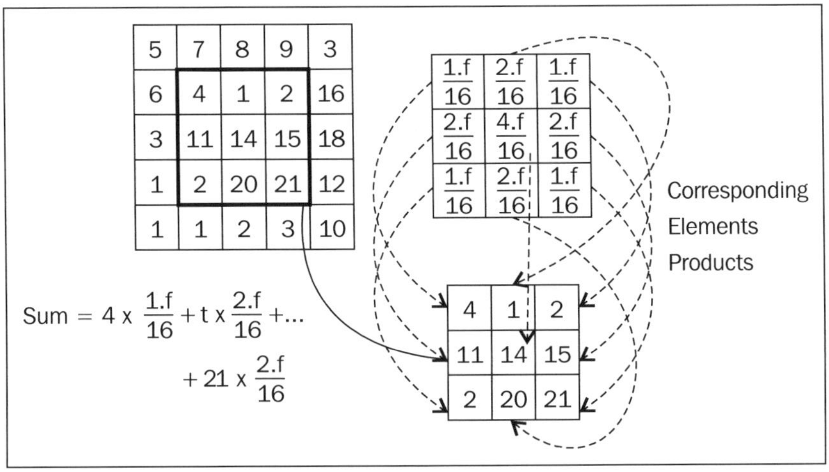

Sobel filter

Sobel filter is one of the most popular filters which can be used for edge detection of an image. Edge detection is important for many algorithms for feature extraction from an image. This is based on the idea that a pixel on an edge in the image, is different from other pixels which are not on any edge, by a unique property. The property is based on the fact that in edge there would be a sudden jump/change in intensity. This is found by computing the derivative along the two directions in a 2D image say Sx and Sy and then magnitude, followed by optional thresholding.

For a 3 x 3 window, this reduces to the following computational steps

1. Let the value of Sx be as follows:

```
            1,  0,  -1
Sx =        2,  0,  -2
            1,  0,  -1
```

   and the value of Sy is as follows:

```
                1,  2,  1
Sy = SxT =      0,  0,  0
               -1, -2, -1
```

2. Now, given an input image `I` take window `A`. For each element in the window `A` multiply it with the corresponding element in the matrix `Sx` and `Sy` to obtain `Tx` and `Ty` matrices as follows:

   Tx = Sx · A and **Ty = Sy · A**

   (· here means convolution)

3. Find the magnitude `T` for each element in the window, using the following formula:

   $T = \text{sqrt}(Tx^2 + Ty^2)$

4. Choose a threshold `Tr`. This threshold value can be selected based on experiment.
5. Finally apply the threshold, that is if `T >= Tr` then this pixel has a characteristic edge, else not. Do this for all the pixels and get all the edge pixels.

OpenCL implementation of filters

Here we discuss how each of the filters is implemented. Similar filters are discussed together. Mean and Gaussian filters are imposed by convoluting with a fixed 3 x 3 matrix.

Mean and Gaussian filter

In our OpenCL implementation of the Mean and Gaussian filters, we write a kernel called `filter_kernel` that can be used for the two filters. We do this by configuring the third argument `filter` so that it can create effects of the corresponding filter. For the Mean filter we send a nine element array, where each element's value is `1/9` and when this is convoluted with the corresponding window, it produces the effect of mean of that window. When the `filter_kernel` kernel is to be called for the Gaussian filter, we pass corresponding coefficients in row major form `(1/16, 2/16, 1/16, 2/16, 4/16, 2/16, 1/16, 2/16, 1/16)`.

So we explain these two filters together. The following code is the common kernel code for these two filters:

```
__constant sampler_t image_sampler = CLK_NORMALIZED_COORDS_FALSE |
  CLK_ADDRESS_CLAMP_TO_EDGE | CLK_FILTER_NEAREST;
```

```
__kernel void filter_kernel(__read_only image2d_t iimage,
  __write_only image2d_t oimage, __constant float *filter,
  int windowSize)
{
  unsigned int x = get_global_id(0);
  unsigned int y = get_global_id(1);
  int halfWindow = windowSize/2;
  float4 pixelValue;
  float4 computedFilter=0.0f;
  int i, j, ifilter, jfilter;

  for(i=-halfWindow, ifilter=0; i<=halfWindow; i++, ifilter++)
  {
    for(j=-halfWindow, jfilter=0; j<=halfWindow; j++,jfilter++)
    {
      pixelValue = read_imagef(iimage, image_sampler,(int2)(
        x+i, y+j));
      computedFilter +=
        filter[ifilter*windowSize+jfilter]*pixelValue;
    }
  }


  write_imagef(oimage, (int2)(x, y), computedFilter);
}
```

This kernel takes four arguments. The first two are input and output images, which are respectively attributed as read and write only, as defined by the attribute specifier `__read_only` and `__write_only`. Then comes the `__global` array of float which mentions the filter in row major form. The fourth argument is window size in a dimension. Hence the `filter` array would contain a total of `windowSize*windowSize` elements.

Within the kernel, based on the `global_id` variable of the work item in the two dimensions, the corresponding element of window of the input image is read using `read_imagef` and then multiplied with corresponding elements of the `filter` array. These products are added to each other and the accumulated sum is stored in the `computedFilter` variable using nested `for` loops. The private variable `halfWindow` is used to get index in left, right, up, and down properly from the current center element identified by the `global_id` of the current work item. Finally `write_imagef` writes back the resulting pixel to the output image.

Note that both the variables `computedFilter` and `pixelValue` are `float4` data types. This is because the `read_imagef` returns a `float4` variable.

```
float4 read_imagef (image2d_t image, sampler_t sampler,
  int2 coord)
```

As of the OpenCL 1.2 specification, there are no OpenCL sampler APIs which return a single float value. All the image sampler routines discussed in Table 6.23 of OpenCL specification 1.2 return vector data types. This is intended to return R, G, B, and A (alpha) image channel data. Now the question arises how one processes a gray scale image? Let's consider the following code snippet:

```
cl_int ImageFilter::setupOCLbuffers()
{
  cl_int status;
  //Intermediate reusable cl buffers
  cl_image_format image_format;
  cl_image_desc image_desc;
  image_format.image_channel_data_type = CL_FLOAT;
  image_format.image_channel_order = CL_R;

  image_desc.image_type = CL_MEM_OBJECT_IMAGE2D;
  image_desc.image_width = image->width;
  image_desc.image_height = image->height;
  image_desc.image_depth = 1;
  image_desc.image_array_size = 1;
  //Note when the host_ptr is NULL row_pitch and
  //slice_pitch should be set to 0;
  //Otherwise you will get a CL_INVALID_IMAGE_DESCRIPTOR error
  image_desc.image_row_pitch = 0;
  image_desc.image_slice_pitch = 0;
  image_desc.num_mip_levels = 0;
  image_desc.num_samples = 0;
  image_desc.buffer= NULL;
  ocl_input_image = clCreateImage(context, CL_MEM_READ_ONLY,
    &image_format, &image_desc, NULL, &status);
  LOG_OCL_ERROR(status, "clCreateImage Failed" );

  //Note when the host_ptr is NULL row_pitch and
  //slice_pitch should be set to 0.
  //Otherwise you will get a CL_INVALID_IMAGE_DESCRIPTOR error
  image_desc.image_row_pitch = 0;
  image_desc.image_slice_pitch = 0;
```

```
    ocl_filtered_image = clCreateImage(context, CL_MEM_WRITE_ONLY,
    &image_format, &image_desc, NULL, &status);
    LOG_OCL_ERROR(status, "clCreateImage Failed" );

    ocl_filter = clCreateBuffer(context,
      CL_MEM_READ_WRITE|CL_MEM_USE_HOST_PTR,
      WINDOW_SIZE*WINDOW_SIZE*sizeof(float), filter, &status);
    LOG_OCL_ERROR(status, "clCreateBuffer Failed" );

    //Create OpenCL device output buffer
    return status;
}
```

In the preceding code, you will observe that the `image_channel_order` value is set to `CL_R` while describing the `image_format` variable. And besides this, the `image_channel_data_type` variable is set to `CL_FLOAT`. Now when the image pixel value is sampled in the kernel using the `read_imagef` function, it will set the value of the first vector component to the pixel value and the remaining are set to `0.0f`. This actually provides an added advantage in our kernel code, that it can take the input images with the `image_channel_data_type` variable set as `CL_RGBA`, `CL_BGRA`, `CL_ARGB` `CL_RGB`, or `CL_RGBx` and so on. The preceding code snippet creates two image buffers, one for the input image `ocl_input_image`, and the other is the output image `ocl_filtered_image`.

Median filter

The `median_filter_kernel` kernel implements the Median filter. This takes three arguments, `__read_only` and `__write_only` input and output images respectively, and the third argument is `windowSize`. Since median is the mid value of a set, when elements are in sorted order, for the Median filter kernel no filter argument is needed, rather we need to find the median from the elements of the current window itself. We find the median of the `windowSize*windowSize` elements. This median value is the result of the current pixel in process. The following code is the OpenCL kernel for the Median Filter, which computes the median value of the neighboring pixels:

```
__constant sampler_t image_sampler = CLK_NORMALIZED_COORDS_FALSE
  | CLK_ADDRESS_CLAMP_TO_EDGE | CLK_FILTER_NEAREST;

__kernel void median_filter_kernel(__read_only image2d_t
  in_image, __write_only image2d_t out_image, int windowSize)
  {
```

```
    unsigned int x = get_global_id(0);
    unsigned int y = get_global_id(1);
    int halfWindow = windowSize/2;
    float4 pixelValue;
    int i, j, ifilter, jfilter;
    float oldPixels[9]; float tmp;
    int index =0;
    //Load the window in oldPixels
    for(i=-halfWindow, ifilter=0; i<=halfWindow; i++, ifilter++){
      for(j=-halfWindow, jfilter=0;j<=halfWindow;j++,
        jfilter++){
        pixelValue = read_imagef(in_image,image_sampler,(int2)(
          x+i, y+j));
        oldPixels[index] = pixelValue.x;
        index++;
      }
    }

    // Find the rank-th element
    int totalNumber = windowSize*windowSize;
    int rank = totalNumber/2 +1;
    for(int i=0; i< rank;++i)
    {
      for(int j=0; j< totalNumber-1 ; ++j)
      {
        if(oldPixels[j] > oldPixels[j+1])
        {
          tmp = oldPixels[j];
          oldPixels[j] = oldPixels[j+1];
          oldPixels[j+1] = tmp;
        }
      }
      totalNumber--;
    }
    //median is oldPixels[rank], update
    pixelValue.x = oldPixels[rank];
    write_imagef(out_image, (int2)(x, y), pixelValue);
}
```

To find the median of the windowSize*windowSize elements (let's keep windowSize=3) we need not sort the data completely. Rather, it is enough to find the top or bottom five elements, which we do and take the central element. The sorting which is implemented in the preceding kernel would be comparison based, and results in too many branches in the code. It is always good to avoid branches and use ternary operators and rely on the compiler to generate a good branchless code. In the case of median filtering we copy the global pixel elements to private memory anyway.

Sobel filter

In the sobel_filter_kernel kernel we can pass the filter operator as a global parameter in the kernel code or as a private variable inside the kernel. In the following kernel code, we have passed the filter operators filter_x_grad and filter_y_grad in global memory. These are the 3 x 3 matrices and are used to operate on each pixel. The other option is to store one matrix and compute the other using transpose within the kernel. The pixel value is read using the read_imagef function. This function returns a float4 pixel value. Since we had created the image in CL_R format, only the intensity value is read from the vector, that is the kernel processes a gray scale image. We compute the x and y gradients of the image pixel using the Sobel filter as in the following code:

```
__constant sampler_t image_sampler = CLK_NORMALIZED_COORDS_FALSE
  | CLK_ADDRESS_CLAMP_TO_EDGE;
__kernel void
sobel_filter_kernel(__read_only image2d_t iimage,
  __write_only image2d_t oimage,
  __global float *filter_x_grad,
  __global float *filter_y_grad,
  int windowSize)
{
  unsigned int x = get_global_id(0);
  unsigned int y = get_global_id(1);
  int halfWindow = windowSize/2;
  float4 pixelValue;
  float gradientX = 0.0f;
  float gradientY = 0.0f;
  float computedFilter  = 0.0f;
  int i, j, ifilter, jfilter;
```

```
    for(i=-halfWindow, ifilter=0; i<=halfWindow; i++, ifilter++)
    {
      for(j = -halfWindow,  jfilter=0;j<=halfWindow; j++,jfilter++)
      {
        pixelValue = read_imagef(iimage, image_sampler,
          (int2)(x+i, y+j));
        gradientX +=
        filter_x_grad[ifilter*windowSize+jfilter]*pixelValue.x;
        gradientY += filter_y_grad[ifilter*windowSize+jfilter]
          *pixelValue.y;
      }
    }
    //gradient and gradient is the image gradient in X and Y axes.
    //Now compute the gradient magnitude
    computedGradient = sqrt(gradientX*gradientX +
      gradientY*gradientY);
    write_imagef(oimage, (int2)(x, y), (float4)(computedGradient,
      0.0f, 0.0f, 1.0f);
}
```

Finally the kernel computes the square root of Tx^2 and Ty^2 which is the magnitude of gradient for that pixel. Finally the computed gradient value is written to the image buffer. Note that the two gradient matrices `Sx` and `Sy` are a transpose of each other. Also one row is negative of the second row. So ideally we could have computed the matrices `Tx` and `Ty` without passing the gradient matrices as an argument to the kernel. As an exercise, modify the `sobel_filter_kernel` to do edge detection without passing the gradient matrices `Sx` and `Sy`.

JPEG compression

Image compression is a huge topic in itself, and we cannot discuss it all here in the context of OpenCL. In the preceding section, we discussed the different kinds of filters which would perform some operation on the raw image data and result in some special effect to give the resultant image. After discussing different kinds of filters we would jump to compressed image data representation. Image representation is a tradeoff between space and quality. The image quality is directly related to the amount of storage required to store it. If we try to have better quality, it would come at the cost of space and if we want to reduce space, the quality is affected. When we capture an image and store it raw pixel by pixel, it is in its maximum size and also in its best natural quality.

In order to decrease the size of the image and retain as much quality as possible there are various compression algorithms. These algorithms are either lossless or lossy image compression.

One such compression technique is **JPEG (Joint Photographic Experts Group)** compression. JPEG is a standard (first approved as ITU-T in 1992) that defines compression and decompression algorithms where compression amount and image quality reduction can be adjusted. With a little perceivable loss of image quality, size can be reduced approximately to one-tenth of the original. It is a lossy compression in the sense that due to compression of an image some original pixel details would be lost, that can never be recovered from the compressed image.

There are many variations of JPEG encoding. Baseline JPEG encoding is one of the most popular techniques among them. Basic outline of the steps are described step by step in the following section. Detailed discussion of each step is out of the scope of this chapter. Those who have basic knowledge of the JPEG decoder can skip this section and move to the following section on OpenCL implementation. For more details readers are requested to refer to the related materials.

Encoding JPEG

JPEG encoding contains multiple steps, each one makes some sort of compression or prepare data for compression at some future step. The steps are as follows:

1. Transform (R, G, B) representation to (Y', Cb, Cr) representation. The Y' image is essentially a greyscale copy of the main image. Cb and Cr are respectively blue and red difference chroma components. The transformation formulae are as follows:

   ```
   Y = 0.299 R + 0.587 G + 0.114 B
   Cb = - 0.1687 R - 0.3313 G + 0.5 B + 128
   Cr = 0.5 R - 0.4187 G - 0.0813 B + 128
   ```

   There is a lot of redundancy in the raw image representation. This redundancy can be removed by subsampling the chroma components. Y' represents the luminosity or gray scale components of the image. Y'CbCr is a color space that separates redundant and non-redundant information from the visual quality perspective.

2. The Cb Cr details provide less visual impact and can be subsampled easily. Resolution of Cb and Cr can be left as it is or it can be reduced to half, that is the Cb and Cr components are down sampled in both the x and y directions. This results in one Cb and Cr 8 x 8 block for every four Y component 8 x 8 blocks. These four 8 x 8 blocks and one each of down sampled Cb and Cr 8 x 8 blocks represents one **MCU (Minimum Coded Unit)** in JPEG.

   The eye is more sensitive to brightness difference than fine color details, loosing less quality we reduce more size here.

3. For each MCU and within each MCU, each 8 x 8 block is applied the **Discrete Cosine Transformation (DCT)** separately. As compared to a data range 0 to 255, DCT works better in the data range -128 to 127. So data is converted to range -128 to 127 by subtracting 128 from each matrix element before performing DCT. In the end of the decoder, 128 must be added back to get the values correspondingly.

   On transformation, the DCT operation converts a spatial domain image to frequency domain image. This saves space while affecting the quality to a lesser extent. Partitioning into small non-overlapping blocks of size 8 x 8 is done to one (reduce the cost of DCT 2) special redundancy is found based on a smaller region which is better for image quality.

4. **Quantization of DCT coefficients**: To scale the DCT coefficient to a smaller value, we use a quantization matrix say Q(i, j) of size 8 x 8. Each element of the coefficient matrix is divided by the corresponding element of quantization matrix, and then the resulting values are approximated to nearest integer to get a smaller suitable integral value. It is this step where one can control the compression level. A bigger value in quantization matrix element result in more compression but less quality and vice versa.
5. After quantization, many elements become zero and they are located towards the right bottom corner of matrix. While transforming the two dimensional matrix in one dimensional array of integers, instead of representing in row major or column major way, scanning is done in a zig-zag way described in the following figure:

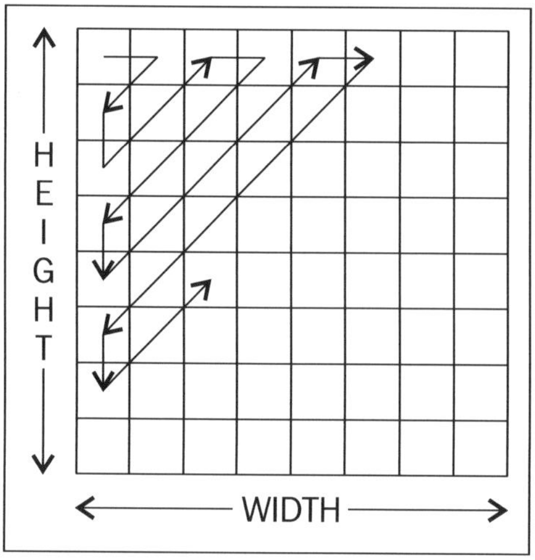

Image showing zig-zag scanning of an 8 X 8 block

This increases the probability of getting most of the zeros at the end of the array because of the fact that zeros are more likely to be located at the right bottom direction of the matrix. With mostly zeros at the end of the zig-zag scan, the trailing zeros can just be discarded, by putting an end of block marker. This results in saving of space.

6. **Run length encoding**: After doing the zig-zag scanning, Run-length encoding is employed on the coefficients to get one level of lossless compression. A run is a successive occurrence of the same symbol, and compression is achieved by replacing the entire run by a tuple of symbol and run-length which is illustrated by the following example:
7. `5,5,5,5,5,5,5,5,5,5,2,2,2,2,2,2,2,3,3,3,3,3,3` becomes `(5,10), (2,7), (3,6)`.
8. **Huffman coding**: This is also a lossless compression algorithm based on entropy encoding. In this step we futher compress based on the strategy that employs lesser bits for representing more frequently occurring data, and gradually more and more bits for less frequently occurring data. Here we create a binary tree called the Huffman tree, where each leaf node represents a symbol (here, an integer representing the output of run-length encoded value). Each non-leaf node represents a letter of code-word. Just concatenating the letters encountered when traversed from root to a leaf would give the code-word for the symbol that the leaf represents. Since the path length to node at lower height from root is less than that to a node at higher height, length of the code-word for more frequently occurring symbols are less, and those for less frequently occurring are more. Leaves at a lower height have more frequency and higher height have lesser frequency. Huffman coding is employed on the data obtained from run-length encoding.

This completes the JFIF version of JPEG compression. The final file format is described in brief as follows.

JFIF stores 16-bit words in big-endian format in a stream of blocks each of which are identified by a marker value. The first two bytes are the **Start of Image (SOI)** marker with values 0FFD8. Then with marker APP0 with value 0xFFE0 a block starts. The APP0 marker refers to the JFIF baseline format encoded image. This block contains length, version, aspect ratio, and so on, header information.

A Quantization table is identified by the marker DQT with value `0xFFDB`. This block, in addition to quantization values, contains table-length, precision, and the destination ID which is 0 or 1, indicating luminance or chrominance respectively. Quantization values form an 8 x 8 matrix Quantization Table. There would be two consecutive blocks of the preceding type one for luminance or chrominance.

This is followed by the Huffman table section. The **DHT (Define Huffman Table)** marker with the value `0xFFC4` identifies this table section and after that the **SOS (Start of Scan)** marker with value `0xFFDA` identifies the block of scan data. End of image is identified by the marker **EOI (End of Image)** with value `0xFFD9`.

In JPEG decoding, JPEG files are read in the reverse order of the encoder algorithm (described in the preceding paragraphs) we transform data to finally get the pixels. In our implementation, we have used the `JPEGdecoder_MCU` kernel to compute DCT. This kernel takes the help of the device function `DCTQuantInv8x8LS_JPEG_16s8u` which in return is taking help of another device function `Idct`.

OpenCL implementation

In this section we will discuss implementation of a JPEG decoder. In a JPEG decoder, when the file is scanned and as the markers arrive one after the other, the different tables are decoded and a data structure is filled, corresponding to the Huffman Table and Quantization table. There is no scope for parallelizing here.

On parsing the DQT and DHT tables from a JPEG file, next arrives the SOS marker, which is the Start of Scan marker. After this all the MCUs are encoded. Each MCU is of variable length and varies for each 8 x 8 block. This is precisely the reason that it is difficult to find parallelism here, as there is no mechanism to predict an MCU boundary for the encoded bits. Only after running a Huffman decode and when a run length is applied we get the 64 element entry which when fills the 8 x 8 block in a zig-zag manner, we get the DCT coefficients of Y, Cb, and Cr components. Finally after multiplying with the Quantization table, we perform an inverse DCT on the 8 x 8 block. The following code snippet computes the IDCT of an 8 x 8 block, which is applied to all the blocks of Y, Cb, and Cr components in an MCU. Only after obtaining the MCUs we can continue with the inverse DCT operation, which can run in parallel. It is this part of the JPEG decoder which we are trying to implement in parallel using OpenCL.

```
void Idct(const short  *pSrc, unsigned char *pDst)
{
 int i, j, k, l;
 float partialProduct;
 float tmp[64];
/*c is the precomputed cosine products from the I-DCT formula*/
  const float c[8][8] = {
    {0.35355338F,  0.35355338F,  0.35355338F,  0.35355338F,
     0.35355338F,  0.35355338F,  0.35355338F,  0.35355338F},
    {0.49039263F,  0.41573480F,  0.27778512F,  0.09754516F,
    -0.09754516F, -0.27778512F, -0.41573480F, -0.49039263F},
    {0.46193975F,  0.19134171F, -0.19134171F, -0.46193975F,
    -0.46193975F, -0.19134171F,  0.19134171F,  0.46193975F},
```

```
    {0.41573480F, -0.09754516F, -0.49039263F, -0.27778512F,
     0.27778512F,  0.49039263F,  0.09754516F, -0.41573480F},
    {0.35355338F, -0.35355338F, -0.35355338F,  0.35355338F,
     0.35355338F, -0.35355338F, -0.35355338F,  0.35355338F},
    {0.27778512F, -0.49039263F,  0.09754516F,  0.41573480F,
    -0.41573480F, -0.09754516F,  0.49039263F, -0.27778512F},
    {0.19134171F, -0.46193975F,  0.46193975F, -0.19134171F,
    -0.19134171F,  0.46193975F, -0.46193975F,  0.19134171F},
    {0.09754516F, -0.27778512F,  0.41573480F, -0.49039263F,
     0.49039263F, -0.41573480F,  0.27778512F, -0.09754516F}
  };

  for (i=0; i<8; i++)
    for (j=0; j<8; j++)
    {
      partialProduct = 0.0F;
      for (k=0; k<8; k++)
        partialProduct+= c[k][j]*pSrc[8*i+k];
      tmp[8*i+j] = partialProduct;
    }

    // Transpose operation is integrated into address mapping
      by switching
    // loop order of i and j

    for (j=0; j<8; j++)
      for (i=0; i<8; i++)
      {
        partialProduct = 0.0F;
        for (k=0; k<8; k++)
          partialProduct+= c[k][i]*tmp[8*k+j];
        l = (int)(partialProduct+0.5F);
        l = l+ 128;
        if(l < 0)
          l = 0;
        if(l > 255)
          l = 255;
        pDst[8*i+j] = l;
      }
}
```

Inverse DCT is an important computational step in decoding a JPEG image. This inverse DCT can be applied to the entire 8 x 8 block in an MCU in parallel. The role of the `Idct()` function is to compute inverse DCT, taking values in `pSrc` and output at `pDst`. It uses an 8 x 8 matrix of constant floats for this transformation. This matrix is the pre-computed cosine products for an 8X8 matrix.

The OpenCL kernel `JPEGdecoder_MCU` takes 11 arguments. For each of the three types (one for luminance and the other two for chrominance) of MCU data there are two parameters. One is the raw data array for which we want to compute the inverse DCT, and the other is the global buffer for the Quantization table for that type. The next parameter is simply the output buffer. The remaining four parameters are total height and width and also MCU height and width. Entire transformations are done just by calling the function void `DCTQuantInv8x8LS_JPEG_16s8u` six times for each 8 x 8 block, followed by nested `for` loops for writing back the data. The first four are computing the luminance data and last two are the chrominance data. The following sample code computes the six 8 x 8 blocks for the luminance and chrominance data given one input MCU. There will be as many instances or work-items in the image as there are MCUs.

```
_kernel void
JPEGdecoder_MCU(__global short *pMCUdata1, __global unsigned
  short *pQuantTable1, __global short *pMCUdata2,
  __global unsigned short *pQuantTable2, __global
  short *pMCUdata3, __global unsigned short *pQuantTable3,
  __global unsigned char * output, const unsigned
  int width, const unsigned int height, const unsigned
  int mcuWidth, const unsigned int mcuHeight)
{

  /* get the block ids in both the directions */
  int bx = get_global_id(0);
  int by = get_global_id(1);
  int tbx = get_global_size(0);
  int tby = get_global_size(1);
  int index = 0;
  int imageSize=0;

  unsigned char dst[64];
  __global short *tempPtr1;
```

The first six parameters are the MCU data and their corresponding Quantization matrices. `pMCUdata1` is the Y component MCU data, `pMCUdata2` is the Cb component MCU data, and finally pMCUdata3 is the Cr component data. These pointers contain the raw decoded DCT coefficients. Each work-item finds the inverse DCT and multiplies it with the quantization coefficients. The following code is the continuation of the above kernel. Note, the `__global` address space qualifier for the `tempPtr1` variable. OpenCL C has a restriction that casting a pointer of one address space to another pointer in a different address space is not allowed. Hence we provide the address space qualifier `__global`. Without that the `tempPtr1` variable would have been defaulted to the `__private` address space.

```
/* get the local ids within the block */
/*Y component*/
tempPtr1 = pMCUdata1 + by * tbx *( sizeof(int) * 64 ) + bx *
  sizeof(int) * 64 ;
DCTQuantInv8x8LS_JPEG_16s8u(tempPtr1,dst,8,(pQuantTable1));
for (int i=0;i<8;i++)
{
  for (int j=0;j<8;j++)
  {
    index = width*by*mcuHeight + bx*mcuWidth + i*width + j;
    output[index] = dst[i*8 + j];
  }
}

tempPtr1 = pMCUdata1 + by * tbx * sizeof(int) * 64 + bx *
  sizeof(int) * 64 +  64;
DCTQuantInv8x8LS_JPEG_16s8u(tempPtr1,dst,8,pQuantTable1);
for (int i=0;i<8;i++)
{
  for (int j=0;j<8;j++)
  {
    index = (width*by*mcuHeight) + (bx*mcuWidth + 8) + i*width
      + j;
    output[index] = dst[i*8 + j];
  }
}

tempPtr1 = pMCUdata1 + by * tbx *(sizeof(int)*64) + bx *
  sizeof(int) * 64 + ( 2 * 64 );
DCTQuantInv8x8LS_JPEG_16s8u(tempPtr1,dst,8,pQuantTable1);
for (int i=0;i<8;i++)
{
  for (int j=0;j<8;j++)
  {
    index = (width*by*mcuHeight) + (bx*mcuWidth) + (i+8)*width
      + j;
    output[index] = dst[i*8 + j];
  }
}

tempPtr1 = pMCUdata1 + by * tbx *(sizeof(int)*64) + bx *
  sizeof(int) * 64 + 3 * 64;
DCTQuantInv8x8LS_JPEG_16s8u(tempPtr1,dst,8,pQuantTable1);
for (int i=0;i<8;i++)
{
```

```
    for (int j=0;j<8;j++)
    {
      index = (width*by*mcuHeight) + (bx*mcuWidth + 8) +
        (i+8)*width + j;
      output[index] = dst[i*8 + j];
    }
  }
```

The preceding four for loops decode the four 8 x 8 Y components and stores the result in the output buffer. Similarly, the input buffer of Cb and Cr coefficients are taken and inverse DCT is applied to get the raw pixel values. The following code shows the decoding of the Cb and Cr components. You can see that a pixel value is copied to four different locations. The baseline JPEG compression which we are trying to evaluate here has a chroma subsampling of 4:1:1.

```
/*Cb component*/
tempPtr1 = pMCUdata2 + by * tbx *(1*64) + (bx * 1 * 64);
DCTQuantInv8x8LS_JPEG_16s8u(tempPtr1,dst,8,pQuantTable2);

imageSize = (width * height);
for (int i=0;i<8;i++)
{
  for (int j=0;j<8;j++)
  {
    index = imageSize + width*by*mcuHeight + bx*mcuWidth +
      2*i*width + 2*j ;
    output[index] = dst[i*8 + j];
    index = imageSize + width*by*mcuHeight + bx*mcuWidth +
      2*i*width + 2*j + 1;
    output[index] = dst[i*8 + j];
    index = imageSize + width*by*mcuHeight + bx*mcuWidth +
      (2*i + 1)*width + 2*j;
    output[index] = dst[i*8 + j];
    index = imageSize + width*by*mcuHeight + bx*mcuWidth +
      (2*i + 1)*width + 2*j + 1;
    output[index] = dst[i*8 + j];
  }
}
```

```
/*Cr component*/
tempPtr1 = pMCUdata3 + by * tbx *(1*64) + (bx * 1 * 64);
DCTQuantInv8x8LS_JPEG_16s8u(tempPtr1, dst, 8, pQuantTable3);
imageSize = 2*(width * height);
for (int i=0;i<8;i++)
{
  for (int j=0;j<8;j++)
  {
    index = imageSize + width*by*mcuHeight + bx*mcuWidth +
      2*i*width + 2*j ;
    output[index] = dst[i*8 + j];
    index = imageSize + width*by*mcuHeight + bx*mcuWidth +
      2*i*width + 2*j + 1;
    output[index] = dst[i*8 + j];
    index = imageSize + width*by*mcuHeight + bx*mcuWidth +
      (2*i + 1)* width + 2*j;
    output[index] = dst[i*8 + j];
    index = imageSize + width*by*mcuHeight + bx*mcuWidth +
      (2*i + 1)* width + 2*j + 1;
    output[index] = dst[i*8 + j];
  }
}
}
```

Role of the function

```
void DCTQuantInv8x8LS_JPEG_16s8u(__global short int *pSrc,
  unsigned char *pDst, int dstStp, __global unsigned short
  pQuantInvTable)
```

The role of the function is to compute the inverse DCT of the input 8 x 8 block pointed by `pSrc`. Once an inverse DCT is found the matrix is multiplied by the Quantization matrix to obtain the raw pixel values which are stored back in `pDst`. The Quantization matrix is given in the input parameter `pQuantInvTable`. For computing inverse DCT it uses the Idct function which was shown earlier in this chapter. All the functions are implemented in the `JPEGDecoder` sample code.

```
void Idct(const short  *pSrc, unsigned char *pDst).
```

Take a look at the JPEG sample code available with the code distribution. Other parts of JPEG decoding are not highly data parallel. So only the data parallel part from the Decode algorithm is extracted to make a parallel implementation using OpenCL. Remaining parts are implemented in host.

Summary

In this chapter we discussed a number of image processing algorithms. First we have discussed four filters namely Mean filter, Median filter, Gaussian filter, and Sobel filter. Then we discussed decoding of an image into a standard and very popular format called JPEG. In image processing, OpenCL is very well suited for point operation, since the operation is highly data parallel in nature. In the following chapter, we would discuss how OpenGL can be used along with OpenCL.

References

Digital image processing and analysis—B.Chandra and D. D. Majumdar, Prentice Hall India.

10

OpenCL-OpenGL Interoperation

In this chapter we will discuss OpenCL and OpenGL interoperation, which in its simple form means sharing of data between OpenGL and OpenCL in a program that uses both. Interoperation is commonly abbreviated as interop.

OpenGL was first released in January 1992 for proving graphics acceleration APIs. OpenCL was first released in December 2008 for accelerating general purpose computing. Both OpenCL and OpenGL use a GPU for their acceleration (OpenCL can use many other devices though). This OpenCL-GL Interoperation feature was introduced from the earliest version of OpenCL, that is, 1.0, but was really improved in OpenCL 1.1 by linking OpenCL and OpenGL events and efficient sharing of image and buffers. The computational part is done by OpenCL and graphics rendering is done by OpenGL without transferring data to and from host. This optimization in memory bandwidth should lead to an increase in efficiency and simplicity in coding.

In this chapter we first provide a brief introduction to OpenGL. Readers who are already familiar with OpenGL programming may like to skip this section. OpenGL itself is a vast course in graphics programming. So its tutorial is out of the scope of the present chapter, as well as this book. OpenCL also supports interoperation with Microsoft's DirectX 3D application programming interface **D3D** (**Direct 3D**).

In this chapter we start with a descriptive definition of OpenCL-OpenGL interoperation. We then gradually move to discuss the actual implementation steps and APIs. This includes detecting if interoperation is supported in the current implementation, initializing OpenCL context for OpenGL interoperation, mapping of a buffer (CL and GL), synchronization techniques, and then using the Texture and Renderbuffer objects of OpenGL.

Introduction to OpenGL

Open Graphics Language (**OpenGL**) is an open standard 2D and 3D graphics library standardized by Khronos group. It is supported on multiple platforms and also with many languages. Multiple vendors like AMD and NVIDIA, provide OpenGL implementation which are accelerated on a **GPU** (**Graphics Processor Unit**). Microsoft provided OpenGL support, for PC, from Windows 95.

There are two parts of an OpenGL program, shown as follows:

- Core OpenGL APIs, which are platform independent. For core API call, the header `<GL/gl.h>` must be included in all the files using OpenGL. It should be linked to `OpenGL32.lib` (part of Windows SDK) in Windows and `libGL.so` in Linux. Another OpenGL utility header `<GL/glu.h>` is included most of the time.
- The windowing and other platform-specific part. There are several libraries like GLX for X Window based system developed by Silicon Graphics, WGL or Wiggle for Windows developed and supported by Microsoft, and Core OpenGL (CGL) or Apple Graphics Library (AGL) for Mac. All these libraries provide APIs for interacting with their respective native Windowing system. There is a cross-platform **OpenGL Utility Toolkit** (**GLUT**) library which provides uniform interface for platform specific tasks. If GLUT is used then, `#include <GL/glut.h>` would include all GL-specific and platform-specific headers like the header required for WGL.

A very simple OpenGL program using GLUT would look like the following code:

```
#include <GL/glut.h>

#define WIN_WIDTH 350
#define WIN_HEIGHT 300

#define WIN_POS_X 150
#define WIN_POS_Y 150


void myDraw()
{
  //Set the color of drawing object with green color
  glColor3f (0.0, 1.0, 0.0);
```

```
  //Draw shape, vertices are enclosed
  //within glBegin(...) and glEnd(...)
  glBegin(GL_TRIANGLES);// Drawing Using Triangles
  glVertex3f( 0.0f, 1.0f, 0.0f);// Top vertex
  glVertex3f(-1.0f,0.0f, 0.0f);// Bottom Left vertex
  glVertex3f( 1.0f, 0.5f, 0.0f);// Bottom Right vertex
  glEnd();// Finished Drawing The Triangle

  //Actual execution of the drawing command is completed.
  glFlush();

}

int main(int argc, char** argv)
{
  //Initializes glut, so must be called before other glut routines
  glutInit(&argc, argv);

  //Sets the display in RGB mode with support of double bufferring
  glutInitDisplayMode (GLUT_RGB | GLUT_DOUBLE);

  //Sets window's size in pizel
  glutInitWindowSize (WIN_WIDTH, WIN_HEIGHT);

  //Sets windows position with respect to top left corner
    of screen
  glutInitWindowPosition (WIN_POS_X, WIN_POS_Y);

  //Only create the window with the given name
  //"myWindowName", but don't display at this point
  glutCreateWindow ("myWindowName");

  //Create read background
  //sets the background color to be used
  glClearColor (1.0, 0.0, 0.0, 0.0);

  //Projection matrix stack is the target for matrix operations
  //default initial value is modelview stack
  glMatrixMode(GL_PROJECTION);
```

```
    //Replace the current matrix with one identity matrix
    glLoadIdentity();

    //Set the co-ordinate system that determines how the drawn
    //image is maped to the screen
    //First four arguments are left, right, bottom, top of
    //the clipping planes
    //Fifth argument is nearValue which is nearer depth clipping
    //planes, it is behind the viewer so negative
    //Sixth argument is farvalue which is farther depth
      clipping planes
    glOrtho(0.0, 1.0, 0.0, 1.0, -1.0, 1.0);

    //Sets the display function
    glutDisplayFunc(myDraw);
    //Enters event processing loop,actually displays the windows
    glutMainLoop();
    return 0;
}
```

The inline comments would explain the role of each API in brief. After setting `myDraw` as a display function, it would be used to draw a scene in an OpenGL window. To understand the detail of the matrix mode and co-ordinate system, readers are requested to refer to some OpenGL manual/book. A series of books are popularly known by the cover colors that is *The Red Book*, *The Orange Book*, *The Blue Book*, *The Green Book*, and *The Alpha Book*. The last two books are specific to X Window System and Windows respectively. An easy start can be *Introduction to C Programming with a little OpenGL Graphics for fun* by Robert P. Cook. For 3D graphics, a good introduction can be *3D Computer Graphics: A Mathematical Introduction with OpenGL* by Samuel R Buss.

Defining Interoperation

Interoperation is a feature that allows an application to share data between OpenCL and OpenGL, without explicitly copying. Precisely, OpenCL-OpenGL interoperation means creating OpenCL memory objects directly from the existing OpenGL data structure without transferring data through the CPU. This saves a lot of data transfer time. It also saves memory in the GPU and solves the problem of data management, since the same data is being used by both OpenGL and OpenCL.

OpenCL applications can access data from two possible objects. They are as follows:

- Image Object
- Buffer Object

On the other hand an OpenGL program can share data with OpenCL with three possible objects. They are as follows:

- **Vertex Buffer Object (VBO)**
- Texture Object
- RenderBuffer Object

The OpenGL Vertex buffer object can be linked to the OpenCL buffer object, as in the following figure:

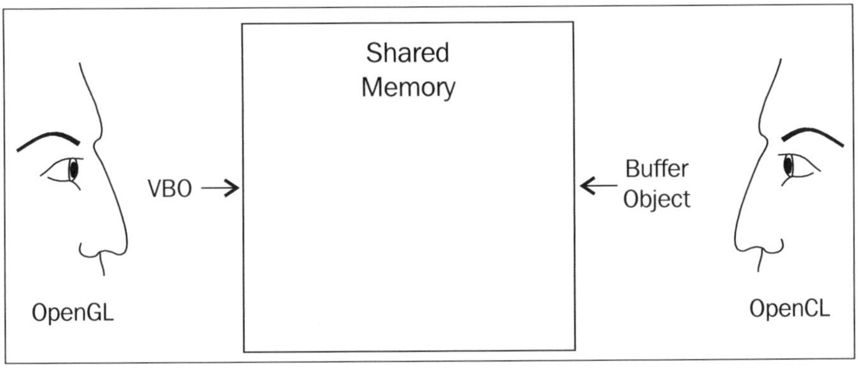

Similarly the OpenGL the texture or render buffer object can be linked to the OpenCL image, as in the following figure:

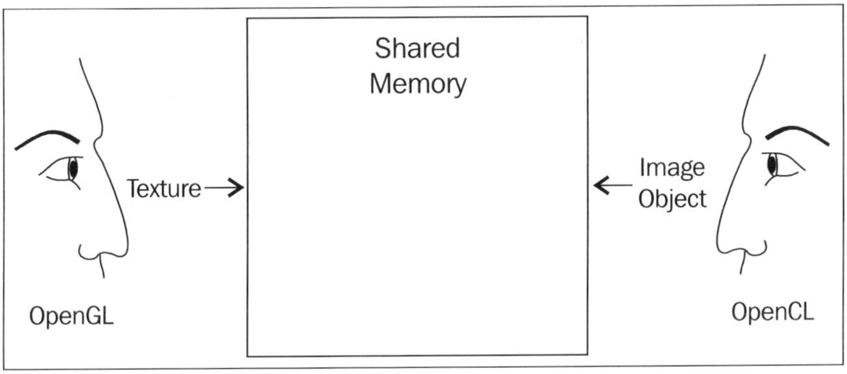

Which kind of application would use both OpenCL and OpenGL and how? The answer is evidently not unique, but we can imagine a typical example of such a program easily. The program should fulfill the following requirements:

- It must have some graphics to render, so that OpenGL is used
- A general purpose data parallel computation should be there,

- where OpenCL would be used
- The OpenCL kernel should be accessing a data buffer of OpenGL, probably updating with its own computation result

Implementing Interoperation

To use the Interoperation function we need to include the `cl_gl.h` header file. This header contains declaration of the required function for interoperation.

Detecting if OpenCL-OpenGL Interoperation is supported

Before discussing other implementation steps, we try to detect whether the current environment supports this interoperation. We use the OpenCL API `clGetDeviceInfo(…)` for this purpose. The first call would get the total size needed to store the string (`char*`) returned by the second call. This string is a list of all the device extensions that are supported by the current environment. We then try to find from this list, whether it has an item called `cl_khr_gl_sharing` for Windows and Linux and `cl_apple_gl_sharing` for Mac. Its presence would indicate the support of OpenCL-OpenGL interoperation, otherwise not.

Find the size of device info string in a variable `sizeOfExtensionString` called which is of type `size_t` as follows:

```
size_t sizeOfExtensionString;
cl_int errorStatus = clGetDeviceInfo(deviceToCheck,
  CL_DEVICE_EXTENSIONS,
  0,
  NULL,
  &sizeOfExtensionString);
```

Here, if `CL_SUCCESS == errorStatus` then `sizeOfExtensionString` gets the proper value. Then we can proceed to get the actual string of device extension. First we allocate sufficient memory to hold this string using the following code:

```
char* extensionString = (char*)malloc(sizeOfExtensionString);
```

On success of this memory allocation, we try to get the extension string into the `extensionString` variable using the following code:

```
errorStatus = clGetDeviceInfo(deviceToCheck,
  CL_DEVICE_EXTENSIONS,
  sizeOfExtensionString,
  extensionString,
  &sizeOfExtensionString);
```

The `extensionString` variable is nothing but a list of space-separated strings, each indicating one extension. In this list we check the existence of the item `cl_khr_gl_sharing` with some code/function as follows:

```
bool isCLGLInteropSupported(char* extensionString)
{
  std::string allStrings(extensionString);
  std::string searchString("cl_khr_gl_sharing");
  std::size_t index = allStrings.find(searchString);
  if(std::string::npos == index)
  {
    return false;
  }
  else
  {
    return true;
  }
}
```

> For Apple the statement `std::string searchString("cl_khr_gl_sharing");` must be replaced with `std::string searchString("cl_apple_gl_sharing");`.

If the preceding function returns `true`, we can continue our experiment of interoperation with the current environment.

Initializing OpenCL context for OpenGL Interoperation

The next task is to create OpenCL context with reference to OpenGL context in Linux and Windows, or to a shared group in Mac. This OpenGL context or shared group establishes a link between the operating system and graphic windows. The context would be created as usual, with the `clCreateContext` OpenCL call, but in addition we set the `cl_context_properties` which is the first argument of the `clCreateContext` function. In the `cl_context_properties` argument we set the corresponding property to mention the current context of OpenGL from which data should be shared. Unfortunately, the actual code varies across different operating systems. Here we present some code for Windows with a brief explanation. In Windows, three properties must be set. They are `CL_CONTEXT_PLATFORM`, `CL_WGL_HDC_KHR`, and `CL_GL_CONTEXT_KHR`. The `CL_CONTEXT_PLATFORM` property specifies the platform. The `CL_WGL_HDC_KHR` property specifies the handle to device context (HDC) for the rendering window. The `CL_GL_CONTEXT_KHR` property specifies an OpenGL rendering context for the X11 or the Windows.

To find the values of the `CL_GL_CONTEXT_KHR` and `CL_WGL_HDC_KHR` properties, we have to use operating system specific calls. For the `CL_CONTEXT_PLATFORM` property we use a standard OpenCL call and determine the platform ID using the function `clGetPlatformId()`. The following code is an example declaration of the `cl_context_properties`:

```
cl_context_properties custom_properties[] =
{
  //set platform
  CL_CONTEXT_PLATFORM,
  (cl_context_properties)currentPlatform,
  //set device context
  CL_WGL_HDC_KHR,
  (cl_context_properties) wglGetCurrentDC(),
  //set current context
  CL_GL_CONTEXT_KHR,
  (cl_context_properties) wglGetCurrentContext(),
  0
}
```

Then, we create the context as in the following code:

```
cl_context contextForInterop = clCreateContext(
  custom_properties,
  1,// number of devices
  pDevice, //pointer to current device id
  NULL,//pointer to pfn_notify
  pUserData, // pointer to user data
  clInt errNumner);
```

The enumeration type `cl_context_properties` specifies one property from a list of enumeration types, each with valid enumeration values. This array should be terminated with 0 to indicate the end.

The first argument `currentPlatform` is of type `cl_platform` structure. This value can be obtained by a call to the OpenCL `clGetPlatformIDs(...)` command as shown in the following code:

```
cl_uint noOfPlatforms;
clGetPlatformIDs (0, NULL, &noOfPlatforms);
cl_platform_id* PlatformIDList;
PlatformIDList =
 (cl_platform_id*)malloc(sizeof(cl_platform_id)*noOfPlatforms);
clGetPlatformIDs(noOfPlatforms, PlatformIDList, NULL);
```

Then select the `cl_platform` in the variable `currentPlatform` from `PlatformIDList`. This `PlatformIDList` is of type `cl_platform_id*`, and on return contains the available list of platforms.

The functions `wglGetCurrentDC()` and `wglGetCurrentContext()` are called wiggle functions which require inclusion of the `windows.h` header. These functions are extensions of OpenGL in windows which allow linking OpenGL to Windows programming.

On Linux, the graphical interface is provided by X11, X Window system. Here the `CL_WGL_HDC_KHR` property is replaced by `CL_GLX_DISPLAY_KHR`. This specifies the display object, which represents a connection to the X server. The remaining enumeration for properties remain the same.

The following code creates the property-list and sets the suitable values for the properties:

```
cl_context_properties custom_properties [] = {
    //Platform
    CL_CONTEXT_PLATFORM,
    (cl_context_properties) platform,
    // Connection to X server
    CL_GLX_DISPLAY_KHR,
    (cl_context_properties) glXGetCurrentDisplay(),
    //Rendering context
    CL_GL_CONTEXT_KHR,
    (cl_context_properties) glXGetCurrentContext(),
    0
};
```

After this, we create the context using the previous property-list as the first parameter in the following call:

```
cl_context contextForInterop = clCreateContext(
  custom_properties,
  1,// number of devices
  pDevice, //pointer to current device id
  NULL,//pointer to pfn_notify
  NULL, // pointer to user data
  clInt_errNumner);
```

On Mac, instead of three properties only one property is to be set. Its data type is `CGLShareGroupObj` and the value is obtained using the function call `CGLGetShareGroup` like in the following code:

```
CGLContextObj cglCtx = CGLGetCurrentContext();
CGLShareGroupObj cglShGrp = CGLGetShareGroup(cglCtx);
```

The enumeration is `CL_CONTEXT_PROPERTY_USE_CGL_SHAREGROUP_APPLE` and the setting is done using the following code:

```
cl_context_properties custom_Properties[] =
{
  CL_CONTEXT_PROPERTY_USE_CGL_SHAREGROUP_APPLE,
  (cl_context_properties)kCGLShareGroup,
  0
};
```

Then create the context using the following code:

```
Ctx = clCreateContext(
  custom_Properties,
  0,
  0,
  NULL,
  NULL,
  clInt_errNumner);
```

Mapping of a buffer

Now we create the OpenCL buffer which is the same as some existing OpenGL buffers. The `clCreateFromGLBuffer` OpenCL command is used for this purpose as shown in the following code:

```
cl_mem clCreateFromGLBuffer (
  cl_context context,
  cl_mem_flags flags,
  GLuint bufObj,
  cl_int * errCode)
```

Here, context is a valid OpenCL context which is created from an OpenGL context as described in preceding section. The `flags` field is a bit field which is similar to the flag used in `clCreateBuffer()` but, in the present `clCreateFromGLBuffer` call, only `CL_MEM_READ_ONLY`, `CL_MEM_WRITE_ONLY`, and `CL_MEM_READ_WRITE` values can be used. The name of the OpenCL Buffer object which is already created using OpenGL API is `bufObj`. The error code in case of error is `errCode`.

The OpenCL memory object should be created before the OpenGL rendering starts but after the corresponding OpenGL VBO has been created, so this `bufObj` must be created before the call of `clCreateFromGLBuffer`, although it may not be initialized and the size of this buffer is used as the buffer object returned by the `clCreateFromGLBuffer` call. The modification of the state of a GL Buffer object using the GL API (such as `glBufferData`) when corresponding to the CL buffer object exist and the buffer is acquired by CL buffer, it will lead to an undefined behavior in subsequent use of the CL Buffer object.

If we create an OpenCL memory object from the OpenGL buffer, the OpenGL object would not get deleted until the OpenCL object is deleted.

Call of the `cl_int clReleaseMemObject (cl_mem memobj)` function decrements the reference count to the memory object. This can be used to release the Buffer object. Similarly call of the `cl_int clRetainMemObject (cl_mem memobj)` function increments the reference count to the memory object, hence it is used to retain the Buffer object.

Now we present a code snippet for illustration. The following code creates a vertex Buffer object called `vBuffObj` and links it to `GL_ARRAY_BUFFER`:

```
#define BUF_SIZE 350
...
GLuint vBuffObj;
glGenBuffers(1, &vBuffObj);
glBindBuffer(GL_ARRAY_BUFFER, vBuffObj);
glBufferData(GL_ARRAY_BUFFER, BUF_SIZE, NULL, GL_STATIC_DRAW);
```

The call `glGenBuffers(...)` generates the Buffer object name. The first argument specifies the number of names to be generated (here only one) and the second is populated with the generated name(s). The generated names are integers, and not necessarily continuous.

The call `glBindBuffer(...)` binds a Buffer object to the specified buffer binding point, here that is the array buffer. Here, the vertex array pointer parameter is interpreted as an offset within the buffer object, measured in basic machine units.

The call `glBufferData(...)` actually creates a new data store for the Buffer object with specified size in bytes and usage (here, static draw).

After all the preceding steps we use the following code to create the corresponding vertex buffer object of OpenCL:

```
cl_mem vboBuff = clCreateFromGLBuffer(ctx, CL_MEM_WRITE_ONLY,
vBuffObj, &err);
```

Hence `vboBuff` is an OpenCL memory object that refers to the OpenGL vertex Buffer object `vBuffObj`.

Listing Interoperation steps

After this creation, the typical steps are as follows:

1. Make sure that all the GL commands that were pending on the buffer are finished.
2. Acquire the Memory object in OpenCL.
3. Call the kernel with a parameter as this memory object, so that the kernel can update the memory buffer.
4. Make sure that kernel has finished.
5. OpenCL releases the acquisition of that buffer, and OpenGL reacquires the buffer and renders the graphics from the buffer.

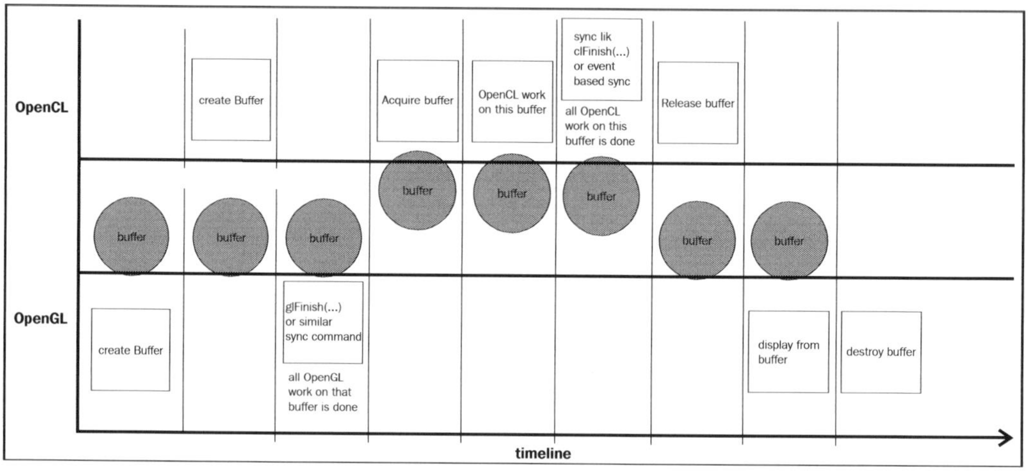

The steps shown in the previous figure are done by the following code:

```
...
glFinish();
clEnqueueAcquireGLObjects(cmdQueue,
  1,
  &vboBuff,
  0,//No event to wait for
  NULL, // Wait event list pointer is NULL
  NULL //Event of this command
  );
clEnqueueNDRangeKernel(
  cmdQueue,
  KernelToWriteOnVBO,
  2,
  NULL,
  globalSize,
```

```
    NULL,
    0,
    NULL,
    NULL);

  clFinish(cmdQueue);
  clEnqueueReleaseGLObjects(cmdQueue,
    1,
    &vboBuff,
    0,
    NULL,
    NULL );
```

Now render the vertex Buffer using OpenGL rendering steps.

When the compiler directive `cl_khr_gl_event` is enabled (also called OpenCL extension)we don't need to make an explicit call to functions `glFinish()` and `clFinish()` because with `cl_khr_gl_event` implicit synchronization is enabled. Hence, `clEnqueueAcquireGLObjects()` acquires only after all corresponding OpenGL's pending commands (that writes on memory object) get finished. A similar thing happens for function `clEnqueueReleaseGLObjects()`.

To check if this extension is available, we can use `clGetDeviceInfo(…)`. To enable it we can use the compiler directive
`#pragma OPENCL EXTENSION cl_khr_gl_event : enable`
or
`#pragma OPENCL EXTENSION all : enable.`

Synchronization

We have already found means to synchronize OpenCL and OpenGL via `glFinish()`, `clFinish(…)`, or using implicit synchronization. Here we discuss some explicit synchronization mechanisms. The synchronization needs two things enabled, extension `cl_khr_gl_event` should be enabled and OpenGL context should support the fence synchronization object (for OpenGL Version 3.2 or greater, or in case the support exists for `ARB_sync` extension). The advantage of explicit synchronization is that it allows more fine-grained synchronization.

The fence synchronization object is created with an OpenGL call shown as follows

```
GLsync fSyncObj = glFenceSync(GL_SYNC_GPU_COMMANDS_COMPLETE, 0);
```

Here `GLsync` is the synchronization object type. Currently only one standard type is supported called `fence`. The first parameter specifies the condition on which it would receive the signal. Right now, the only supported option is `GL_SYNC_GPU_COMMANDS_COMPLETE`, which is used here. The second parameter is bit based flags. No flag is supported right now so 0 is used.

The function `glFenceSync(…)` not only creates a sync object of type `fence` but inserts it into the GL command stream. So at the location of the call of this function a fence is placed. This fence is signaled when the GPU completes all its vertex Buffer operations which were invoked before it. But it is non-blocking in the sense that the CPU can proceed with next command. Only the `glWaitSync(…)`, and `glClientWaitSync(…)` commands are blocking commands.

This `fence` object created by calling the `glFenceSync(…)` function can be used to create an OpenCL event so that the event is completed when fence object is signaled. That way we would able to get the OpenGL signal at OpenCL context, the command for which is as follows:

```
cl_event fenceEvent = clCreateEventFromglsyncKHR (
  ctxCreatedFromGL,
  fSyncObj,
  NULL);
```

The first parameter `ctxCreatedFromGL` is a valid context that is created from OpenGL context. The second parameter is the fence sync object. The third parameter is `cl_int*` error code to be returned which is set to `NULL` here for the sake of simplicity.

This `cl_event` called `fenceEvent` generated from the `clCreateEventFromglsyncKHR()` call would have a few special characteristics. The `clCreateEventFromGLsyncKHR` command implicitly performs a `clRetainEvent( )` call on this CL event object, and creates a reference on the fence sync object. When an event is deleted the reference is deleted. The value of `CL_EVENT_COMMAND_TYPE` (of type `cl_event_info`) would be `CL_COMMAND_GL_FENCE_SYNC_OBJECT_KHR`, and the value of `CL_EVENT_COMMAND_QUEUE` (of type cl_event_info) would be `NULL`, since it's not directly associated with any command queue of OpenCL. The value returned by a call to `clGetEventInfo` with parameter `CL_EVENT_COMMAND_EXECUTION_STATUS` is either `CL_SUBMITTED` or `CL_COMPLETE`, but never `CL_QUEUED` or `CL_RUNNING`. `CL_SUBMITTED` which means that the event has not completed yet. `CL_COMPLETE` means it is completed. All these values can be queried and verified with a `clGetEventInfo()` call. Due to the singular nature of the CL event created by `clCreateEventFromglsyncKHR()`, this `cl_event viz. fenceEvent` can only be used in a waitlist of events of `clEnqueueAcquireGLObjects`. The following code is a sample call

```
clEnqueueAcquireGLObjects(cmdQueue,
  1,
  &vboBuff,
  1, //Number of events in wait-for list
  &fenceEvent, //GL event to wait for
  NULL //Event of this command
  );
```

We have discussed how to get an OpenCL event from an OpenGL sync object. Now we discuss the opposite process. We will now see how to get an OpenGL sync object from an OpenCL event that is, `cl_event`. For this we need to have enabled the OpenGL extension `ARB_cl_event`.

Suppose we have a valid `cl_event` called `eventFromCl`, as follows:

```
cl_event eventFromCl; eventFromCl;
```

To get a corresponding fence object we use the `glCreateSyncFromCLeventARB()` OpenGL call. This call returns a `GLsync` object, so that waiting on this object is the same as waiting on the corresponding `cl_event`, and can be used with `glWaitSync()`, `glClientWaitSync()`, and `glFenceSync()`. This call takes three parameters. The first parameter would be a valid context of OpenCL. The second parameter is the corresponding `cl_event` object which is linked with. The third parameter is a bit-field.

Creating a buffer from GL texture

Similarly to create a an OpenCL buffer from 2D and 3D texture memory we used the following calls respectively on OpenCL1.0 and OpenCL1.1:

```
cl_mem clCreateFromGLTexture2D (cl_context ctx,
  cl_mem_flags flg,
  GLenum txtr_target,
  GLint miplevel,
  GLuint texture,
  cl_int * errcode_ret)
```

The preceding API creates an OpenCL 2D object from an OpenGL 2D texture object and the following code is for corresponding 3D:

```
cl_mem clCreateFromGLTexture3D (cl_context ctx,
  cl_mem_flags flg,
  GLenum txtr_target,
  GLint miplevel,
  GLuint texture,
  cl_int * errcode_ret)
```

Both take a similar set of arguments. Parameter `flg` is a valid OpenCL context that is created from OpenGL context or OpenGL 3D context in respective cases.

The second parameter that is `flg`, is `cl_mem_info` enumeration whose permitted values here are limited to `CL_MEM_READ_ONLY`, `CL_MEM_WRITE_ONLY`, and `CL_MEM_READ_WRITE` only for both the APIs.

The third parameter is GLenum texture_target. For the 2D texture GLenum texture_target, it specifies the image type of texture without creating any reference to a bound GL texture object. GL_TEXTURE_2D, GL_TEXTURE_CUBE_MAP_POSITIVE_X, GL_TEXTURE_CUBE_MAP_POSITIVE_Y, GL_TEXTURE_CUBE_MAP_POSITIVE_Z, GL_TEXTURE_CUBE_MAP_NEGATIVE_X, GL_TEXTURE_CUBE_MAP_NEGATIVE_Y, GL_TEXTURE_CUBE_MAP_NEGATIVE_Z are the permitted values. Value GL_TEXTURE_RECTANGLE is also permitted but only for Version 1.3 or higher . For 3D the only permitted value is GL_TEXTURE_3D.

The fourth parameter miplevel gives the mipmap level to be used. Mipmaps are pre-computed sets of images, which come with main texture for faster rendering. This value is mostly set to 0 because the implementations report error for higher values.

The fifth parameter GLuint texture is name of a texture object. In respective cases 2D and 3D texture objects. According to the rules of texture completeness in OpenGL, a texture object must be a complete texture.

The last parameter is as error code which may be one of the CL_OUT_OF_HOST_MEMORY, CL_INVALID_MIPLEVEL, CL_INVALID_GL_OBJECT, CL_INVALID_CONTEXT, CL_INVALID_IMAGE_FORMAT_DESCRIPTOR, or CL_INVALID_VALUE (for invalid flags or texture target).

OpenCL 1.2 introduces a new API, as follows:

```
cl_mem clCreateFromGLTexture (cl_context ctx,
  cl_mem_flags flg,
  GLenum txtr_target,
  GLint miplevel,
  GLuint texture,
  cl_int * errcode_ret)
```

The meaning of the parameters are similar, except the parameter texture should be the name of a OpenGL 1D, 1D array, 2D, 2D array, 3D, rectangle, cubemap or buffer texture object, and txtr_target can be the corresponding supported values.

Renderbuffer object

Renderbuffer are another type of OpenGL objects which are optimized for use as render targets, especially when the user doesn't need to sample from the produced image. Functions glGenRenderbuffers(), glDeleteRenderbuffers(), and glBindRenderbuffer() are there respectively for the creation , deletion, and binding of the Renderbuffer object (refer to the OpenGL manual for detail).

To create an OpenCL memory object from a Renderbuffer object we use the following function:

```
cl_mem clCreateFromGLRenderbuffer (cl_context cxt,
  cl_mem_flags flg,
  GLuint buff,
  cl_int * errcode_ret);
```

The function `clCreateFromGLRenderbuffer` was introduced in OpenCL 1.0. The first parameter is an OpenCL context, created from OpenGL context. The second parameter is a bit-field flag. The values it can take are `CL_MEM_READ_WRITE`, `CL_MEM_READ_ONLY`, and `CL_MEM_WRITE_ONLY`. The third parameter is a Renderbuffer object's name. The Renderbuffer dimension and format would be used to create an OpenCL 2D image object.

The OpenGL internal format of a Renderbuffer object can be `GL_RGBA8I`, `GL_RGBA8I_EXT`, `GL_RGBA16I`, `GL_RGBA16I_EXT`, `GL_RGBA32I`, `GL_RGBA32I_EXT`, `GL_RGBA8UI`, `GL_RGBA8UI_EXT`, `GL_RGBA16F`, `GL_RGBA16F_ARB`, and so on. When an OpenCL object is created from a Renderbuffer object, the channel order and the channel data type is as given in the table below.

Internal format of Renderbuffer Object in GL	**Image Channel Data Type in CL**	**Image Channel order in CL**
GL_RGBA16	CL_UNORM_INT16	CL_RGBA
GL_RGBA8	CL_UNORM_INT8	CL_RGBA or CL_BGRA
GL_RGBA32I	CL_SIGNED_INT32	CL_RGBA
GL_RGBA16I	CL_SIGNED_INT16	CL_RGBA
GL_RGBA8I	CL_SIGNED_INT8	CL_RGBA
GL_RGBA32UI or GL_RGBA32UI_EXT	CL_UNSIGNED_INT32	CL_RGBA
GL_RGBA16UI or GL_RGBA16UI_EXT	CL_UNSIGNED_INT16	CL_RGBA
GL_RGBA8UI or GL_RGBA8UI_EXT	CL_UNSIGNED_INT8	CL_RGBA
GL_RGBA32F or GL_RGBA32F_ARB	CL_FLOAT	CL_RGBA
GL_RGBA16F or GL_RGBA16F_ARB	CL_HALF_FLOAT	CL_RGBA

The function `clCreateFromGLRenderbuffer` returns an image object or `NULL` respectively on success or failure to create the buffer object. The error code `CL_SUCCESS` is returned in the fourth parameter `cl_int * errcode_ret`; and in the second case error-code `CL_INVALID_CONTEXT`, `CL_INVALID_VALUE` (if `flg` is not valid), `CL_INVALID_GL_OBJECT`, `CL_INVALID_IMAGE_FORMAT_DESCRIPTOR` (if for current internal format of OpenGL there is no corresponding map in the OpenCL image), or `CL_OUT_OF_HOST_MEMORY` is returned.

After creating the OpenCL image object, if the format or dimension of the source OpenGL Renderbuffer object is modified (using OpenGL APIs such as `glRenderbufferStorage(...)`), then the behavior of the created OpenCL object is undefined in subsequent use. To release the image object we use the `clReleaseMemObject` function.

Summary

In this chapter we have covered the topic of CL-GL interoperation. After giving a brief description of OpenGL, we defined OpenCL-OpenGL interoperation and the required steps of implementation (including detection of interoperation support, initializing OpenCL context for OpenGL interoperation, mapping of Buffer (CL and GL), synchronization techniques, and then using the Texture and Renderbuffer objects of OpenGL). In the following chapter we will discuss application of OpenCL in some algorithms from various fields such as statistics, machine learning, and so on.

11
Case studies – Regressions, Sort, and KNN

In this chapter we present more examples to illustrate the capability of OpenCL in different domains. For each example, we present a very brief introduction to the problem and algorithm before discussing the implementation using OpenCL kernel. Readers who are already well-versed with any particular problem may like to directly jump to the discussion of kernel. It is worth remembering the fact that all the kernels are not going to give some performance benefit for all ranges of data and on every GPU. Here instead of discussing optimization techniques on these algorithms (which is already discussed in the section *Case study – matrix multiplication* of *Chapter 8, Basic Optimization Techniques with Case Studies*) we aim to make the reader more comfortable to convert sequential algorithms from various domains into one that exploits the data parallel part of it to write OpenCL kernels.

We will discuss four problems in this chapter. The first two are from the statistics domain. The third one is the parallel sorting algorithm. The fourth, KNN classification will use the sorting algorithm. The following are the case studies discussed here:

- Curve Fitting with least squares Method
    - Straight Line approximations
    - Parabolic Approximations
- Sorting Algorithm – Bitonic Sort
- K-Nearest Neighborhood Classification Algorithms

Regression with least square curve fitting

In least square curve fitting (line and parabola), we are given two interdependent scalar quantities described by two variables say X and Y, but the exact relationship between them is not known in terms of a function like $Y = f(X)$. But instead we are given N pair of values (x_i, y_i) for i equals 1,2,..., N, which exactly means that when X takes the value x_i, then Y takes the value y_i. Generally X is called the independent variable and Y is called the dependent variable. We have to construct a function like $Y = f(X)$ which approximates the exact relationship between X and Y. This function $f(X)$ would be constructed using the given set of value pairs (x_i, y_i). Since function f is approximating the original function and choice of function f is in our hand, we choose a polynomial function for simplicity and also are motivated by a theorem in mathematical analysis called *Stone Weierstrass Theorem*. Informally speaking this theorem states that in every closed interval, any continuous function can be approximated by a polynomial sufficiently well as desired just by increasing the degree and adjusting the coefficient of the terms.

Linear approximations

First we consider a polynomial of degree one, which is the linear approximation. So the function f takes the form as the following:

$$\boxed{y = a_0 + a_1 x}$$

Our task is to find the value of a_0 and a_1. To find these two values we use the given (x_i, y_i) for i equals 1,2,..., N and a technique called method of least square. This method states to find a straight line $y = a_0 + a_1 x$, that is, find the values of a_0 and a_1 such that the sum of the square of vertical distance of all points (x_i, y_i) from the line is minimized.

As described in the following figure, we are using basic analytical geometry knowledge to find the sum which is equal to $\sum_{i=1}^{n} d_i$, where d_i equals vertical distance between the line and the point (x_i, y_i), which is $(y_i - a_0 - a_1 x_i)^2$. So we have to optimize the $\sum_{i=1}^{n} (y_i - a_0 - a_1 x_i)^2$ by suitable choice of a_0 and a_1.

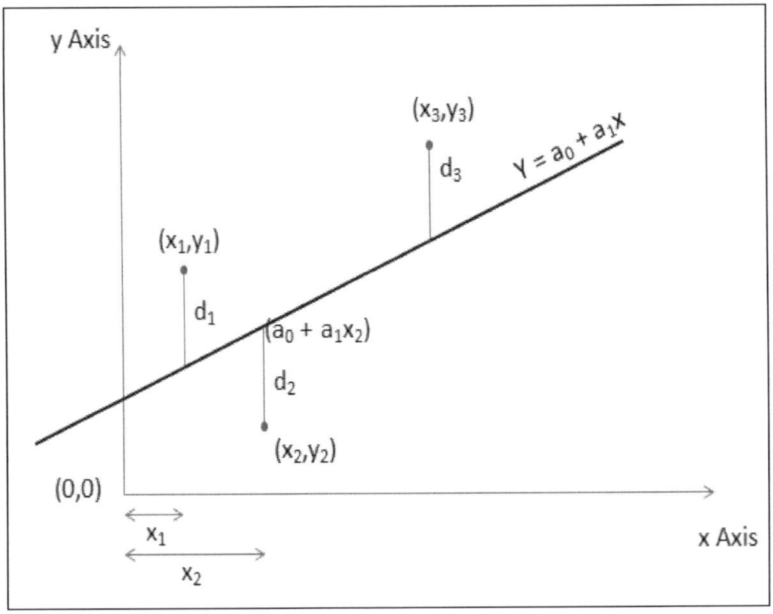

$$\sum_{i=1}^{N}\left(y_i - a_0 - a_i x_i\right)^2 = \sum_{i=1}^{n} d_i^2 = F\left(a_0, a_1\right)$$

Using optimization techniques (which is out of the scope of this book), we arrive at the result that the mentioned sum takes minimum value as shown in the following equations:

$$a_0 = \frac{\left(\sum_{i=1}^{N} y_i\right)\left(\sum_{i=1}^{N} x_i^2\right) - \left(\sum_{i=1}^{N} x_i\right)\left(\sum_{i=1}^{N} x_i y_i\right)}{N\sum_{i=1}^{n} x_i^2 - \left(\sum_{i=1}^{N} x_i\right)^2}$$

$$a_1 = \frac{N\sum_{i=1}^{N} x_i y_i - \left(\sum_{i=1}^{N} x_i\right)\left(\sum_{i=1}^{N} y_i\right)}{N\sum_{i=1}^{N} x_i^2 - \left(\sum_{i=1}^{N} x_i\right)^2}$$

Parabolic approximations

Secondly we consider the polynomial of degree two like $y = a_0 + a_1x + a_2x^2$ and use the same least square technique. This approximation is called the parabolic approximation. Here we need to find the values of three variables a_0, a_1, and a_2. Using the minimization technique, we arrive at the following three equations:

$$\sum_{i=1}^{N} y_i = a_0 N + a_1 \sum_{i=1}^{N} x_i + a_2 \sum_{i=1}^{N} x_i^2$$

$$\sum_{i=1}^{N} x_i y_i = a_0 \sum_{i=1}^{N} x_i + a_1 \sum_{i=1}^{N} x_i^2 + a_2 \sum_{i=1}^{N} x_i^3$$

$$\sum_{i=1}^{N} x_i^2 y_i = a_0 \sum_{i=1}^{N} x_i^2 + a_1 \sum_{i=1}^{N} x_i^3 + a_2 \sum_{i=1}^{N} x_i^4$$

These three equations are solved to get the desired values of *a0, a1,* and *a2*. The solution is done using *Cramer's Rule* in the following way:

$$\begin{pmatrix} p_1 & q_1 & r_1 \\ p_2 & q_2 & r_2 \\ p_3 & q_3 & r_3 \end{pmatrix} \begin{pmatrix} a_0 \\ a_1 \\ a_2 \end{pmatrix} = \begin{pmatrix} s_1 \\ s_2 \\ s_3 \end{pmatrix}$$

$$\text{and } D = \begin{vmatrix} p_1 & q_1 & r_1 \\ p_2 & q_2 & r_2 \\ p_3 & q_3 & r_3 \end{vmatrix}, \quad D_1 = \begin{vmatrix} s_1 & s_1 & s_1 \\ s_2 & s_2 & s_2 \\ s_3 & s_3 & s_3 \end{vmatrix}, \quad D_2 = \begin{vmatrix} p_1 & s_1 & p_1 \\ p_2 & s_2 & p_2 \\ p_3 & s_3 & p_3 \end{vmatrix}$$

$$D = \begin{vmatrix} p_1 & q_1 & r_1 \\ p_2 & q_2 & r_2 \\ p_3 & q_3 & r_3 \end{vmatrix} \quad \text{then } a_0 = \frac{D_1}{D}, \; a_1 = \frac{D_2}{D}, \; a_3 = \frac{D_3}{D}$$

$$\text{provided } D \neq 0$$

Implementation

We start with a sequential implementation using two functions called `linearApproximation` and `parabolicApproximation`. Both take the first three arguments as inputs. First argument is the size of array `N` and second and third arguments are two arrays `pX` and `pY` (each of size `N`) containing the given values of coordinates *X* and *Y*. The remaining parameters are output parameters. For the `linearApproximation` function there are two output parameters, namely, `pA0` and `pA1`. Pointers are passed to get the values. As explained in the following code:

```
void linearApproximation( size_t N,
                          float* pX,
                          float* pY,
                          float* pA0,
                          float* pA1)
{
  float sumX = 0.f;
  float sumY = 0.f;
  float sumXY = 0.f;
  float sumXX = 0.f;
  for(int i=0; i < N; ++i)
  {
    sumX += *(pX+i);// *(pX+i) is same as pX[i] in meaning
    sumY += *(pY+i));
    sumXY += ( *(pX+i) )*( *(pY+i)) );
    sumXX += ( *(pX+i) )*( *(pX+i)) );
  }

  *pA0 = (sumY*sumXX - sumX*sumXY)/(N*sumXX - sumX**2 );
  *pA1 = (N*sumXY - sumX*sumY)/(N*sumXX - sumX**2 );
}
```

For the `parabolicApproximation` function there are three output parameters, namely, `pA0`, `pA1`, and `pA2`. To get the values pointer to those are passed. Finding the values in the `parabolicApproximation` function is not straightforward as with the `linearApproximation` function, since we finally have to use *Cramer's Rule*.

```
void parabolicApproximation(size_t N,
                            float* pX,
                            float* pY,
                            float* pA0,
                            float* pA1,
                            float* pA2)
{
```

```
    float sumX = 0.f;
    float sumY = 0.f;
    float sumXY = 0.f;
    float sumXX = 0.f;
    float sumXXY = 0.f;
    float sumXXX = 0.f;
    float sumXXXX = 0.f;

    float XX = 0.f;
    float XXX = 0.f;
    for(int i=0; i < N; ++i)
    {
      sumX += *(pX+i); // *(pX+i) is same as pX[i] in meaning
      sumY += *(pY+i));
      sumXY += ( *(pX+i) )*( *(pY+i)) );
      XX = ( *(pX+i) )*( *(pX+i)) );
      sumXX += XX;
      sumXXX += ( *(pX+i) )*XX );
      sumXXXX += XX*XX;
    }

    //compute *pA0, *pA1, *pA2
    Bool result = true;
    findParabola(pA0, pA1, pA2, N, sumX,sumXX,sumXXX,sumXXXX,sumY,
      sumXY, sumXXY, &result);
}
```

Observe that this function uses the routine `findParabola` which in turn uses the function `determinant3By3`. The function `findParabola` merely implements *Cramer's Rule* to solve simultaneous equations of the three variables. When the determinant of the co-efficient matrix is zero, then we really don't have the solution of the equation system. The last parameter `bool* resultValid` indicates whether the solution could be found or it does not exist.

```
void findParabola(//Output parameters
                   float* pA0,
                   float* pA1,
                   float* pA2,
                   //Input parameters
                   int    N,
                   float sumX,
                   float sumXX,
                   float sumXXX,
                   float sumXXXX,
                   float sumY,
```

```
                        float sumXY,
                        float sumXXY,
                        bool* resultValid
                        )
{
  //compute detA
  float detA = determinant3By3((float)N, sumX,    sumXX,

                                          sumX,     sumXX,  sumXXX,
                                          sumXX,    sumXXX, sumXXXX);
if( 0.f == detA)
{
  *resultValid = false;
  return;
}
float detA0 = determinant3By3(sumY, sumX,    sumXX,
                                   sumXY,    sumXX,  sumXXX,
                                   sumXXY,   sumXXX, sumXXXX);
float detA1 = determinant3By3((float)N, sumY,    sumXX,
                                   sumX,     sumXY,  sumXXX,
                                   sumXX,    sumXXY, sumXXXX);

float detA2 = determinant3By3((float)N, sumX,    sumY,
                                   sumX,     sumXX,  sumXY,
                                   sumXX,    sumXXX, sumXXY);
  *pA0 = detA0/detA;
  *pA1 = detA1/detA;
  *pA2 = detA2/detA;
}
```

To compute the three by three matrix's determinant, we use the function `determinant3By3` which takes all the nine elements of the determinant in a row-major way as shown below.

```
float determinant3By3(float a1, float b1, float c1,
                      float a2, float b2, float c2,
                      float a3, float b3, float c3
                      )
{
  float det = a1*b2*c3 - a1*b3*c2;
  det += a3*b1*c2 - a2*b1*c3;
  det += a2*b3*c1 - a3*b2*c1;
  return det;
}
```

Now we describe the kernel implementations. First kernel is for linear approximation and is `linear_regression_kernel`. This takes eleven parameters and is used to compute the different sums. The first two parameters `X` and `Y` are input arrays.The next four are different summations `sumX`, `sumY`, `sumXX` and `sunXY` which is computed by the OpenCL kernel. These summations are used to compute `a0` and `a1`. All these values are kept in global memory. The data type here is described using a macro called `DATA_TYPE`. This macro is defined to be float. The advantage of using such a macro is flexibility. With very little effort we can change the type from float to double or some other suitable type. For that we only need to change the `#define DATA_TYPE` float to `#define DATA_TYPE` double, and so on.

Another macro used here is called `SUM_STEP`. The kernel first loads the 64 elements each of *X* and *Y* into a local memory before hitting a local memory barrier. The `SUM_STEP` macro computes the sum of each of the local memory `localSumX`, `localSumY`, `localSumXX`, and `localSumXY`. Take a look at the following diagram which shows how the sum is calculated for 16 elements and shows the four `SUM_STEP`:

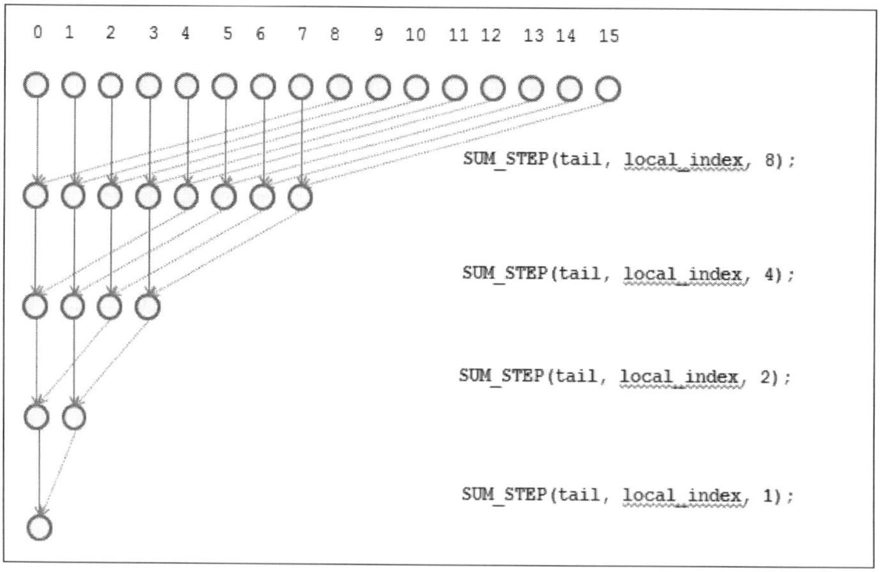

The SUM_STEP operation

The kernel first initializes the `accumulatorX` and `accumulatorY` two private variables with the array elements. Then it initializes the local variables which store the partial sums within a work group. Using local memory fence we make sure that all local data are properly initialized before we proceed further. Then using six consecutive `SUM_STEP(...)` calls we accumulate the sum of 32 elements into a single element. Lastly, we write the result in output variables. This creates a sum per work group.

```
#define DATA_TYPE float
#define  SUM_STEP(LENGTH,  INDEX,  _W)                              \
  if  ((INDEX  <  _W)  &&  ((INDEX  +  _W)  <  LENGTH))  {          \
    localSumX[INDEX]    = localSumX[INDEX]  +  localSumX[INDEX + _W]; \
    localSumY[INDEX]    = localSumY[INDEX]  +  localSumY[INDEX + _W]; \
    localSumXY[INDEX]   = localSumXY[INDEX] +  localSumXY[INDEX + _W];\
    localSumXXY[INDEX]  = localSumXXY[INDEX] +                      \
                          localSumXXY[INDEX + _W];                  \
    localSumXX[INDEX]   = localSumXX[INDEX] +                       \
                          localSumXX[INDEX  + _W];                  \
    localSumXXX[INDEX]  = localSumXXX[INDEX] +                      \
                          localSumXXX[INDEX + _W];                  \
    localSumXXXX[INDEX] = localSumXXXX[INDEX] +                     \
                           localSumXXXX[INDEX + _W];                \
    }                                                               \
  barrier(CLK_LOCAL_MEM_FENCE);

__kernel
void linear_regression_kernel(
                  __global DATA_TYPE *X,
                  __global DATA_TYPE *Y,
                  __global DATA_TYPE *sumX,
                  __global DATA_TYPE *sumY,
                  __global DATA_TYPE *sumXX,
                  __global DATA_TYPE *sumXY,
                  __local  DATA_TYPE *localSumX,
                  __local  DATA_TYPE *localSumY,
                  __local  DATA_TYPE *localSumXX,
                  __local  DATA_TYPE *localSumXY,
                           int       length )
{
    //Get the index of the work-item
    int index = get_global_id(0);
    int gx = get_global_id (0);
    int gloId = gx;

    //  Initialize the accumulator private variable with data from the
input array
    //  This essentially unrolls the loop below at least once
    DATA_TYPE accumulatorX;
    DATA_TYPE accumulatorY;
    if(gloId < length){
       accumulatorX = X[gx];
       accumulatorY = Y[gx];
```

```
    }


    //  Initialize local data store
    int local_index = get_local_id(0);
    localSumX[local_index] = accumulatorX;
    localSumY[local_index] = accumulatorY;
    localSumXY[local_index] = accumulatorX*accumulatorY;
    localSumXX[local_index] = accumulatorX*accumulatorX;
    barrier(CLK_LOCAL_MEM_FENCE);

    //  Tail stops the last workgroup from reading past the end of the
input vector
    uint tail = length - (get_group_id(0) * get_local_size(0));

    // Parallel reduction within a given workgroup using local data
store
    // to share values between workitems
    SUM_STEP(tail, local_index, 32);
    SUM_STEP(tail, local_index, 16);
    SUM_STEP(tail, local_index,  8);
    SUM_STEP(tail, local_index,  4);
    SUM_STEP(tail, local_index,  2);
    SUM_STEP(tail, local_index,  1);

     //  Abort threads that are passed the end of the input vector
    if( gloId >= length )
        return;

    //  Write only the single reduced value for the entire workgroup
    if (local_index == 0) {
        sumX[get_group_id(0)] = localSumX[0];
        sumY[get_group_id(0)] = localSumY[0];
        sumXX[get_group_id(0)] = localSumXX[0];
        sumXY[get_group_id(0)] = localSumXY[0];
    }
};
```

To get the final sum we accumulate them from all the workgroups. The following host code does this job:

```
clStatus = clEnqueueReadBuffer(command_queue,
                               psumX_clmem,
                               CL_TRUE,
                               0,
```

```
                                num_of_work_groups * sizeof(float),

                                psumX,
                                0,
                                NULL,
                                NULL);
clStatus = clEnqueueReadBuffer(command_queue,
                                psumY_clmem,
                                CL_TRUE,
                                0,
                                num_of_work_groups * sizeof(float),
                                psumY,
                                0,
                                NULL,
                                NULL);
clStatus = clEnqueueReadBuffer(command_queue,
                                psumXX_clmem,
                                CL_TRUE,
                                0,
                                num_of_work_groups * sizeof(float),
                                psumXX,
                                0,
                                NULL,
                                NULL);
clStatus = clEnqueueReadBuffer(command_queue,
                                psumXY_clmem,
                                CL_TRUE,
                                0,
                                num_of_work_groups * sizeof(float),
                                psumXY,
                                0,
                                NULL,
                                NULL);
    float sumX  = 0.0f;
    float sumY  = 0.0f;
    float sumXX = 0.0f;
    float sumXY = 0.0f;
    for(int i=0;i<num_of_work_groups;i++)
    {
        sumX  += psumX[i];
        sumY  += psumY[i];
        sumXY += psumXY[i];
        sumXX += psumXX[i];
    }
```

Finally, the values of `a0` and `a1` (respectively in the variables `A0` and `A1`) are computed using the obtained sums.

```
A0 = (sumY*sumXX - sumX*sumXY)/(NUM_OF_POINTS*sumXX - sumX*sumX );
A1 = (NUM_OF_POINTS*sumXY - sumX*sumY)/(NUM_OF_POINTS*sumXX -
sumX*sumX );
```

Kernel for parabolic approximation works in exactly the same way except it takes extra arguments for the extra computational parameter. This kernel is listed in the following code:

```
#define DATA_TYPE float

__kernel
void parabolic_regression_kernel(
                    __global DATA_TYPE *X,
                    __global DATA_TYPE *Y,
                    __global DATA_TYPE *sumX,
                    __global DATA_TYPE *sumY,
                    __global DATA_TYPE *sumXY,
                    __global DATA_TYPE *sumXXY,
                    __global DATA_TYPE *sumXX,
                    __global DATA_TYPE *sumXXX,
                    __global DATA_TYPE *sumXXXX,
                    __local  DATA_TYPE *localSumX,
                    __local  DATA_TYPE *localSumY,
                    __local  DATA_TYPE *localSumXX,
                    __local  DATA_TYPE *localSumXY,
                    __local  DATA_TYPE *localSumXXY,
                    __local  DATA_TYPE *localSumXXX,
                    __local  DATA_TYPE *localSumXXXX,
                             int        length )
{
    //Get the index of the work-item
    int index = get_global_id(0);
    int gx = get_global_id (0);
    int gloId = gx;
    DATA_TYPE XX;

    //  Initialize the accumulator private variable with data from the
input array
    //  This essentially unrolls the loop below at least once
    DATA_TYPE accumulatorX;
    DATA_TYPE accumulatorY;
    if(gloId < length){
```

```
        accumulatorX = X[gx];
        accumulatorY = Y[gx];
    }

    //  Initialize local data store
   int local_index = get_local_id(0);
    localSumX[local_index] = accumulatorX;
    localSumY[local_index] = accumulatorY;
    XX = accumulatorX*accumulatorX;
    localSumXY[local_index]   = accumulatorX*accumulatorY;
    localSumXXY[local_index]  = XX*accumulatorY;
    localSumXX[local_index]   = XX;
    localSumXXX[local_index]  = XX*accumulatorX;
    localSumXXXX[local_index] = XX*XX;
    barrier(CLK_LOCAL_MEM_FENCE);

    //  Tail stops the last workgroup from reading past the end of the
input vector
    uint tail = length - (get_group_id(0) * get_local_size(0));

    // Parallel reduction within a given workgroup using local data
store
    // to share values between workitems
    SUM_STEP(tail, local_index, 32);
    SUM_STEP(tail, local_index, 16);
    SUM_STEP(tail, local_index,  8);
    SUM_STEP(tail, local_index,  4);
    SUM_STEP(tail, local_index,  2);
    SUM_STEP(tail, local_index,  1);

     //  Abort threads that are passed the end of the input vector
    if( gloId >= length )
        return;

    //  Write only the single reduced value for the entire workgroup
    if (local_index == 0) {
        sumX[get_group_id(0)]     = localSumX[0];
        sumY[get_group_id(0)]     = localSumY[0];
        sumXY[get_group_id(0)]    = localSumXY[0];
        sumXXY[get_group_id(0)]   = localSumXXY[0];
        sumXX[get_group_id(0)]    = localSumXX[0];
        sumXXX[get_group_id(0)]   = localSumXXX[0];
        sumXXXX[get_group_id(0)]  = localSumXXXX[0];
    }
};
```

The preceding kernel takes the help of the following macro which computes the step sum:

```
#define  SUM_STEP(LENGTH,  INDEX,  _W)                                \
  if  ((INDEX  <  _W)  &&  ((INDEX  +  _W)  <  LENGTH))  {            \
    localSumX[INDEX]   = localSumX[INDEX]   +  localSumX[INDEX + _W]; \
    localSumY[INDEX]   = localSumY[INDEX]   +  localSumY[INDEX + _W]; \
    localSumXY[INDEX]  = localSumXY[INDEX]   +  localSumXY[INDEX +
_W];\
    localSumXXY[INDEX] = localSumXXY[INDEX] +                         \
                         localSumXXY[INDEX + _W];                     \
    localSumXX[INDEX]  = localSumXX[INDEX]  +                         \
                         localSumXX[INDEX + _W];                      \
    localSumXXX[INDEX] = localSumXXX[INDEX] +                         \
                         localSumXXX[INDEX + _W];                     \
    localSumXXXX[INDEX] = localSumXXXX[INDEX] +                       \
                          localSumXXXX[INDEX + _W];                   \
    }                                                                 \
  barrier(CLK_LOCAL_MEM_FENCE);
```

After the computation of summations in the OpenCL kernel. The data is transferred to the host using the clEnqueueReadBuffer function as shown below. Finally a for loop computes the final summations.

```
clStatus = clEnqueueReadBuffer(command_queue, psumX_clmem,
             CL_TRUE, 0,
             num_of_work_groups * sizeof(float), psumX, 0, NULL,
             NULL);
clStatus = clEnqueueReadBuffer(command_queue, psumY_clmem,
             CL_TRUE, 0,
             num_of_work_groups * sizeof(float), psumY, 0, NULL,
             NULL);
clStatus = clEnqueueReadBuffer(command_queue, psumXY_clmem,
             CL_TRUE, 0,
             num_of_work_groups * sizeof(float), psumXY, 0, NULL,
             NULL);
clStatus = clEnqueueReadBuffer(command_queue, psumXXY_clmem,
             CL_TRUE, 0,
             num_of_work_groups * sizeof(float), psumXXY, 0, NULL,
             NULL);
clStatus = clEnqueueReadBuffer(command_queue, psumXX_clmem,
             CL_TRUE, 0,
             num_of_work_groups * sizeof(float), psumXX, 0, NULL,
             NULL);
```

```
clStatus = clEnqueueReadBuffer(command_queue, psumXXX_clmem,
            CL_TRUE, 0,
            num_of_work_groups * sizeof(float), psumXXX, 0, NULL,
            NULL);
clStatus = clEnqueueReadBuffer(command_queue, psumXXXX_clmem,
            CL_TRUE, 0,
            num_of_work_groups * sizeof(float), psumXXXX, 0, NULL,
            NULL);

    float sumX    = 0.0f;
    float sumY    = 0.0f;
    float sumXY   = 0.0f;
    float sumXXY  = 0.0f;
    float sumXX   = 0.0f;
    float sumXXX  = 0.0f;
    float sumXXXX = 0.0f;
    for(int i=0;i<num_of_work_groups;i++)
    {
        sumX    += psumX[i];
        sumY    += psumY[i];
        sumXY   += psumXY[i];
        sumXXY  += psumXXY[i];
        sumXX   += psumXX[i];
        sumXXX  += psumXXX[i];
        sumXXXX += psumXXXX[i];
    }
```

After this we use the function called `findParabola` to find the values of `a0`, `a1`, `a2`. This function and the function `determinant3By3` which it uses to find determinant are briefly described in the preceding section with the descriptions of sequential implementation of `parabolicApproximation`.

Bitonic sort

Bitonic sort is a parallel sorting algorithm devised by *Ken Batcher*. A sequence of numbers from *a(1), a(2), a(3), …, a(n)* is called monotonic increasing or decreasing, if *a(i)* >= *a(i+1)* or *a(i)* <= *a(i+1)* respectively for all *i* equals 1,2,3,…, *n-1*. Sequence is monotonic if it is either monotonic increasing or monotonic decreasing.

A bitonic sequence is one that is monotonically increasing (or decreasing) up to some point where it reaches the maximum (or minimum) value of the sequence, and then it becomes monotonically decreasing (or increasing) up to the end. A sequence that can be converted to the aforementioned bitonic sequence by cyclic shifting is also called a bitonic sequence.

Given a bitonic sequence, bitonic split is an operation on it which scans for *i* equals 1 to n/2, and if $a(i+n/2) < a(i)$ then swap $a(i+n/2)$ and $a(i)$. This operation produces two bitonic subsequences say *L* and *R* where *L* and *R* are left and right parts of the transformed sequence and all elements of *L* are less than all elements of *R*. The following is an illustrative example:

Index to elements	0	1	2	3	4	5	6	7	8	9
Bitonic sequence	5	9	24	39	65 (max)	60	45	19	4	3
Increasing -------------------------------------> Decreasing -->										

Index to elements	0	1	2	3	4	5	6	7	8	9
Split	5	9	19	4	3	60	45	24	39	65
Subsequence	L (smaller Bitonic sequence)					R (smaller Bitonic sequence)				
All elements of L are less than all elements of R										

By repeatedly using bitonic split we can convert a bitonic sequence into a sorted sequence. But here initially we need a bitonic sequence. So if given any other sequence we first convert that into a bitonic sequence using the following technique.

Given an arbitrary sequence we first swap elements pair-wise if they are not in proper order (a proper order is a bitonic sequence of length four) and after the first pass we get several bitonic sequences, each of length four. The process is illustrated with the following example. Here we take an arbitrary sequence of number (not bitonic) and using the method of pair-wise exchange and split. First pairwise exchange making sure that given arbitrary sequence is converted into small bitonic sequences each of size four. So in a group of four elements to be converted to a bitonic sequence (like first four elements) we compare the first and the second elements. If first element is greater than the second element we exchange them. Then we compare third and fourth elements. If third is smaller than fourth, then we exchange. The following figure shows the same:

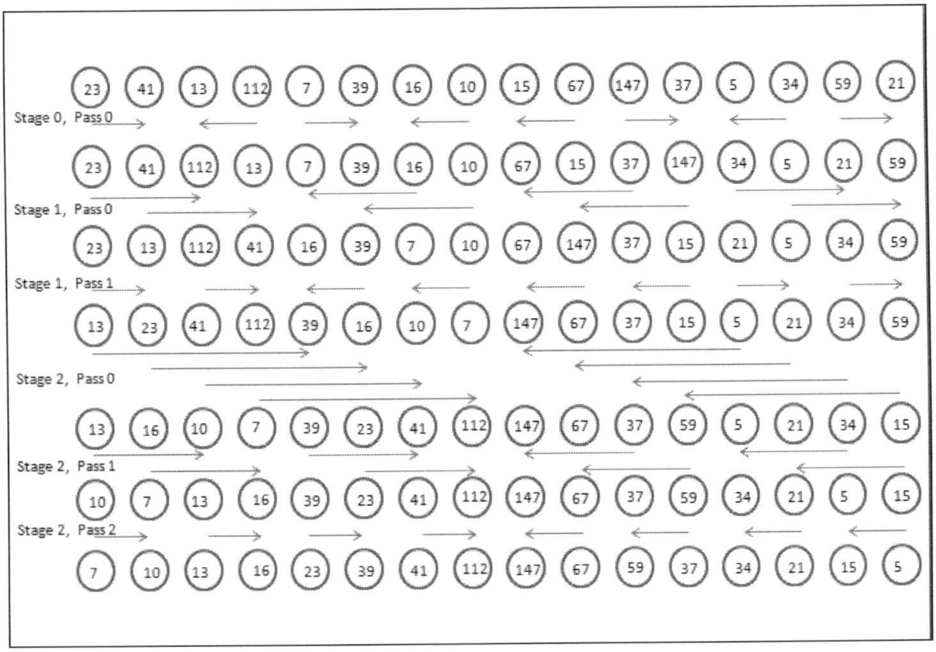

Thus we get a bitonic sequence of all elements. Now we use our previous split method and merge method to get the sorted sequence.

First we use sort (by bitonic split on current bitonic subsequences) and finally at last stage swap if needed.

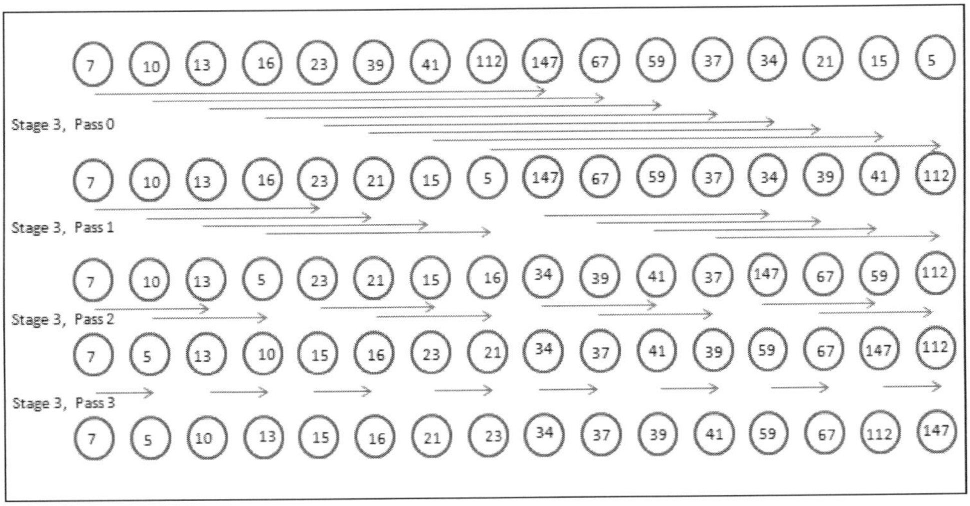

With the preceding explanation and illustration of bitonic sort, we introduce the kernel in the following code:

```
#define DATA_TYPE int

//The bitonic sort kernel does an ascending sort
kernel
void bitonic_sort_kernel(__global DATA_TYPE * input_ptr,
                          const uint stage,
                          const uint passOfStage )
{
    uint threadId = get_global_id(0);
    uint pairDistance = 1 << (stage - passOfStage);
    uint blockWidth   = 2 * pairDistance;
    uint temp;
    bool compareResult;
    uint leftId = (threadId & (pairDistance -1))
    + (threadId >> (stage - passOfStage) ) * blockWidth;
    uint rightId = leftId + pairDistance;

    DATA_TYPE leftElement, rightElement;
    DATA_TYPE greater, lesser;
    leftElement  = input_ptr[leftId];
    rightElement = input_ptr[rightId];

    uint sameDirectionBlockWidth = threadId >> stage;
    uint sameDirection = sameDirectionBlockWidth & 0x1;

    temp    = sameDirection?rightId:temp;
    rightId = sameDirection?leftId:rightId;
    leftId  = sameDirection?temp:leftId;

    compareResult = (leftElement < rightElement) ;

    greater       = compareResult?rightElement:leftElement;
    lesser= compareResult?leftElement:rightElement;

    input_ptr[leftId]  = lesser;
    input_ptr[rightId] = greater;
};
```

This kernel takes three arguments. First one is the pointer to input buffer which is to sorted. Data type is defined by a macro so that it can be changed easily. Currently it is chosen to be int. Second and third parameters are respectively the stage and pass of stage which determine the state of the entire sort process. Stage value is initially set to log of array size to the base 2. As shown in the figure we just saw, there are four stages and those 1, 2, 3, and 4-th stages have respectively 1, 2, 3, and 4 passes. Outputs are shown after each pass of each stage.

Variables `leftElement, rightElement;` hold the two elements of the selected subsequence to be compared and exchanged if needed. The statement `compareResult = (leftElement < rightElement);` compares the left and right elements and accordingly selectes the greater and lesser elements `greater = ompareResult?rightElement:leftElement; lesser = compareResult?leftElement:rightElement;`. Finally the updated values are dumped in the original data structure by the statements `input_ptr[leftId]  = lesser;` and `input_ptr[rightId] = greater;`. Input pointer values are exchanged at the same time.

First part of the kernel determines the position and length of the bitonic subsequence. Left position is indicated by `leftId` and length is by `pairDistance`. Last element of the subsequence is `rightId`.

The following is the host code:

```
int main(void) {
    // Basic initialization and declaration...

    // Execute the OpenCL kernel on the list

  // Each work item shall compare two elements.
    size_t global_size = DATA_SIZE/2;
  // This is the size of the work group.
    size_t local_size  = WORK_GROUP_SIZE;
  // Calculate the Number of work groups.
    size_t num_of_work_groups = global_size/local_size;

    //Allocate memory and initialize the input buffer.
    DATA_TYPE *pInputBuffer = (DATA_TYPE*)malloc(
                          sizeof(DATA_TYPE)*DATA_SIZE);
    for(int i =0; i< DATA_SIZE; i++)
    {
        pInputBuffer[i] = DATA_SIZE - i;
        printf("pInputBuffer[i] = %4d\n",pInputBuffer[i]);
    }
    //Create memory buffers on the device for each vector
    cl_mem pInputBuffer_clmem = clCreateBuffer(
                                    context,
                                    CL_MEM_READ_WRITE|
                                    CL_MEM_USE_HOST_PTR,
                                    DATA_SIZE * sizeof(DATA_TYPE),
```

```
                                    pInputBuffer,
                                    &clStatus);

    // Create kernel...

    clSetKernelArg(bitonic_sort_kernel,
                   0,
                   sizeof(cl_mem),
                   (void *)&pInputBuffer_clmem);

    unsigned int stage, passOfStage, numStages, temp;
    stage = passOfStage = numStages = 0;
    for(temp = DATA_SIZE; temp > 1; temp >>= 1)
        ++numStages;
    global_size = DATA_SIZE>>1;
    local_size  = WORK_GROUP_SIZE;
    for(stage = 0; stage < numStages; ++stage)
    {
        // stage of the algorithm
        clSetKernelArg(
           bitonic_sort_kernel,
           1,
           sizeof(int),
           (void *)&stage);
        // Every stage has stage + 1 passes
        for(passOfStage = 0; passOfStage < stage + 1; ++passOfStage) {
            // pass of the current stage
            std::cout << "Pass no "<< passOfStage << std::endl;
            clStatus = clSetKernelArg(bitonic_sort_kernel,
                                      2,
                                      sizeof(int),
                                     (void *)&passOfStage);
            //
            // Enqueue a kernel run call.
            // Each thread writes a sorted pair.
            // So, the number of  threads (global) should be half the
length of the input buffer.
            //
            clEnqueueNDRangeKernel(
                                   command_queue,
                                   bitonic_sort_kernel,
                                   1,
                                  NULL,
                                  &global_size,
                                  &local_size,
                                  0,
                                  NULL,
                                  NULL);
            LOG_OCL_ERROR(clStatus, "enqueueNDRangeKernel() failed for
sort() kernel." );
            clFinish(command_queue);
```

```
        }//end of for passStage = 0:stage-1
    }//end of for stage = 0:numStage-1

    DATA_TYPE *mapped_input_buffer =
  (DATA_TYPE *)clEnqueueMapBuffer(
                command_queue,
                pInputBuffer_clmem,
                true,
                CL_MAP_READ,
                0,
                sizeof(DATA_TYPE) * DATA_SIZE,
                0,
                NULL,
                NULL,
                &clStatus);
    // Display the Sorted data on the screen
    for(int i = 0; i < DATA_SIZE; i++)
        printf( "%d  ", mapped_input_buffer[i] );

    // cleanup...

    return 0;
}
```

As an example to understand Bitonic sort take an input array of numbers and try to calculate using Bitonic sort manually which will help you understand the amount of parallelism involved. We take a data array of numbers 16, 15, ..., 3,2,1. This is not a bitonic sequence and is in descending order (we would sort in ascending order). We have four stages (four values of the input parameter stage namely, 0, 1, 2, and 3). At stage 0, we covert the given sequence to four bitonic sequences each of size four. In the next two stages (stage equals 1 and 2) we merge stage 2 of the bitonic sequences of previous stages and double its size (hence reduce the number of sequences by a factor of two in each stage). So, after stage 1 we get two bitonic sequences each of size 8 and after stage 2, we get a single bitonic sequence of size 16. At stage 3, we finally get the monotonic sequence, that is, a sorted sequence.

k-Nearest Neighborhood (k-NN) algorithm

In machine learning classification is the problem of identifying class/type of a given input quantity. Formally the problem can be stated like, we have a set of classes/types represented by:

```
C={t(1), t(2),…, t(m)}.
```

We have a set *P* of objects, each of which is described by a vector. All the objects of *P* have a unique class from *C*. From *P* we are given n objects (that is their representative vectors) *p(1), p(2), …, p(n)* (each *p(i)* is d-dimensional vector) and for each one of them *p(i)* the class is also given *c(i)*. These *n* vectors with their classes *(p(i) , c(i))* are called as the training data. We are given a distance measure *d(p1 , p2)* that gives the relevant distance between two vectors of *P*. Now, we are presented an arbitrary point from *P* say *p* whose class is not known. The problem is to find the class of *p* (using each given data and distance).

To find the class of *x* we use the following algorithm called k-nearest neighborhood algorithm.

1. Fix a positive integer *k*. (choice of *k* is dependent on dataset size and other factors, which are out of scope of this discussion, rule of thumb is *k* is nearest integer of square root of *n*).
2. For each *p(i)* in *P*, compute distance *d(p, p(i))*.
3. Find lowest *k* distances from the preceding distances. Let those lowest *k* distances correspond to the points *z(1), z(2),…, z(k)* where each of the points are from *P*. Suppose the classes of *z(1), z(2),…, z(k)* are respectively *q(1), q(2),…, q(k)* where each of *q(1), q(2),…, q(k)* belongs to *Y*.
4. Find the class/type that appears the most times in those list *q(1) ,q(2) ,…, q(k)*. Predict *x* belongs to that class/type. A tie occurs when more than one class/type has maximum frequency (same frequeny which is maximum among all the frequencies). The tie is broken by some strategy like choose the class that has the lower array index.

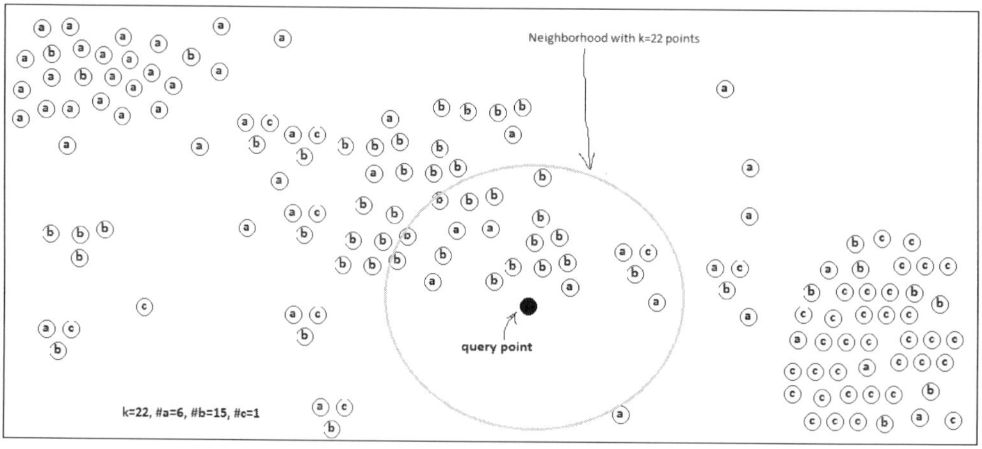

k-Nearest Neighbourhood

The figure we just saw illustrates the k-NN algorithm for three classes, namely, *a*, *b*, *c*. Here we fix k equals 22. The dark point is the query point and all other points are labeled with their classes. We find all the distances from the query point and choose the nearest k equals 22 points. Those 22 points are shown within the green border. Then we find the number of occurrences of each of the classes *a*, *b*, *c* within that green border. The occurrence of *a*, *b*, *c* are respectively 6, 15, 1 times. Since class b occurs maximum number of times among these three classes, we infer that class of the query point is *b*.

The following is the sequential implementation of the k-NN algorithm followed by its explanation:

```
int KNearestNeighbourhoodAlgorithm(
            size_t trainingSetSize,
            float* pX,
            const int noOfClasses,
            int* pY,// class of X
            const int k,
            float queryPoint
            )
{
  // Compute all the distances from the queryPoint
  float* distances =  new float[trainingSetSize];
  for(int i = 0; i < trainingSetSize; ++i )
  {
    distances[i] = distanceF(queryPoint, pX[i]);
  }

  //Find nearest k points
  int* nearestK =  new int[k];
  for(int i=0;i<k;++i)
  {
    int index = -1;
    float min = FLT_MAX;
    //Find i-th minimum
    for(int j=0;j<trainingSetSize;++j)
    {
      if( min > distances[j])
      {
        min = distances[j];
        index = j;
      }
    }
    nearestK[i] = index;
            // so that is distance is not consider next time
```

```
        distances[index] = FLT_MAX;
      }
      delete distances[];

      //find the frequencies of each classes among those k chosen data
      int* frequencyOfClasses =  new int[noOfClasses];
      //initilize frequency array
      for(int i = 0; i < noOfClasses; ++i )
      {
        frequencyOfClasses[i] = 0;
      }
      //now compute the actual frequencies
      for(int i=0;i<k;++i)
      {
        frequencyOfClasses[pY[nearestK[i]]]++;
      }
      delete nearestK[];

      //find max frequency among them
      int maxFreq = INT_MAX;
      int maxFreqIndex = 0;
      for(int i=0;i<k;++i)
      {
        if(maxFreq < frequencyOfClasses[i])
        {
          maxFreqIndex = i;
          maxFreq = frequencyOfClasses[i];
        }
      }
      delete frequencyOfClasses[];

      //report the corresponding index
      return maxFreqIndex;
    }
    float distanceF(float pointX, float pointY)
    {
          float x = pointX - pointy;
      return sqrt(x*x);
    }
```

To explain the code we start with the `distanceF` function. This computes the distance between two points. This we use in the following algorithm where we have a fixed value of *k* (integer). The main function `int KNearestNeighbourhoodAlgorithm` returns the integer representing class of the `queryPoint`, the sixth parameter to the function. Number of classes is given by the third parameter `const int noOfClasses`. We have `trainingSetSize` number of data points stored in `pX` and `pY` stores the corresponding class.

First the for loop computes all the distances from the `queryPoint` function and stores them in dynamic array distances. Then we find the k nearest points from the `queryPoint` function using the nested for loops. First we find for *i* equals 0 the lowest value, then excluding that we find the second lowest value for *i* equals 1, then similarly exluding these two we find third lowest value for *i* equals 2 and so on. Now, we find the frequencies of those *k* nearest points and store them in the dynamic array `frequencyOfClasses`. Lastly, we find the class with maximum frequency and returns that class.

One of the most time consuming and complex parts of the preceding algorithm is finding the nearest *k* points. In OpenCL version that part is done a bit differently. We just sort the entire distance list and then take the bottom *k* items from that list. To sort we use the OpenCL kernel bitonic sort which is described earlier in *Bitonic sort* section.

The same kernel is reused with some small enhancement to the kernel according to the requirement of k-NN algorithm. The following is the listing of kernel:

```
kernel
void knn_bitonic_sort_kernel(__global DISTANCE_TYPE * input_ptr,
                  __global POINT *data_set,
                  const uint stage,
                  const uint passOfStage )
{
    uint threadId = get_global_id(0);
    uint pairDistance = 1 << (stage - passOfStage);
    uint blockWidth   = 2 * pairDistance;
    uint temp;
    uint leftId = (threadId & (pairDistance -1)) + (threadId >>
      (stage - passOfStage) ) * blockWidth;
    bool compareResult;
    uint rightId = leftId + pairDistance;

    DISTANCE_TYPE leftElement, rightElement;
    DISTANCE_TYPE greater, lesser;
    POINT      leftPoint, rightPoint;
    POINT      greaterPoint, lesserPoint;
    leftElement  = input_ptr[leftId];
    leftPoint    = data_set[leftId];
    rightElement = input_ptr[rightId];
    rightPoint   = data_set[rightId];

    uint sameDirectionBlockWidth = threadId >> stage;
    uint sameDirection = sameDirectionBlockWidth & 0x1;
    temp    = sameDirection?rightId:temp;
```

```
        rightId = sameDirection?leftId:rightId;
        leftId  = sameDirection?temp:leftId;

        compareResult = (leftElement < rightElement) ;

        greater      = compareResult?rightElement:leftElement;
        greaterPoint = compareResult?rightPoint:leftPoint;
        lesser       = compareResult?leftElement:rightElement;
        lesserPoint  = compareResult?leftPoint:rightPoint;

        input_ptr[leftId]  = lesser;
        data_set[leftId]   = lesserPoint;
        input_ptr[rightId] = greater;
        data_set[rightId]  = greaterPoint;
    }
```

This kernel takes four arguments. Argument one is the distance array. And the second is the corresponding point array. As we sort the distance we need to maintain the distance point pair. The first two are the arrays it is supposed to sort. To keep the data type easily changeable we have used the macro `DISTANCE_TYPE` and typedef-ed structure `POINT` as data type.

```
#define DISTANCE_TYPE float
typedef struct _point {
    int x;
    int y;
    int classification;
} point;
typedef point POINT;
```

Third and fourth arguments are stages and `passOfStage` which tell the kernel about the state of the algorithm so that length and location of bitonic subsequence can be determined.

As we discussed, to add flexibility we have taken the macro `DISTANCE_TYPE` and typedef'd structure POINT as data type. In addition to bitonic sort kernel we here use one device function called `point_distance` which takes two `POINTS` and computes the distance between them and another kernel called `knn_distance_kernel`.

This kernel `knn_distance_kernel` uses the distance function `point_distance` and computes the distance between the query point and all the elements of training data array. First parameter is the query point and second is the training data array pointer. Third parameter is output array pointer where the distances are dumped.

```
__kernel
void knn_distance_kernel(
                    POINT match,
                   __global POINT *data_set,
                   __global DISTANCE_TYPE *distance_data)
{
    //Get the index of the work-item
    int gid   = get_global_id (0);
    POINT read_point = data_set[gid];
    DISTANCE_TYPE computed_distance = point_distance (
                                       read_point,
                                       match );

    distance_data[gid] = computed_distance;
}
```

Based on global ID of the kernel instanc we select an element of the data array and using the distance function find the distance and finally update the computed distance to output the array's corresponding element.

Here we list the main program that implements the complete algorithm of k-NN. Trivial parts like declarations, basic memory allocation, and so on are just skipped to focus on the core algorithm.

```
int main(void) {
  // declare clStatus, point *pPoints and allocate
  // memory and load data for the second.
  // Set up the Platform etc.

  // Process all points. Each work item shall process a point
  size_t global_size = NUM_OF_POINTS;
  // This is the size of teh work group.
  size_t local_size  = WORK_GROUP_SIZE;
  // Calculate the Number of work groups.
  size_t num_of_work_groups = global_size/local_size;
  //Allocate memory for storing the sumations
  float *pDistance = (float*)malloc(
                   sizeof(float)*NUM_OF_POINTS);

    //Create memory buffers on the device for each vector
    cl_mem pPoints_clmem = clCreateBuffer(
                      context,
                      CL_MEM_READ_WRITE|CL_MEM_USE_HOST_PTR,
                      NUM_OF_POINTS * sizeof(point),
                      (void *)pPoints,
```

```
                          &clStatus);
    cl_mem pDistance_clmem = clCreateBuffer(
                             context,
                             CL_MEM_READ_WRITE,
                             NUM_OF_POINTS * sizeof(float),
                             NULL,
                             &clStatus);

    // Create a program from source and build and create kernels
distance_kernel and bitonic_sort_kernel
    // Set the arguments of the distance kernel
    clStatus  = clSetKernelArg(distance_kernel, 0,
                            sizeof(point), &matchPoint);
    clStatus |= clSetKernelArg(distance_kernel,
                               1,
                               sizeof(cl_mem),
                               (void *)&pPoints_clmem);
    clStatus |= clSetKernelArg(distance_kernel,
                               2,
                               sizeof(cl_mem),
                               (void *)&pDistance_clmem);
    LOG_OCL_ERROR(clStatus, "Kernel Arguments setting failed." );
    cl_event distance_event;
    clStatus = clEnqueueNDRangeKernel(command_queue,
                                      distance_kernel,
                                      1,
                                      NULL,
                                      &global_size,
                                      &local_size,
                                      0,
                                      NULL,
                                      &distance_event);
 clStatus = clWaitForEvents(1, &distance_event);
    //Sort the distance buffer using Bitonic Sort.
    clStatus = clSetKernelArg(bitonic_sort_kernel,
                              0,
                              sizeof(cl_mem),
                              (void *)&pDistance_clmem);
    clStatus |= clSetKernelArg(bitonic_sort_kernel,
                              1,
                              sizeof(cl_mem),
                              (void *)&pPoints_clmem);
    unsigned int stage, passOfStage, numStages, temp;
    stage = passOfStage = numStages = 0;
```

```
for(temp = NUM_OF_POINTS; temp > 1; temp >>= 1)
    ++numStages;
global_size = NUM_OF_POINTS>>1;
local_size  = WORK_GROUP_SIZE;
for(stage = 0; stage < numStages; ++stage)
{
    // stage of the algorithm
    clStatus = clSetKernelArg(bitonic_sort_kernel,
                              2,
                              sizeof(int),
                             (void *)&stage);
    // Every stage has stage + 1 passes
    for(passOfStage = 0;
        passOfStage < stage + 1;
        ++passOfStage) {
        // pass of the current stage
        clStatus = clSetKernelArg(bitonic_sort_kernel,
                                  3,
                                  sizeof(int),
                                  (void *)&passOfStage);
    // Enqueue a kernel run call.
    // Each thread writes a sorted pair.
    // So, the number of  threads (global)
  //should be half the length of the input buffer.
    clStatus = clEnqueueNDRangeKernel(command_queue,
                                      bitonic_sort_kernel,
                                      1,
                                      NULL,
                                      &global_size,
                                      &local_size,
                                      0,
                                      NULL,
                                      NULL);
        clFinish(command_queue);
    }//end of for passStage = 0:stage-1
}//end of for stage = 0:numStage-1

float *mapped_distance =
  (float *)clEnqueueMapBuffer(command_queue,
                              pDistance_clmem,
                              true
                              CL_MAP_READ,
                              0,
                              sizeof(float) * NUM_OF_POINTS,
```

```
                                   0,
                                   NULL,
                                   NULL,
                                   &clStatus);
    point *mapped_points   =
    (point *)clEnqueueMapBuffer(command_queue,
                                pPoints_clmem,
                                true,
                                CL_MAP_WRITE,
                                0,
                                sizeof(point) * NUM_OF_POINTS,
                                0,
                                NULL,
                                NULL,
                                &clStatus);
    // Display the Sorted K points on the screen
    for(int i = 0; i < K_CLASSIFICATION_POINTS; i++)
        printf( "point(%d, %d, %d) = %3.8f \n",
                  mapped_points[i].x,
                  mapped_points[i].y,
                  mapped_points[i].classification,
                  mapped_distance[i] );
    //select class with max frequency
    // Finally release all OpenCL allocated objects and host buffers.
    return 0;
}
```

Following are the macros which are used to indicate different parameters of algorithm and kernel.

```
#define NUM_CLASSES 3

#define NUM_OF_POINTS 1024
#define WORK_GROUP_SIZE 64
#define K_CLASSIFICATION_POINTS 16
```

First we calculate the number of stages required. The nested for loops of stages and passOfStages launches the kernel knn_bitonic_sort_kernel at every loop. Finally the sorted distance array and the corresponding points array are the output of this multiple call.

Summary

In this chapter we have discussed OpenCL implementation of several commonly occurring algorithms from different fields. Simple algorithms like linear regression to complex algorithms like k-NN could be explored to find the data and task parallel portion within this. Those are the scope of applying OpenCL. As shown in the case of k-NN algorithm, multiple kernels can be implemented and as shown in the case of Bitonic sort same kernel can be invoked multiple times within a loop. OpenCL is already applied to accelerate algorithms in diverse fields, such as Computational Finance, Computational Biology, Image Processing, Numerical Methods, Dense and Sparse linear algebra, mathematical or statistical modeling, simulation, spectral methods like weather forecasting, and computational fluid dynamics. More areas as well as more applications are yet to be explored for applicability of heterogeneous computing based on OpenCL.

Index

C

D

E

F

G

H

L

M

N

O

P

Q

R

S

T

U

V

W

[PACKT] PUBLISHING

Thank you for buying OpenCL Programming by Example

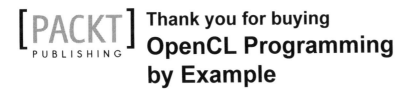

About Packt Publishing

Packt, pronounced 'packed', published its first book "*Mastering phpMyAdmin for Effective MySQL Management*" in April 2004 and subsequently continued to specialize in publishing highly focused books on specific technologies and solutions.

Our books and publications share the experiences of your fellow IT professionals in adapting and customizing today's systems, applications, and frameworks. Our solution based books give you the knowledge and power to customize the software and technologies you're using to get the job done. Packt books are more specific and less general than the IT books you have seen in the past. Our unique business model allows us to bring you more focused information, giving you more of what you need to know, and less of what you don't.

Packt is a modern, yet unique publishing company, which focuses on producing quality, cutting-edge books for communities of developers, administrators, and newbies alike. For more information, please visit our website: `www.packtpub.com`.

Writing for Packt

We welcome all inquiries from people who are interested in authoring. Book proposals should be sent to `author@packtpub.com`. If your book idea is still at an early stage and you would like to discuss it first before writing a formal book proposal, contact us; one of our commissioning editors will get in touch with you.

We're not just looking for published authors; if you have strong technical skills but no writing experience, our experienced editors can help you develop a writing career, or simply get some additional reward for your expertise.

[PACKT]
PUBLISHING

OpenCL Parallel Programming Development Cookbook

ISBN: 978-1-849694-52-0 Paperback: 302 pages

Accelerate your applications and understand high-performance computing with over 50 OpenCL recipes

1. Learn about parallel programming development in OpenCL and also the various techniques involved in writing high-performing code

2. Find out more about data-parallel or task-parallel development and also about the combination of both

3. Understand and exploit the underlying hardware features like processor registers and caches that run potentially tens of thousands of threads across the processors

---

OpenGL Development Cookbook

ISBN: 978-1-849695-04-6 Paperback: 326 pages

Over 40 recipes to help you learn, understand, and implement modern OpenGL in your applications

1. Explores current graphics programming techniques including GPU-based methods from the outlook of modern OpenGL 3.3

2. Includes GPU-based volume rendering algorithms

3. Discover how to employ GPU-based path and ray tracing

4. Create 3D mesh formats and skeletal animation with GPU skinning

Please check **www.PacktPub.com** for information on our titles

[PACKT]
PUBLISHING

OpenGL 4.0 Shading Language Cookbook

ISBN: 978-1-849514-76-7 Paperback: 340 pages

Over 60 highly focused, practical recipes to maximize your use of the OpenGL Shading Language

1. A full set of recipes demonstrating simple and advanced techniques for producing high-quality, real-time 3D graphics using GLSL 4.0
2. How to use the OpenGL Shading Language to implement lighting and shading techniques
3. Use the new features of GLSL 4.0 including tessellation and geometry shaders

---

.NET 4.5 Parallel Extensions Cookbook

ISBN: 978-1-849690-22-5 Paperback: 336 pages

80 recipes to create scalable, task-based parallel programs using .NET 4.5

1. Create multithreaded applications using .NET Framework 4.5
2. Get introduced to .NET 4.5 parallel extensions and familiarized with .NET parallel loops
3. Use new data structures introduced by .NET Framework 4.5 to simplify complex synchronisation problems
4. Practical recipes on everything you will need to create task-based parallel programs

Please check **www.PacktPub.com** for information on our titles

9360643R00172

Made in the USA
San Bernardino, CA
12 March 2014